# UNCONVENTIONAL

## A Combat Engineer's Road to Afghanistan

by
John Hallett

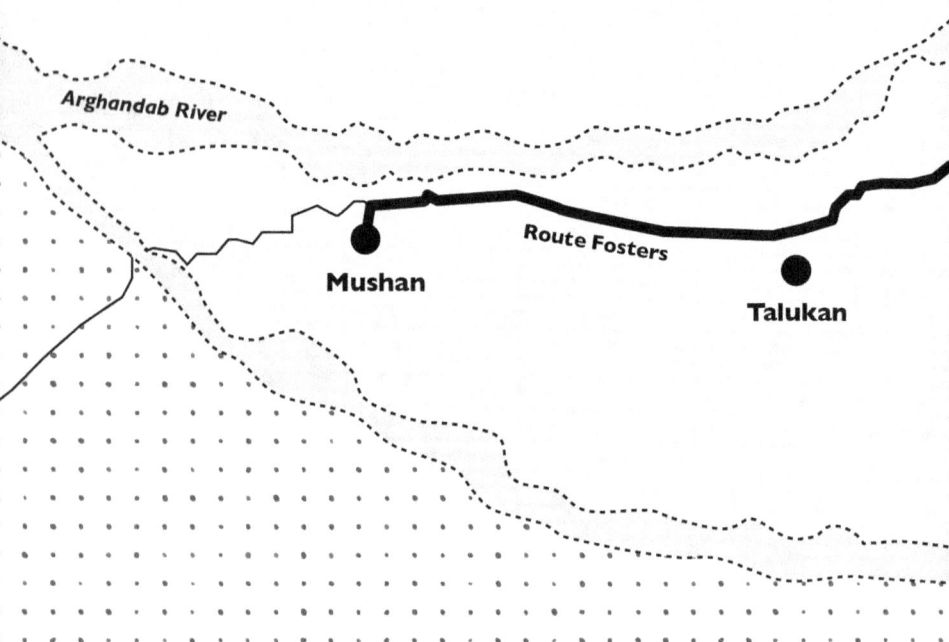

# Area of Operations
# Kandahar Province

Arghandab River

Route Fosters

**Mushan**

**Talukan**

**Registan Desert**

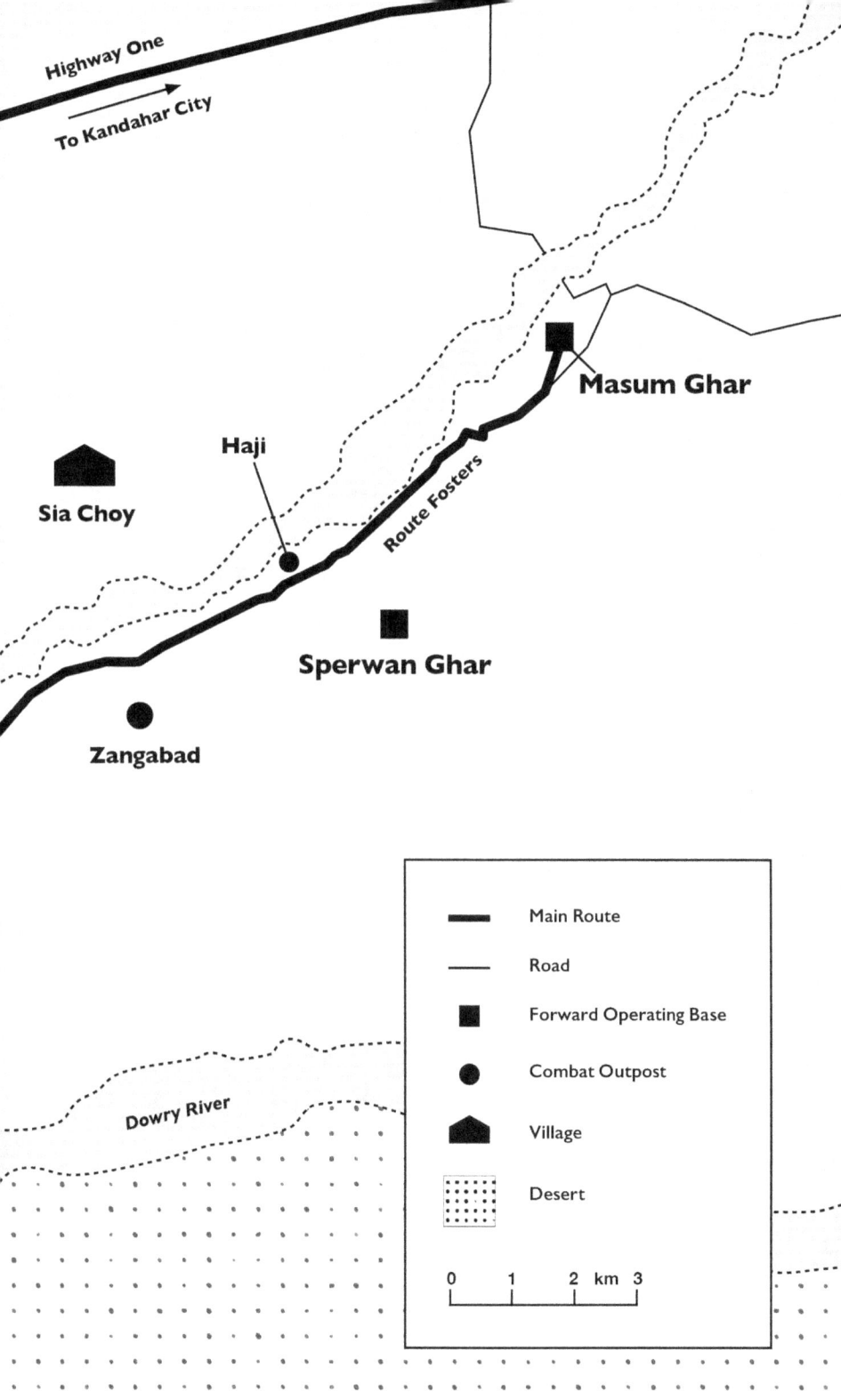

Library and Archives Canada Cataloguing in Publication
Hallett, John, author
Unconventional/John Hallett

Issued in print and electronic formats.

ISBN: 978-1-998501-62-5 (paperback)
ISBN: 978-1-998501-63-2 (ebook)

Cover Design: Axel Peralta
Interior Design: Richa Bargotra

Double Dagger Books
Toronto, Ontario, Canada
www.doubledagger.ca

# Table of Contents

# Note to the Reader

Between 2001 and 2014, Canada was actively engaged in the war in Afghanistan as part of its NATO and UN commitments to global security and counterterrorism in the wake of September 11, 2001. Over the course of the mission, more than 40,000 Canadian Armed Forces members—along with countless civilians and contractors—deployed in a wide range of roles. Among them, Combat Engineers played a critical role: enabling the military to live, move, and fight by clearing routes, constructing infrastructure, and countering explosive threats.

The chapters that follow trace the making of a Combat Engineer—from civilian life through the demands of trades training, deployment preparation, and ultimately, combat operations in Afghanistan in 2008. The early sections of the book focus on training—a rigid, heavily scripted system where meeting the standard sometimes took precedence over realities on the ground. For military readers, this world will feel familiar. For civilian readers, it offers necessary context.

Understanding the doctrinal, bureaucratic training processes is key to appreciating the deeper tension between preparation and military operations. Once deployed, we faced an adversary who studied our routines, exploited our patterns, and adapted faster than our doctrine could respond. Many times our training saved us. Other times, it became a liability—forcing us to adapt quickly or risk becoming casualties of our own procedures. In contrast to the structured world of garrison, sometimes success in Afghanistan depended on adaptability, initiative, and the willingness to challenge what we'd been taught—in essence, we learned when to follow and when to become unconventional.

# Glossary

**Hesco Bastion** - A collapsible wire mesh container lined with heavy-duty fabric. They come in multiple sizes and become like building blocks. They are filled with in-situ material such a soil or sand to create rapid barriers in flood situations or to create blast-resistant walls for protection in combat zones.

**In theatre** - Refers to being in the area of active military operations or deployment.

**Initial Counselling** - The first formal remedial measure taken when a Canadian Armed Forces member demonstrates a conduct of performance deficiency. Although meant to be corrective in nature, if the underlying issues aren't addressed, they form the first step in the progressive administrative process that could lead to career-impacting administrative actions that limit promotion, training opportunities, or even release from the service.

**Nine-liner** - A standardized radio format used to request medical evacuation (MEDEVAC) for casualties, covering nine essential pieces of information.

**PMN Anti-Personnel Mine** - A Soviet-era landmine designed to injure or kill dismounted personnel. Known for its low metal signature which made it hard to detect, it was the preferred device to initiate the main charge of IEDs in Afghanistan.

**Ramp Ceremony** - A solemn military ritual held on the tarmac as fallen soldiers are loaded onto an aircraft for repatriation.

**Stand-to** - A term used by troops to prepare for immediate action. It is a routine defensive posture taken at dawn and dusk, when attacks are most likely.

**Stick-time** - A colloquial term for hands-on experience operating a vehicle or piece of equipment, particularly in training.

# Prologue

It all began with an unconventional decision. Instead of following the traditional path of getting an education, finding a good job, and purchasing a place to settle down, I stopped short of buying a house. Something wasn't right. It felt off. So, I decided to change course.

Sliding the company Chevrolet truck keys across the bespoke oak desk, a perplexed look crossed my boss's face. A first-generation Italian immigrant to Canada after World War II, he started with less than ten dollars in his pocket and made a fortune in the concrete business. A straight shooter who valued a job, hard work, and dedication, he looked up from the key's gleaming reflection on the desk.

"Are you sure you want to quit?"

The building vibrated slightly as a concrete truck rumbled from the rear garage.

"Yes, boss."

In the distance, the batch plant siren sounded. It rang out hundreds of times daily, signalling "load complete" for the concrete truck. Trained as a concrete batcher, I'd spent countless hours in the plant over the past two years, watching the concrete mixer revolve as I loaded trucks with what my boss called "grey gold." My first job out of university, it was interesting in the beginning; however, it became more monotonous with each concrete load. Although the pay was exceptional, I'd wiped out my student loans in less than a year and saved up a house downpayment; it lacked adventure. Gradually, the initial thrill of the job transformed into a stale grind for a paycheck. I became bored with the routine. Then one day during a lull, I read a newspaper article advertising that the Canadian Armed Forces required combat engineers. For some reason, that article sparked an idea that created a relentless itch. I struggled to articulate my reasoning as my boss tempted me with new opportunities.

"John, you know we plan on making a new concrete plant. We want you to help build and operate it."

The batch plant siren shrieked again. After two years of hearing it hundreds of times daily, the high-pitched wail had wormed its way into my subconscious.

"I know, boss. It sounds great," I replied unconvincingly. Shifting in his chair, the slight sound of leather on cloth broke the silence.

"So, John, are you sure you want to *quit*?"

This time, the word *quit* pierced as I tended to finish what I started. But from his perspective, the word *quit* was apropos as he felt a deep, unwavering loyalty to his family and the business he had spent most of his life building. From my perspective, a better word to describe the situation was *growth*. Comparable to a root-bound potted plant, I needed a new environment with more opportunities than simply making grey gold. Sure, I could help build a new concrete plant, but I knew how that movie would end. Once built, it wouldn't be long before I was sitting in front of another concrete mixer with my feet on the desk, batching by the sight and sound of the plant versus the aggregate weight scales while talking on the phone, and playing solitaire on the computer, bored out of my gourd.

I still didn't know what I wanted to make of my life; however, I knew I didn't want that.

Struggling to find the right words, I blurted out, "Boss, I just have an itch to do more while I'm still young. I know it's a cliché, but joining the military is the best way to get the most experience in the least amount of time."

Pensive, he glanced at the *Calgary Herald* newspaper beside the truck keys. The world news section featured multiple headlines about the 2004 Iraq War and America's fight against terrorism.

He pointed to the paper. "John, you have an *itch* to take a fifty percent pay cut and become part of *this?*"

A wise, sometimes irascible man, he remained surprisingly calm through his inquisition. Looking down at the war pictures depicting blown-up buildings, refugees, and burning trucks, the scenes could not have been more different than my peaceful office and a high-paying job. The only sirens I heard were part of the monotonous concrete batch process, not signalling an emergency but rather another truckload complete. This change came with a lot of risk; however, deep in my gut, I knew I'd regret staying. Resolved to live with no regrets, I summoned the courage to give him a categorical response.

"Yes, boss. I want to give it a try."

He took a deep, audible breath. Maybe he realized that it was fruitless to question the logic of a naive and idealistic twenty-four-year-old.

"John, that's an odd choice to make."

He was right. But little did I know it would be the first of many unconventional choices.

# 1

# Sergeant Six Inches

A few days after quitting my job, I arrived in Saint-Jean-sur-Richelieu, a small town just outside Montreal. Home of the General-Jean-Victor-Allard building, commonly known as "the MEGA," it was the site for basic recruit and officer training in the Canadian Armed Forces. The MEGA's massive structure loomed on the horizon, a concrete monolith that looked less like a military training facility and more like an abandoned Cold War mental institution.

Typically, military bases are sprawling complexes spread over acres of land, allowing space for unit lines, training facilities, housing, and administrative buildings. Designed as part of a weird social experiment, the MEGA designers wanted to see if an entire military base could be predominately housed in a single structure. It resulted in a bizarre building. Being cooped up in one building and hardly ever stepping outside further strained recruits' psyches. Although a bustling French-Canadian community surrounded the MEGA, it felt strangely isolated. As our bus, packed with recruits from Pierre Elliott Trudeau International Airport, rolled through the gates, I took in the imposing chain-link fence. Bold signs reinforced the boundary: Department of National Defence – No Trespassing. As I surveyed the ominous setting, I wondered whether the wired enclosure was meant to keep trespassers out or trap the recruits in.

Once inside the MEGA, pandemonium ensued. Standing against the corridor wall with luggage strewn all over the floor as if a bomb went off, the scene would have given the most passive fire marshall a heart attack. As we commenced the in-clearance process, the freshly arrived busload of recruits could not do anything right. Similar to the movies, even the slightest misstep resulted in severe reprimands from a diverse spectrum of military drill sergeants. As a direct entry officer who obtained a Civil Engineering degree at the University of Calgary and not from a military college, everything was new to me. I didn't know the military ranks, drill commands, or how to address the course staff properly. To remain incognito while adjusting to the new environment, I kept my eyes and ears open, and my mouth shut.

In the tumultuous scene, drill sergeants materialized from all angles, barking orders like a pack of enraged Dobermans. The air was thick with the scent of nervous sweat, as every few seconds, someone got verbally vaporized for existing incorrectly. A slight relief in the onslaught came when we began to corral through the intake process like cattle. I quickly learned that the military ran on paperwork. The in-clearance process required us to fill out copious amounts of forms regarding dietary restrictions, medical limitations, and emergency contact information. To increase the tension of an already tedious process, drill sergeants yelled at us throughout it all, outraged that we didn't complete the forms before arrival. One nerdy-looking recruit wearing coke bottle glasses protested that the forms were previously unavailable. His comment resulted in a choir of drill sergeants berating him from all sides for having the audacity to question the process. Up to that point, I had a genuine question about service numbers, the employee number of Canadian Armed Forces members. Being so fresh to the military, I didn't know the term or if I had one. However, to avoid being the next victim of the verbal carnage, I didn't ask. I handed my forms in with the service number line blank.

With my initial paperwork mostly complete, they assigned me to a platoon composed of thirty-five other recruits. Moments later, I met my course instructor, Sergeant Cook. A fit, six-foot infanteer, he spoke with a stutter that became distinctively pronounced when irritated. Having recently returned from Afghanistan, he asked for a training school posting to strike a better work-life balance and get a break. But after witnessing his temperament towards our endless infractions, the school offered no reprieve. He screamed so much during our first hour together I began to take mental bets when he would suffer from an aneurysm.

After failing to provide my completed forms upon arrival and mistakenly addressing him as 'sir,' Sergeant Cook's voice boomed at my impertinence.

"Hallett, my name is Sergeant Cook! I work for a living!"

I didn't understand the customary military jab between non-commissioned members and officers who are addressed as ma'am or sir.

"You seem to be struggling today. If you don't sort yourself out, I will be your new best friend!"

The comment seemed rather presumptuous, given that we'd just met. After chastising one of my platoon members for wearing an inappropriately coloured pink hair elastic and another for wearing Velcro shoes, implying an inability to tie shoelaces, Sergeant Cook gave us our first order.

"Troops, move your luggage to your rooms on the sixth floor. Elevators are out of bounds!"

I inferred from the way he paused that elevator use by recruits was a common infraction.

"For the duration of the course, you will only use the stairs."

The elevator ban concluded the in-clearance process and signalled the start of the trek to the sixth floor. In a discombobulated gaggle, we manually moved all our luggage up the stairs to our new home, the first of countless trips that would occur over the course.

Basic training for officers lasted twelve weeks. The first week's learning curve was steep as instructors outlined expectations and our daily routines. The instructors taught us military comportment through a jammed schedule and pedantically walked us through various orientation classes that covered a myriad of topics ranging from marching drills, military ranks and protocols, weapons handling, and physical fitness. Intermixed with lectures, we received copious amounts of military kit that had to be carried manually to the sixth floor. Raised in the construction industry, where I worked through high school and university to pay for my education, it had been ingrained in me that time is money. Consequently, it baffled me that we walked past perfect elevators to haul hundreds of pounds of kit up the stairs. Even more puzzling were the ensuing rebukes for being too slow.

On the ground floor, instructors yelled, "Hurry up, you're supposed to be in shape!"

While we hustled up the stairs, the instructors took the elevator. Upon arriving at the sixth floor, they criticized us again, asking, "What took you so long?"

Stunned by the insanity of the process, I had to exercise great restraint not to say, "If only this building had elevators."

I became frustrated with the relentless pace and make-work approach because there was an easier way to accomplish the task. In what world is it expected to walk by a perfect elevator while moving hundreds of pounds of kit to the sixth floor? It was ludicrous. On my fourth trip up the stairs one day, struggling under the weight of rucksacks, boots, and uniforms, I contemplated how all the items would fit into my tiny, university-sized dorm room. I didn't have to wonder long. When we finished hauling all our kit up the stairs, Sergeant Cook began his lecture on room standards.

In a common room immediately adjacent to our dorms, I quickly learned that there is a standard for everything in the military; this included dress, deportment, and our room layout. For example, the standard room layout required dress shirts to be ironed correctly and placed equidistantly apart in a specific order in the closet; each shelf held precisely folded items such as socks or t-shirts. The volume of details was a bit overwhelming. Thankfully, the instructors provided multiple 8 ½ X 11 photos that captured the standard. Although a bit excessive, the expectations seemed manageable until Sergeant Cook taught us how to make a bed. He emphasized the importance of folding the white bed sheet back over the grey fire blanked by precisely six inches in the most excruciating detail. He also showed us the techniques of using a Black & Decker clothing iron to get the white bedsheet as flat as a countertop.

The process struck me as exceptionally bizarre. What sane person irons their bed?

After making the bed to standard, Sergeant Cook demonstrated how to display our polished boots, shoes, and rifle. To prepare our weapons for inspection, they needed to be stripped and placed in a specific manner in the center of the bed. At the end of the lecture, Sergeant Cook produced another photo that would guide us for the remainder of the course.

"Troops, this is the room layout standard. Your first inspection will be tomorrow at 0700."

After a gruelling day of hauling gear in which I'd made multiple extra trips up the stairs to help some unfit platoon members, I prepared my room for inspection. While climbing into my bed, it dawned on me that the demands of the morning routine would make it challenging to make my bed to standard. I pondered the predicament as a I fell asleep.

The following morning, Sergeant Cook corrected my insolence. He came barging into my room at precisely 0700. I came to attention and presented myself as instructed.

"Officer Cadet Hallett, ready for inspection, Sergeant!"

Sergeant Cook stood so close I could smell his old spice. His beady eyes meticulously inspected me while transitioning from my boots to my uniform to my hair.

"Hallett, did you shave with a hot rock?"

The remark took me by surprise. No one had ever questioned me about shaving before.

"Uh, no, Sergeant, a Gillette Mac III, a gift from my mom."

Disgusted, he barked, "You missed a hair on your chin!"

Regretting the mom comment more than missing a hair on my chin, I listened to his footsteps on the linoleum floor as he went to my bed.

"Hallett, did you iron your white bed sheet?"

"Uh, yes, Sergeant," I stammered, confused by the question.

"Was the iron plugged in? It looks like you slept in your bed!"

I remained silent. Of course I slept in my bed; why else would a bed be in a bedroom? While I pondered the absurdity of the question, the inspection continued. Standing beside my bed, Sergeant Cook placed a metal, six-inch ruler on my white bed sheet. His foot began to tap similar to a countdown timer.

"Hallett, your bed sheet is only folded over five and seven-eighths! The standard is six inches! You're an engineer. Aren't you supposed to be good with numbers?"

Before I could respond, Sergeant Cook returned to my grill; his face was only six inches from mine. As anger inflamed his speech impediment, he could barely speak. He started to stutter so fast he sounded like a car that wouldn't start in winter because the words couldn't come out.

Eventually, he calmed down enough to spit out his rebuke.

"H-a-llett, little details are a big detail!" in a rapid, staccato cadence at 133 decibels.

He paused to regain control of his speech. He continued slowly but with the same passion as before.

"If-f-f you can't make your be-e-d-d and shave properly with your mom's razor, how are you supposed to be trusted to lead tr-o-o-o-ps in battle?"

I felt his stinging stare as he paused to let the message sink in: *trusted to lead troops in battle.* I respected his opinion as an Afghanistan veteran, but it didn't make sense. I didn't join the army to learn how to make my bed.

I thought "Sergeant Six-Inches" was ridiculous as he departed for the next room. What is the big deal? Undoubtedly, there had to be more critical items to worry about. It's just a bed.

Although I failed to see the importance of making an immaculate bed each morning, I schemed for ways to meet the standard and avoid further reprimands. Speaking with my peers, I discovered they were also equally inept at making their beds. Based on the morning routine of a five-kilometre run, showers, and eating breakfast, we didn't have enough time to make our beds unless we got up in the middle of the night. Brooding my predicament while walking up the stairs one afternoon, I stopped at the fifth floor to use the toilet. Since the entire floor was vacant, I could avoid the bathroom wait lines on the sixth floor, and by using another can, I helped keep our washroom clean for morning inspections. While enjoying some peace from the bustle of the sixth floor, I found a tri-wall box full of grey fire blankets in the hallway. An idea struck. Making my bed to standard was only a problem if I slept in it. So, I decided to commandeer two blankets and try something new.

Before going to bed that night, I prepared my room for inspection. I mopped the floor, dusted the window and made my bed precisely to standard. After lights out, I made a makeshift place to sleep with my freshly acquired fire blankets on the floor beside my actual bed. In the morning, I arose to an already "met standard" room. Instead of running around like a chicken with my head cut off to prepare for inspection, I just placed my fire blankets in the civilian lock-up, a spare room designated for storing civilian luggage that was excluded from room inspections. My pod mate, Mark, found my approach ingenious and followed suit. My other pod mate, Ryan, thought it was preposterous to sleep on the floor and that trouble would follow if we got caught. Getting caught sleeping on the floor seemed like the lesser of two evils, so Mark and I gladly accepted the risk. Soon after "Operation Makeshift Bed" was in full swing, Mark and I listened to Sergeant Six-Inches go nuclear on Ryan during the routine inspection one morning.

"Week two! You still can't make your bed!"

Not slowing down to control his stutter, he continued.

"Y-y-ou n-n-need to work with Hallett. He has it figured out!"

During week two, Sergeant Six-Inches began inspecting weapons for cleanliness. As a hunter with several rifles, I confidently knew how to clean a weapon. But once again, I grossly underestimated the standard. During an inspection, Sergeant Six-Inches barged into my room.

"Hallett, let's see if your rifle is clean."

In an overly dramatized move, he donned a white glove in front of me before inspecting my issued C7 rifle. Though I'd been around firearms most of my life, I'd never used a white glove to clean one. After rubbing it all over the exterior of my rifle with the flourish of a magician about to pull a rabbit from a hat, the glove remained snow-white. Sergeant Six-Inches then contorted his finger like a miniature Olympic gymnast into the breech and produced a minuscule amount of black grime. He proceeded to hold it in front of my face as if it was evidence in a murder trial.

"Hallett, your weapon is filthy! How do you expect this to work in battle?"

I thought, "I bet you a $100; the rifle will work just fine. Let's try."

However, I knew it was another rhetorical question, so I remained silent.

Staring at the gnat size spot on his white glove, I concluded that Sergeant Six-Inches was ridiculous. It was a misleading statement to say the rifle wouldn't function. But to avoid friction, I conformed to the military inspection standard. From that day forward, before, during or after a range, my rifle never saw oil. I kept my bolt and breech as dry as a popcorn fart.

The rest of basic training was relatively inconsequential to me. The weeks were filled with more practical training like physical fitness classes, weapons handling, and field exercises, which ultimately met the course's aim of orienting me to the military. Outside the course curriculum, I also learned that bureaucracy is part of the job and that sometimes it is not about agreeing with the organizational standard but conforming to it. Consequently, I received an introduction to the check-in-the-box notion, a phrase used repeatedly throughout the course that emphasized a perfunctory approach, completing a task merely just to comply with the standard rather than focusing on meaningful results. Over time, it became like a game; sometimes, you had to play along to survive. For example, the game with my bed. Untouched since the first week when I began to sleep on the floor, the inspection feedback was predicated on the instructor's mood, ranging from "nice bed" to "your bed looks like crap." The concept of playing a game to pass a course didn't bother me, but something seemed off in a military context. I didn't want to play a game in places where the military might send me. Consequently, a nagging feeling ensued that the check-in-the-box mentality wasn't right.

Although Sergeant Six-Inches and I didn't become best friends as he insinuated when we first met, we built a rapport over time. Deep down, I learned he genuinely had my best interests in mind.

For my last inspection, he barged into my room exactly the same as day one.

"Hallett, let's see if your rifle is clean."

Having gained confidence and a deeper understanding of the bureaucracy, I toyed with the process. To precede the inspection, I yelled out:

"Clean as a whistle, Sergeant. So clean she squeaks!"

After conducting the standard acrobatic moves with his fingers in search of a speck of dust, he found nothing.

"Great work. Your rifle meets the standard."

His tone indicated that he knew it was insane to have an unoiled rifle with an audibly squealing action; he was just inspecting it against the organizational standard.

"Your bed looks okay too."

For the last time on that course, he stood in front of me, face to face.

"All the best on your next course," he said with some civility, congratulating me on receiving my check-in-the-box for basic training. For a moment, he became human.

That was the last time I ever saw him.

# 2

# What's a Chimo?

After basic training, I moved to Canadian Forces Base Gagetown in New Brunswick. It's the only place where you can dig a fire trench on top of a hill and still somehow hit water. At the same time, Canada's involvement in Afghanistan continued to deepen with significant combat engagements like Operation MEDUSA. Every day, as I read the national news, I became acutely aware that I could deploy to Afghanistan in a little over a year.

The first part of combat engineer training is the Common Army Phase called "CAP." As a secondary duty of combat engineers is to fight as infantry, we learned baseline army skills such as advanced weapons handling, field craft, and section-level infantry tactics before moving to the Canadian Forces School of Military Engineering. Upon arrival at the engineering school, I learned the proud history of the Canadian Military Engineers. Combat engineers have been called *sappers* for generations, a term rooted from medieval times when armies laid siege to fortifications. A trench, referred to as a "sap," was dug up to and under the wall so it could be brought down with explosives. The French Army named this perilous task "driving a sap," and those brave enough to do it became known as *sappers*. Thus, the term continues to live on, and the legacy of the sapper is inseparable from that of military engineers.

We also learned the unique greeting and toast of Canadian Military Engineers: *Chimo*. More than just a word, Chimo is derived from the Inuktitut greeting "saim," meaning hello, goodbye, or peace be with you. After helping to develop Canada's North, engineers adopted the phrase Chimo, reflecting our friendly, helpful nature. Throughout my schooling at CFMSE, to acknowledge orders or to say farewell for the day, the students, in unison, often shouted Chimo!

Beyond the trade history and cultural norms, I learned that the role of the combat engineer is to ensure that troops can live, move, and fight on the battlefield while denying the same to the enemy. To perform this role, our training covered topics such as explosives, bridging, theories of landmine warfare and unexploded ordnance removal. However, it wasn't engineering doctrine or textbook instruction from the standard training plan that left the deepest mark. Instead, the indelible lessons came from a few unforgettable instructors.

Once armed with a basic understanding of dismounted engineering skills through hours of dull lectures, we deployed to the field on training exercises, eager to put theory into practice. Since we always needed to be ready to fight as infantry, our backpacks overflowed with gear. The extra weight of engineering gear piled onto standard infantry loads of ammunition, crew-served weapons, food, and water made it feel comparable to dragging small mountains on our backs.

On one of these exercises early in the course, we found ourselves under the frosty, hawk-eyed gaze of Captain Battey, a slim exchange officer from the United Kingdom's Royal Engineers. His cold, calculating gaze swept over us like a factory inspector trying to decide which parts of the assembly line to shut down. I was never quite sure if he had been born this way or if Gagetown's swampy wilderness had leached the warmth from his soul. Throughout the course, I kept my distance from him because he always seemed angry, ready to explode without warning.

While he kept mainly to himself in garrison, Captain Battey came to life in the field, scrutinizing us with laser focus as we stumbled through the dense foliage, attempting to conduct section attacks. Our first few attempts fell short of expectations. Some of us attacked with ferocious zeal, while others struggled to move, burdened under the weight of our gear and ensnared in Gagetown's unforgiving terrain. From where I stood, our section attacks resembled a drunken rugby team chasing a greased pig. Some guys charged forward like rabid wolverines, others got tangled in the underbrush, and at least one sapper fell so far behind that he disappeared for a couple of minutes, only to reappear looking confused and covered in twigs.

During a smoke break after one particularly abysmal assault, we reviewed the situation. To facilitate control and sustain a line-abreast formation, the student section commander suggested we slow down the more aggressive soldiers so the others could keep up. Captain Batty leapt out from the shadows like a scaled cat and roared.

"Slow down?" Batty's voice cracked through the afternoon air like a gunshot.

"Not on your bloody life!"

Startled by his sudden and rather explosive entrance, we froze, still as statues, as he tore into us with a ferocity none of us had seen before.

"You show me a soldier who plods on a battlefield, and I'll show you a corpse in a uniform!"

His voice carried like cannon fire as it echoed through the trees.

"*Speed and aggression* are what you should live and breathe on the assault!"

His scolding cut to the point.

"As leaders, your job is not to hobble the men but to spur them on! Do you think Nelson would have told his sailors to *steady on* when charging into battle?"

He paused momentarily before driving home his message.

"Never step on enthusiasm!"

His face flushed a violent shade of red, his hands trembling as he fought to rein in his temper. He took a deep breath, stalking back and forth like a caged tiger, ready to pounce. Despite the outrage, he genuinely wanted to knock some sense into us.

"If anything," he spat with utter disgust, "you bloody *harness* that enthusiasm!"

Up to that point, slowing down so others could keep up had been the standard response. It followed the logic that the strong uplift the weak, forging a team greater than the sum of its parts. Until that moment, I thought it was the right approach. However, refocusing the leader's attention to motivate the laggards was a fresh, counterintuitive perspective to my leadership training. Upon further reflection, I'd witnessed this many times in my construction jobs. I'd just never realized it until then. My old bosses came down with fire and hades to motivate laggard employees. On the contrary, they never slowed the top performers or hard workers down; they found a way to exploit them. They intuited the maxim, never step on enthusiasm.

Similar to the magnetic pull of iron to lodestone, the engineering school attracted a diverse cast of instructors. Another one of note was Sergeant Kruse, our gangly, mustachioed explosive trainer. With an unrivalled enthusiasm for explosives, he keenly stressed the minutia of basic charge preparations and had a reverence for duct tape. During lectures, he'd often quip, "Troops, nothing sticks to duct tape like duct tape." This expression became a running joke amongst the students, so much so that we'd often conclude every task involving duct tape by parroting, "Nothing sticks to duct tape like duct tape."

While instructing us how to prepare a basic charge of C4 explosives, Sergeant Kruse belaboured each step with a pedantic, physical demonstration. He took so long that I thought we would reach the explosive's expiry date before he finished. After Captain Battey's urging to use violent aggression to close with and destroy the enemy, Sergeant Kruse's meticulous demonstrations and lengthy screeds felt misplaced, and became unbearable.

With our weapon-handling drills, speed demonstrated competency. For example, you needed to rectify a stoppage in a certain amount of time to meet the standard; this made perfect sense. In combat, weapons systems must function, so rapidly rectifying a stoppage showed proficiency in a critical skill. I couldn't believe there were no equivalent time-related standards for creating a basic charge. Throughout history, sappers placed charges under enemy fire. Consequently, quickly creating a basic charge should have been seen as a critical skill as well. I couldn't fathom a scenario where I would take my sweet time to prepare explosives while embroiled in a gunfight.

Believing that speed would be seen as an asset, I moved with alacrity while rehearsing my charge preparations. When it came time for my one-on-one practical session, Sergeant Kruse immediately pulled in the reins.

"Slow down, Hallett. You must do it correctly. We don't want a misfire."

He didn't even look at my basic charge. Instead, he blindly assumed it contained errors because I prepared it quickly. Who says you can't make a basic charge in under two minutes? It's not rocket science.

"Hallett, let me show you again."

As if I missed the entire class demonstration, he started from scratch.

"First, you take the block of C4."

He slowly reached for an explosive training block. The rhythmic ticking of the wall clock filled the silence, each second stretching as he carefully progressed through the demonstration, his movements deliberate and unhurried.

"Now you cut the det cord so you can wrap your charge."

As the demonstration slowly proceeded, I fought the urge to crawl out of my skin. After reviewing knife safety as part of the process, reminding me to always cut away from myself, he finally proceeded to cut a piece of det cord for his presentation.

"Now, watch closely."

By this point, I gripped my det cord so tightly that my knuckles went white as I fought the urge to tie it into a noose – either for him or myself. He was so focused on strict adherence to the standard that he could only see my rapid pace as failing to understand what he was teaching. From my perspective, swiftly making a charge demonstrated competence. I wanted to interject but didn't because it would have only drawn out the process. Comparable to a government-automated voice message system with multiple options, if you pressed the buttons too fast to speed up the process, you'd often consume more time because you'd cause the system to restart. To avoid the risk of resetting his instructions back to the beginning again, I stood in silence while the demonstration played out at the same pace as a receding glacier.

The deliberate instructional approach frustrated me and butted up directly against my results-focused, time-is-money attitude. Adding insult to injury, when the second demonstration finally concluded, I remained unconvinced there were any problems with my original explosive charge. I thought I hid my irritation as I numbed myself to the process; I simply played the game of going through the motions to get my check-in-the-box for basic charge preparation so I could progress on the course. However, Sergeant Kruse asked me to remain behind the next day after dismissal.

"Hallett, have a read of this," presenting me with a brown folder.

The folder contained a red chit, a written reprimand for deficient performance and a poor attitude toward explosive handling standards. It was a slap on the wrist and a reminder to obey policy without question. I wanted to protest. However, as I sat in a sterile classroom devoid of critical thinking outside the standard, I figured that arguing about having a poor attitude only demonstrated a poor attitude. Moreover, I couldn't imagine anything more painful than a drawn-out conversation about the red chit.

"Where do I sign?"

Prepared for a skirmish, Sergeant Kruse had even brought a candy bar for a snack. My *let's get this over with* approach surprised him.

"Uh, at the bottom of the page."

I signed the document with the same velocity as I made my explosive charges and departed.

I left feeling torn. On one hand, speed and aggression were the standard for section attacks and weapon handling drills. On the other hand, systematic adherence to the process was the standard for explosive charge preparation. Since all three tasks might need to occur under enemy fire, I assumed proficiency and speed would be equally valued. I never imagined my hustle and verve to create a basic charge quickly would be viewed as a deficiency that required performance management. Even though I didn't have any experience to back up my thoughts about explosive preparations in the field, innately, the precise textbook approach felt wrong. Irrespective of the red chit, Sergeant Kruse and I just operated on different tempos. Like two machine components with different harmonics, we never got into sync for the remainder of my time at the school.

Fortunately, one instructor, Major Eric Noe, was a blast of fresh air that left a deep, enduring mark on me. A cheerful United States Army Corps of Engineers exchange officer who loved poker, he championed two mantras: "Know the threat" and "Ensure you are fit to fight." Due to his personality, recent deployment experience to Iraq, or a combination of the two, Major Noe had an unorthodox teaching approach. Compared to other instructors who focused on teaching the approved training plans, his instruction focused on contemporary needs, which often clashed with our curriculum's cold, rigid structure. Early on, he took issue with our weapon drills and provided sacrilegious direction to help prevent negligent discharges.

"Folks, your weapons will always be placed on safe."

A palpable ripple passed through the course as this edict contracted all engrained weapons handling drills. One of the sharper students protested.

"But sir, our weapon clearing drill manual doesn't support that."

Major Noe further elaborated on the reasoning for the order.

"Listen, negligent discharges are unacceptable. So, I also want to know the state of your weapon. I want to be able to see that it is on safe."

Another course candidate submitted that to put our weapons on safe, we would have to add an additional step to our weapons-clearing standards. He implied that amending the procedure would require higher-level approval from someone. Nobody knew how or where to find that someone. Major Noe remained unmoved.

"Folks, if anyone has an issue with it, tell them to come see me. My cubical is the one with the big American flag."

It never bothered me to breach the weapons handling policy. During some hunting trips growing up, we'd stretched the rules a few times with firearms. I didn't like putting my weapon on safe because it required readying the C7 before the safety mechanism would engage; however, pragmatically, it made sense, so without protesting, I complied. But overtly challenging the standard made a lasting impression. Up to that point in my military training, I'd never been exposed to that *modus operandi*. Major Noe didn't hesitate to challenge the system to mitigate a risk. With the ink still drying on my red chit for challenging the status quo, I found it refreshing to see an instructor challenging a standard. Maybe my thought process wasn't so out of line. Deeply intrigued, I started paying much closer attention to our American exchange officer.

Major Noe didn't take long to provide additional examples of challenging the standard. One morning during our physical training session, he created an exercise regime that involved a leopard crawl on a Gagetown league soccer field to compensate for shortcomings in our field craft abilities. The subsequent damage to the sacrosanct grass caused a base-wide inquest. Granted, he could have picked a better spot for the exercise, his intentions were genuine. But if you'd asked base leadership, you'd have thought he committed a war crime. As a bystander to the outrage, none of it made sense. The base appeared to have skewed priorities as the kerfuffle gave the impression that the soccer field turf was more critical than training soldiers for war. Meanwhile, casualty reports from Afghanistan routinely topped the national news.

Despite the grass inquisition, Major Noe sustained a steadfast resolve toward his two mantras: "Know the threat" and "Ensure you are fit to fight." The next lesson on Major Noe's curriculum was casualty evacuation training. Lacking resources because casualty evacuation was not a large part of the training standard, he procured a World War II vintage stretcher of his own volition. The thing was so old it looked as if he requisitioned it from the military museum. One morning, as we formed up for a morning run, Major Noe stood by his black Dodge Ram truck. Once we were all within earshot, he dropped the tailgate.

"Folks, you will take this stretcher and barrack box for a walk this morning."

Sensing our confusion, he elaborated.

"This is a stretcher. This box represents a casualty. Proceed to evacuate the casualty."

As a course, we humped a stretcher with roughly sixty pounds of boots in an oversized barrack box around Canadian Forces Base Gagetown. To avoid the soccer fields, we hiked around buildings and in wood lines mixed with spruce and pine trees to simulate casualty evacuation from the battlefield. Throughout the morning, I became increasingly irritated with the ad hoc process because, up until that point, PT had been relatively easy for me. Drenched in sweat, I struggled with the evacuation drill as the uneven terrain made the stretcher shift constantly—sometimes rising to chest level, other times dropping below my knees.

Cussing while carrying a cumbersome load through a circuitous course, Major Noe drilled us on the nine-liner; the term is a military lexicon for a standardized medical evacuation request that transmits critical information in nine brief lines over the radio to ensure a rapid and accurate medical response. To simulate battlefield chaos, Major Noe beat his chest similar to a deranged orangutan while making loud chopper noises with his mouth. I can only imagine what morning base commuters thought of the spectacle. We must have looked comparable to a low-budget nature documentary as twenty-five troops struggled to carry a box of boots around on an old stretcher while an American officer was yelling and beating his chest like a Neanderthal.

"Send your nine-Liner, over!"

By this point, the exercise utterly confused me. Why did we need to carry a loaded stretcher for so long? Without any combat experience, I thought there was no way a casualty evacuation could be this discombobulated and physically challenging. Every muscle in my arms screamed as I gritted my teeth while the rough wooden stretcher handles bit into my palms. The barrack box lurched with every uneven step, slamming against our waists. Finally, after an hour of tortuous walking, we turned towards the barracks, but Major Noe had another sadistic idea. As we proceeded to stop at our traditional spot, he provided a twist.

"Who said stop? The helicopter can't land here to pick up your casualty. You need to keep going!"

Now I was furious. A few of the physically fitter members of the course, like me, had carried the stretcher for a significantly disproportionate amount of time. I'd also become habituated to the morning schedule, a standard. Physically exhausted, Major Noe challenged me mentally with a simple trick of walking past the traditional stopping point. After a ten-minute encore, we stopped by Major Noe's black truck. With a devious grin, he spoke.

"Folks, you must also always have a casualty evacuation plan to properly care for your soldiers."

Sensing the last-minute walk extension required acknowledgement, he continued.

"And never forget, it isn't over until it is over. Stay ready to fight."

He paused to let his message sink in. Too tired to speak, I got his point.

"Now, get my boots back into the truck!" he barked.

As the tailgate slammed shut, the enlightening class, which was entirely outside the standard training plan, concluded.

Back in the classroom, Major Noe provided fresh insights into our training based on current events and his experience from Iraq. These insights often contrasted starkly with many Cold War tactics in the approved training plan. Furthermore, he stressed the fundamental requirement for officers to read. His candid input from contemporary books further encouraged us to think beyond doctrine. Detecting that we were not avid readers, he unilaterally added reading to the course training plan and assigned each student a military history book or military biography to read that would require a summary presentation towards the end of the course. Up until that time, I'd been a sporadic reader at best. However, the combination of Major Noe's advice and the Afghanistan war updates regularly appearing in the news made me see the value of reading, so I got a library card. In addition to course materials, I began to read books such as *The Other Side of the Mountain* and *The Bear Went Over the Mountain*, two books on the Soviet challenges with the Mujahideen, to prepare for a likely deployment to Afghanistan.

After nearly a year at the engineering school, we finally graduated. Just before the graduation parade, I received my posting to 1 Combat Engineer Regiment in Edmonton. Soon after, I learned I would deploy to Afghanistan within a few months as a combat engineer field troop commander. During the grad parade, my gaze drifted past the rigid ranks of freshly minted engineers as the guest speaker extolled about all we had learned at the school. I reflected on the lessons I had learned in addition to the mandated curriculum. Items like the importance of reading and a few guiding maxims: never step on enthusiasm, know the threat, and ensure you are fit to fight. On a much deeper level, I also learned that sometimes you must challenge convention for the right reasons. The critical nuance became knowing the right reasons, a risk management skill set that required further development. Armed with a mixture of knowledge regarding infantry tactics, engineering skills, and military standards, as well as examples of when to challenge the standard, I departed the Royal Canadian Engineering School of Excellence feeling a mix of trepidation and excitement for my first posting. *Chimo!*

# 3

# Opportunity Costs

In August 2007, after a rapid cross-country move, I reported to my new home unit, 1 Combat Engineer Regiment. The hallways buzzed with activity as troops prepared for deployment to Afghanistan as part of Operation ATHENA. I would be part of Roto 5, supporting the 2nd Battalion, Princess Patricia's Canadian Light Infantry battlegroup from Shilo, Manitoba.

With deployment scheduled for February, I arrived midway through the high-readiness training cycle, which typically lasted between twelve and eighteen months. Consequently, I didn't have time to ease in—I had to hit the ground running. After a brief welcome from the Commanding Officer, Lieutenant Colonel Ed Izatt, I dove into my duties.

I began by receiving a detailed handover from the outgoing troop commander. During the brief, I received an exhaustive overview of vehicle serviceability, personnel administration, and the upcoming training. Surprisingly, almost no white space remained in the calendar before deployment. With a packed schedule of individual training for vehicle qualifications, career courses, and exercises in Wainwright, plus leave, there was no room for errors. We had one chance to get the training right before deploying to Afghanistan.

Since I hadn't taken the traditional Royal Military College route into the Canadian Armed Forces, much of the administrative jargon and processes, such as unit employment records, leave management, and personnel files, were new. Although I understood paperwork would be part of the job, nothing in my training prepared me for the sheer volume or the relentless expectations to complete it. At the conclusion of my handover brief, the outgoing troop commander stated that I needed to meet the Squadron Second in Command (2IC) as he had additional administrative questions.

As I stared at the mountain of paperwork, I felt less like a combat engineering officer and more like an archivist working in the bowels on a national archive. Between forms requiring more signatures than a ceasefire treaty and personnel files thick enough to stop a bullet, my intuition told me that administrative work would be my real battle despite current events in Afghanistan. In the summer of 2007 alone, Canada suffered ten casualties. Despite this horrible fact about our future operating environment, our efforts continued to be primarily directed to completing administration, one file after another, instead of discussing contemporary threats. This focus made it feel as if I was more likely to drown in a sea of forms than get taken out by the Taliban. Slightly stunned by the deluge of files and training charts, I strode to the 2IC's office to continue the discussion on administration.

Walking into the 2IC's office resembled stepping into a shrine dedicated to the gods of bureaucracy. Towering stacks of manila folders lined the room like pillars of the Parthenon. To help him manage the massive paper structures, a clerk worked in the common area immediately adjacent to his office. Hundreds of precisely organized files in massive pelican cases surround him on the linoleum tile floor. Based on all the papers they used, they must have single-handedly deforested a British Colombia county. Sitting behind the paper fortress was Captain Bret Parlee, a commissioned-from-the-ranks fitness fanatic who looked like a dead ringer for Spider-Man's boss, Jonah Jameson.

"Hi John, I'm Bret. Welcome to the squadron."

His frank demeanour instantly won me over.

"I wish I had your job instead of this soul-sucking paperwork. Have a seat."

Bret got right to the point, briefing me on the squadron's operations and upcoming milestones for our forthcoming deployment. My first task was reviewing personnel files.

"John, you've got thirty files to chew through, top to bottom. It's your crash course in knowing your troops – and our chance to catch slip-ups before they bite us."

Correct administrative errors? I didn't even know about half of the forms and what they entailed. Now, I was responsible for correcting mistakes. I thought to myself, oh-boy, as Bret continued.

"For instance, Paul's will is from a do-it-yourself drugstore kit, which is about as legally binding as a pirate's treasure map."

A smile crossed my face as I tried not to laugh at the frugal attempt to meet the minimum legal benchmarks of a will. Although many sappers took the administration seriously, for some it was an after thought. Bret hardly paused before he highlighted another problem.

"Wayne needs to respect the Memorial Cross."

His Majesty's Canadian Government grants the Memorial Cross as a memento of personal loss and sacrifice for military personnel who lay down their lives for their country. Common recipients are the widows and mothers of Canadian sailors, aviators, and soldiers who died for their country.

"John, see here," Bret said, quickly pulling out a file and opening it to the document.

"I've got a hunch that the name on Wayne's Memorial Cross form is Lee's sister, another sapper in the unit he is trying to court. Untangle this mess!"

In an act of unparalleled romantic optimism, Wayne used military administration as a dating strategy – an approach so wildly inappropriate that it was almost impressive. I heard that troops got into shenanigans; however, being this cavalier with documents before a combat deployment was concerning. Bret was right. Beyond fixing paperwork, I had to ensure the troops were mentally prepared. Their mindset seemed questionable if they were hesitant to complete a will before going to war but bold enough to use government forms to pick up chicks.

"John, swing by at day's end to grab your files. Until then, dig into the ELAV training plan and get to know your troop warrant officer."

I replied enthusiastically, "Chimo!" despite not fully understanding the term ELAV. Having recently been trained on a Light Armoured Vehicle (LAV), I left to discover what the extra letter meant.

Beside Bret's office, a conference room hummed with squadron staff wargaming the upcoming training schedule. The world's most extensive Gantt chart filled an entire wall, with "Engineering Light Armoured Vehicle" (ELAV) being one of the many line items. Warrant Officer Merriam chaired the planning session. Affectionately known as Hollywood, he looked like a Marine recruiting poster with a crisp buzz cut. His no-nonsense energy radiated off him like static electricity. With a couple of decades of experience in the military, he became a savvy planner with a penchant for detail. After a quick introduction, Hollywood brought me up to speed on the ELAV training.

"Sir, we're the first squadron to roll out with ELAVs."

He went on to explain the key distinctions of the new vehicle in comparison to the LAV. The ELAV had a remote 7.62mm weapons system instead of the 25mm Bushmaster cannon. It also has a blade on the front to help dig in fighting positions and a hydraulic system to power various engineering tools. During the discussion, I learned that the vehicle would help revive engineering skill sets that had faded because we predominantly used armoured vehicles intended for infantry. However, I still didn't grasp the training concerns. Hollywood read my mind and explained the problem.

"Sappers are qualified LAV, but that won't cut it. We need to run conversion training to get them ELAV qualified."

Growing up, I learned to drive anything with wheels, sometimes without the unnecessary formality of a license. To me, the chassis of the two vehicles looked similar enough. Concerning the turret, the ELAV remote weapon system looked comparable to other machine guns in the Canadian Armed Forces. I couldn't grasp the severity of the problem. In my mind, it was no different than transitioning between different makes of concrete trucks – yet somehow, we were treating this transition as if it required a PhD in armoured vehicle operations. Granted, there are nuances between a MAC and a Western Star concrete truck, but a one-day orientation period for an already qualified driver should suffice. Missing the severity of the issue, I pried.

"Hollywood, how long is the conversion training?"

"Sir, we're still hammering out the conversion training standard. I guess it will be a few weeks before it's ready."

Again, it came back to meeting the standard.

Flabbergasted by the seemingly self-imposed problem set, I inquired further.

"We're in charge of creating a conversion training standard for a vehicle we're mostly qualified to use. Yet, we're concerned that our conversion training will take too long?"

Hollywood instantly understood my implication as a smile crossed his face.

"Sir, it doesn't work like that."

I didn't understand. Throughout my orientations to the squadron, everyone expressed concern about insufficient time to complete all our training. Yet here we were, consuming copious amounts of time on conversion training between similar vehicle platforms. At the time, I didn't know enough to rebuttal further; however, I immediately started wondering about the opportunity costs of the conversion training.

Capitalizing on my visit to the office, Hollywood sought clarification on my qualifications.

"Sir, do you have 404s?"

404s are military terminology for a driver's license with the Department of National Defence. Typically, officers don't drive vehicles; however, Hollywood was in a pinch. Based on all the other squadron commitments, he didn't have enough drivers to move all the vehicles for the upcoming exercise. I proudly pulled out my license thinking my previous civilian experiences could help.

"I don't have 404s, but I have a commercial trucking license in Alberta."

He chuckled. Thinking he misunderstood, I elaborated.

"I drove trucks in industry before joining the military. I can drive anything on the road."

Hollywood just grinned.

"Sir, you are wet behind the ears. It doesn't work like that. I'll figure something out. Big Chi, little Mo, Sir!"

This was Hollywood's affectionate customization of the word "Chimo." In this context, it meant "goodbye, your greenhorn pragmatic suggestions aren't helpful. Go away." I felt discouraged witnessing the expenditure of resources to solve seemingly self-imposed problems. Perplexed, I departed to meet my troop warrant.

Our troop office consisted of several desks in a common area with some adjoining offices to allow for private conversations. As I rounded the corner, the office was alive with chatter.

"I'm just waiting to meet the new sprog. Then, I'm going home for *date night* with the wife."

As I entered the room, several sergeants were chuckling at what the warrant officer implied by date night.

"Hi, I'm Lieutenant John Hallett, the new sprog."

After this slightly awkward entrance, the warrant jumped up to greet me. His name was Terence Wolaniuk, but he commonly went by Wally.

"Hey, Sir, we're all excited to meet you."

In his mid-thirties, he had a strong, rugged build, a let's get after it attitude, and a great sense of humour. Outside the military, he was an avid outdoorsman who enjoyed spending time with his family at their lake lot. I didn't know then, but he'd become the perfect command team partner.

After energetically introducing me to several section commanders, Wally suggested we walk around the unit compound to get acquainted. During our stroll, Wally exuded unparalleled passion for his job. If there was a quintessential combat engineer, it was him. Happily married with two sons, Wally had proudly deployed at every rank; his most recent deployment was as a recognizance Sergeant in Afghanistan. He passionately shared concerns about the contemporary explosive threats in Kandahar from reading the news, which was a breath of fresh air after drowning in paperwork throughout the morning. It quickly became apparent that we were like-minded. As the day wound down in the troop office, Wally brought up some seemingly trivial matters.

"Sir, for the upcoming exercises, I'm fighting to get pockets on our sleeves, kicking boot bands to the curb, and a shaving exception."

After a few follow-up questions, I learned these minor issues had sparked heated debates with the squadron sergeant major. Even on exercise, the standard dress code remained the same. I could live with wearing boot bands and shaving, but not addressing the pocket issue hindered our ability to function. Once we donned our body armour, we covered all the traditional pockets on our tunic, which made it hard to access simple items like paper and a pen without getting half undressed. Pockets on our sleeves solved this problem. But the squadron sergeant major held steadfast to the standard and prohibited the tailoring of military clothes to make them more functional in the field.

His ears must have been burning as he happened to pass by the office door at that exact moment.

"Wally, don't corrupt your new boss with ragged dress code ideas!"

I turned to see who barked the remark and saw a corpulent man filling the doorway. He looked anything but fit to fight. After quick introductions and a brief chinwag, we all departed for home.

Walking to my car, which I could drive in civilian life but not in the military, I reflected on my first day. The national headlines continued to contain Afghanistan casualties, yet only Wally mentioned the word threat. His focus also aligned with my priority of ensuring the troops were fit to fight. Though I didn't fully understand the rationale behind his concerns about shaving and boot bands, I admired his moxie and passion. Without a doubt, he had an enthusiasm that could be harnessed.

Unfortunately, the refreshing conversation with Wally was short-lived. The following month became a whirlwind of ceaseless administration and planning for exercises in Wainwright. Every time we completed a piece of administration, two more pieces of paperwork came to the funeral. Beyond wills and Memorial Cross forms, there were troop movement manifests, feeding plans, and vehicle transportation requests. Furthermore, we needed to take rules of engagement briefs, complete medical screenings, receive medical vaccinations, and submit power of attorney forms and life insurance documents; it was endless. Exacerbating the challenge of forming a cohesive unit, half of the troop was scattered across the country attending career courses or critical qualification training required to go to Afghanistan. To an outside observer, it would be next to impossible to see how my daily grind in the office prepared a troop to deploy on a combat mission to Afghanistan. Even I started to doubt whether I was on the right path.

I couldn't drive a car in the military with a commercial trucking license, and the ELAV conversion training consumed an exorbitant amount of time. As I wrestled with the bureaucratic frustrations, my civilian friends were thriving and making small fortunes in Alberta's booming oil and gas industry. I never dared share my frustrations with them; they'd laugh me out of the room and remind me that I had volunteered to go. Far more comfortable in the field than in garrison, the cumbersome military bureaucracy became my worst nightmare.

To make time for additional training, such as live-fire ranges, physical fitness, and in-depth reviews of actual post-IED reports with the troop, I looked for ways to streamline tasks. Having little agency over the training schedule, the only item I truly controlled was the amount of time spent on paperwork. Therefore, I naively took a minimum standard approach to administrative duties to free up time to read, study, and pass on information about the contemporary threats in Afghanistan. Comparable to an Olympic high jumper who just needed to clear the bar so they could progress to the next round, I felt the same about paperwork in the context of going to war. Any additional effort expended to exceed the bar created an opportunity cost by using unnecessary energy that may be required in later rounds of the competition. If we just met the standard with our administration, we could free up some time and energy to address training shortfalls.

For example, before dismissing the troops each day, Wally and I would address them in our lines and pass on upcoming training milestones and objectives. With the bit of extra time freed up with my new approach to administration, we were able to study and highlight germane points from newspaper articles, passages from books or recent intelligence reports from Afghanistan. As I had never deployed, I had no experience to offer on many of the points raised by our research. However, raising points catalyzed senior non-commissioned officers with real experience to speak up and share their knowledge with the young sappers. We regularly tossed different ideas at the troops, like throwing mud at a wall so some would stick. I learned this approach from the work of Lieutenant Colonel Dave Grossman, who wrote *On Killing* and *On Combat*. To help soldiers endure combat's corrosive psychological and physical effects, he championed a simple but powerful principle: forewarned is forearmed. That line resonated with me deeply, and I made it a daily goal to forewarn the sappers about an item they may face in Afghanistan. I didn't realize it then, but years later, I came to see forewarned is forearmed as one of the most profound phrases—one I might have never learned if I had focused on perfecting administration instead of simply meeting the administrative standard.

Unfortunately, my minimum standard approach for paperwork clashed horrifically with the organizational requirement. In retrospect, I lowered the bar too much in certain areas, resulting in some frank mentoring sessions from Bret. Although on the surface it appeared to be a clash about the administrative standard, it actually came down to priorities between contingent and preventative actions. In the event of a casualty, the military needed accurate paperwork to respond with contingent actions. On the other hand, I had a bias towards preventative actions to try and prevent the casualty from happening. One approach focused on keeping the sapper alive while the other dealt with the unfortunate circumstances if they became a casualty.

At the time, without the hindsight of experience, the administrative clash weighed heavily on me and kept me up at night. Buried under layers of red tape with no reprieve, I began questioning my decision to leave the hot Alberta economy for a deployment to Afghanistan. With my doubts nearing a breaking point, I needed to talk to someone I trusted— someone who understood and could offer sound advice. So, I turned to my grandfather, Grandpa Bill. A stoic World War II signals veteran, we formed a close bond during my university years. To save money while earning my engineering degree, I lived in his basement while attending school. During that time, he became more than just my grandfather, he became a mentor and a close friend. The time we spent together became one of the most formative periods of my life. At eighty-eight years of age, I knew he'd offer candid answers to my questions.

Over coffee at his veneered kitchen table, I vented about the military's obsession of means over ends and how disconnected the deployment preparations felt from the national headlines I read about the war. Grandpa Bill listened patiently as the momentum of my monologue slowly waned. He didn't say anything, but by his slight nods and smiles, it felt as if I'd just described the military he joined during World War II. Holding his cup of coffee, Grandpa didn't have much to add.

"John, go."

He took a sip of java before he concluded his thought.

"Just don't be scared to shoot first."

He never said much, but his words always packed a punch. In two simple comments, Grandpa Bill helped my mind untie the Gordian knot I had created. His terse answer cut through my anxiety as I remembered that I had joined the military for an experience; it just differed from my expectations. His short response also reminded me to keep things simple and to remain grounded in the basics: know the threat and ensure you are fit to fight.

As a result of that conversation, I earnestly returned to my duties with a renewed vigor and confidence in my decision to join the military. To ensure that I was ready to go, I met with my boss, Major Nathan Packer the week before a series of back-to-back three-month-long exercises in Wainwright. He was a short, redheaded, boisterous man with a taste for expensive art and worldwide liquor. He also wasn't afraid to speak his mind - a trait that often clashed with the more prosaic expectations of an officer and frequently landed him in trouble.

"Morning, John. Your writing skills suck, and administration isn't exactly your strong suit, but you're a solid fit with the squadron. I like how you've meshed with your warrant."

I took engineering to avoid writing because I found it challenging. Now, I needed to write daily. Ironically, the job description advertising combat engineering did not mention that writing skills were essential for almost every garrison task beyond getting a coffee or going to the bathroom. Major Packer took a moment to put a wad of chew in his mouth before continuing.

"You've already had a section commander and a sapper quit because they weren't committed. Some operational reserve officers would give their left nut to be in your spot as they want to deploy to Afghanistan. If we need to tap into the operational reserve because you have doubts about the deployment, we should do it now. So, are you in?"

Still getting used to his blunt approach, I chuckled at his candid comments about my detest for paperwork. Despite concerns about training priorities creating some opportunity costs we couldn't afford to pay, I remained resolved to see my commitment through. With a litany of unanswered questions lingering in my head about some of the forthcoming challenges, I kept it simple.

"Sir, I'm in."

# 4

# Relevancy

Canadian Forces Base Wainwright is located a couple hundred kilometres east of Edmonton. Once a buffalo national park, it was leased by the Department of National Defence during World War II to establish a training facility. The base is home to the Canadian Manoeuvre Training Centre, a formation responsible for delivering immersive collective training to the Canadian Armed Forces.

From the outset, Alberta's prairies seemed to be an odd choice to prepare for a deployment to Afghanistan. With its wide-open fields, scattered clops of deciduous trees, and gently rolling terrain, the area bore little resemblance to Afghanistan's dust, heat, and canalizing terrain of adobe compounds and grape fields. Some previous battlegroup rotations had opted to conduct collective training on bases in the United States that offered desert-like terrain. Due to financial restraints or unavailability of alternative locations, all our training for a predominately summer deployment to Afghanistan occurred during the fall in Wainwright.

Military training generally follows the progression of "crawl, walk, run." Until Wainwright, our preparation focused primarily on individual "crawling" skills such as weapons systems, advanced first aid and explosives. Concurrently, folks like Hollywood worked tirelessly to ensure we had enough qualified drivers, gunners, and crew commanders for our pack of vehicles. Wainwright would be the first time our squadron came together to provide close engineering support to the 2nd Battalion, Princess Patricia's Canadian Light Infantry-led battlegroup. The next few months would offer us ample opportunities to work together as the training plan consisted of three consecutive exercises. Each one increased in complexity, culminating in a collective all-arms live fire range that involved hundreds of soldiers. Comparable to an orchestra composed of wind, percussion, and brass sections, the Wainwright exercises allowed us to practice together to form a symphony of destruction.

A sprawling temporary camp was established inside the training area to support the legions of training troops. Dozens of green modular tents stood in tight rows, each crammed with aluminum cots. The air was thick with the mingling scents of sweat, boots, and vehicles while the distant hum of generators filled the background. A massive dining facility churned out steaming plates of food, and rows of portable toilets lined the outskirts like silent sentinels. At the centre of it all, the headquarters pulsed with radio chatter and the constant movement of troops.

From the onset of communal living with the battlegroup, we started learning each other's rhythms and formed relationships with our respective rifle companies and armoured squadrons. The advantages of living with engineers quickly became apparent to our combat arm peers as we received random requests to improve life around the camp.

"Hey, Chimo, can you fix the tent line generator?"

Simple requests such as this could take hours for a response from a garrison-based technician but only took minutes with one living a few tents away. Before long, random requests became common as folks witnessed our skill sets with tools. On another occasion, a company sergeant major inquired about a project.

"Hey, Chimos, can you build a table for the smoking area?"

In our downtime, we'd drudge up lumber from various sources to build picnic tables and smoke shelters, transforming austere portions of the camp into a more habitable space with power, smoking shacks, and seating. As we were augmented by reservist sappers, soldiers who left their day jobs to deploy to Afghanistan on our rotation, we had further skill sets to draw upon, such as trades-qualified carpenters. Additionally, heavy equipment assets significantly eased the traditional grunt work of filling sandbags to help secure bivouacs from the gale-force winds that had the propensity to blow modular tents across the prairies. Through completing small party tasks around camp, we showcased some tasks engineers could do to help the army live, move and fight.

Unfortunately, my introduction to Wainwright started with a bang, literally. While preparing the LAV for a range, one of our sergeants tried to power the auxillary systems. While poking around the driver compartment, attempting to start the engine, he erroneously pushed the manual activation button for the Automatic Fire Extinguishing System (AFES), a critical fire safety component in armoured fighting vehicles. This launched halon gases and carbon dioxide into vehicle compartments to suffocate the fire. At first, I didn't think much about it until Major Packer summoned me to the command post.

"John, what the hell? Why is a non-qualified driver poking around the driver's hatch?"

I was momentarily confused about why you needed to be qualified to be in the driver's hatch, as I'd often slept in it because the seat reclined nicely. Then, I recalled not being able to drive a staff car. I explained that we were learning to live out of the vehicle and had an accident.

"John, you can't be so cavalier with qualifications, or somebody will get hurt! AFES systems consume oxygen to put out fires – it could have suffocated soldiers."

Major Packer paused as radio chatter filled the command post. I never imagined a simple mistake could turn the armoured vehicle into a death trap.

"This incident also created a pile of paperwork because troops were exposed to the AFES gases. Be smarter going forward!"

Major Packer's rebuke hit me like a gut punch and caused a stern self-assessment. I'd been so focused on learning to fight the enemy that I hadn't considered the dangers lurking in our equipment–the tools meant to keep us alive. At that moment, I realized it wasn't just about enemy bullets and bombs; sometimes, deadly threats came from our mistakes. I hadn't fully grasped, considered, or appreciated these potential risks and their ramifications.

We also had to contend with Canada's environmental regulations designed to mitigate risks to the training area. Though vital for protecting the environment in Canada, sometimes these rules felt absurd in a military training scenario. For example, you wouldn't stop a river crossing in a theatre of war because you didn't have a permit. Environmental limitations also prohibited engineering operations in certain zones to prevent habitat damage. In some cases, the rules became so overzealous they became a joke amongst the troops.

"Watch out for fornicating frogs!"

Although environmental limitations were essential to protect waterways and species at risk, they clashed in the context of training for war. Consequently, and unintentionally, they severely limited our ability to practice and demonstrate crucial skill sets. The starkest example of this occurred while we assisted with the remediation of a bridge abutment over the Battle River. Significant preparatory work occurred by Wainwright staff behind the scenes before we arrived to capitalize on the resources available during the exercise. By doing so, the base could repair their crossing site, and we could receive realistic training. The symbiotic project worked great except for the deviations from doctrine because of environmental policies. For instance, tasking sappers to monitor spill kits and place secondary containment devices was required to meet environmental laws, not military doctrine. I didn't think too much about it until Wally commented disapprovingly.

"It's tough to be tactical with rooster dink pink buoys."

In the event of a spill, prepositioned containment kits of all shapes, sizes, and colours lined the river edge to comply with environmental regulations. As a result, our tactical river crossing felt less like a military exercise and more like a children's birthday party. With bright floats ready for deployment in the water and snow-white absorption materials lining the shore that resembled decorations, the only thing missing was a clown to make balloon animals.

Furthermore, the environmental administration required to work around Canadian waterways, plus the risks of a mishap such as a soldier drowning, precluded the physical crossing of a water feature. To ensure we received our obstacle crossing check-in-the-box, exercise staff improvised by creating a makeshift crossing site out of white mine tape and metal pickets in an open field. With white tape representing the water feature, we progressed through crossing site requirements on the radio.

"Security forces set."

Engineers proceeded to create a safe lane by removing a section of mine tape before transmitting on the radio.

"Breach open."

With an open lane across the fictitious obstacle, the infantry and armoured assets poured through like water racing by a busted dam to form a bridgehead. A laudable effort to represent an obstacle, the idea of fording a river defined by metal pickets and reflective tape in an open field misrepresented reality. Although the simulation allowed commanders to practice critical obstacle-crossing coordination, it didn't simulate mishaps - failed breaches on real obstacles have consequences.

On one occasion while breaching the white tape obstacle, the ELAV broke down before creating a lane. Instead of assets piling up on the near side of the obstacle, a keen infantry section simply created a lane by moving the mine tape themselves. Being just as qualified as us to move mine tape, the failed crossing site became a momentary glitch. But in reality, a broken piece of engineering equipment could be a showstopper, causing the breach to fail entirely. If engineers could not clear a path through an obstacle, commanders required a more robust contingency plan than relying on the infantry. Already disappointed with the scenario, Wally expressed frustration on the vehicle intercom after witnessing the infantry seamlessly substitute for engineers.

"The setup is so bad. We can't even do it right the wrong way."

At the time, I believed the risk was misemploying engineers due to exercise restraints; however, it started to become apparent that the real risk was misunderstanding engineers. The Armoured Engineering Vehicle (AEV) provided a stark example. Built upon a tank chassis, the AEV is heavily protected and equipped with a dozer blade and a mechanical excavation arm that allows the operators to clear and maintain passageways through obstacles under fire. As crossing sites deteriorate with vehicle passage, AEVs are a critical asset for expediently repairing lanes through obstructions. But when your obstacle is represented by a piece of tape on firm ground, there is no requirement to repair or maintain breach lanes. As a result, folks started questioning the requirement for an AEV as it consumed just as much fuel as a tank without demonstrable results. During one serial, this escalated into a heated exchange during a scenario hotwash.

"The AEV is just a tow truck. It's not worth the fuel."

The comment from an armoured officer was justified in the training scenarios. With environmental limitations, the AEV contributions were limited to being another recovery vehicle instead of a critical mobility asset. Hearing the comment, Major Packer detonated.

"The AEV is not a tow truck!"

He then vehemently extolled the vehicle's capabilities when not restrained by the exercise limitations and Canadian environmental laws. In the end, we continued to receive fuel. However, I felt it was more to placate Major Packer's boisterous comments than because they valued the AEV's unique capabilities.

In addition to environmental laws, Wainwright's status as a long-standing training ground provided further restraints. Range standing orders prohibited digging in most areas without extensive clearance operations or the use of certain armoured assets due to the high risk of unexploded ordnance (UXOs) scattered throughout the terrain. Without this safety measure, a heavy equipment operator could become gravely injured or killed if they detonate a legacy munition while digging. This safety restraint, combined with a comprehensive oil and gas pipeline network crisscrossing the area, made it almost impossible to dig in most locations without completing paperwork to receive dig clearances. The industry standard of "call before you dig" applied in the range training area to ensure the health and safety of the troops, but it also created another unrealistic requirement in the context of war.

For example, in Afghanistan, I would never say, "Sorry, sir, we can't dig. I need to speak with the call before you dig crew first."

As a result of the dig permit challenges, instead of physically digging in defence positions, we hypothetically outlined what we would create if permitted to dig. The conversation between me and the Officer Commanding (OC) of the infantry company or armoured squadron became rather hollow as imaginary usage of heavy equipment sufficed to get the "build a defensive position" check-in-the-box.

"Sir, we could dig a couple of hull-down positions here and here. We could also create a few shell scrapes."

"Great work, John! Nice to have the engineers here."

This cordial but borderline fruitless conversation frustrated me because millions of dollars of equipment sat idle while we could only talk about their capabilities. Academically, during trades training, we conducted "Tactical Exercises Without Troops" or TEWT, which means exactly as the name implies. We discussed options about what would occur if troops and equipment were present. It irritated me to continue the TEWT-like conditions while we could physically hear and smell the heavy equipment's diesel engines. I knew we could offer much more, but we were forced to tell what we could do instead of show results.

On a much deeper level, this verbal-only approach removed a primordial aspect of engineering work: tangibility. Without the ability to physically dig, we missed training opportunities to gauge the time and effort required to build a defensive position. The absence of hands-on physical work also compromised our comprehension of logistical requirements. Factors such as having mechanical technicians available and ordering unique heavy equipment parts and maintenance schedules were overlooked because they were not required; however, this would become a critical necessity to sustain heavy equipment in Afghanistan's harsh operating environment. Much more concerning, our infantry and armoured counterparts never physically witnessed or experienced what engineers could contribute.

In all fairness, exercise planners did their best within their limitations by making ample "stick-time" opportunities available for heavy equipment operators. Unfortunately, it occurred in a rear-area sandbox away from the main body of troops. Though it simplified administration for getting dig permits and provided an excellent environment for operators to hone their skills, the isolated environment did little to educate fellow combat arms about the capabilities and challenges of working with heavy equipment. As a result of all these challenges and a predominantly verbal-only approach to many tasks, engineering input became increasingly superficial as the exercise progressed.

Despite the physical limitations to engineering employment, the initial weeks of the exercise provided outstanding opportunities for cross-training between different combat arms trades. The infantry taught room-clearing drills while the armoured troops familiarized us with the Leopard 1 and Leopard 2 tanks. In exchange, we conducted basic explosive training, giving everyone a taste of our trade. Most importantly, we formally taught Explosive Threat Hazard Awareness Training (ETHAR), a critical course given that IEDs were the leading threat in Afghanistan.

ETHAR aimed to give soldiers training to react to a variety of explosive threats such as mines, unexploded ordinances, or Improvised Explosive Devices (IEDs). As ETHAR instructors, Wally and I were proud of our work, though we continually faced requests to compress the course timeline. Due to jammed-packed training schedules, what started as a five-day training package was whittled down to less than a day. I found the incessant demands to reduce the course alarming and dangerous because I thought ETHAR training was vital based on the explosive threats in Afghanistan. I distinctly recall one officer asking about expediting the training.

"Hey John, can we make this happen quicker? I don't want to miss cultural awareness training."

I couldn't believe my ears based on the explosive threats I continually read about in the national news. Instead, this captain prioritized an orientation course to educate soldiers on Afghanistan's values, attitudes, basic language and history over

ETHAR. I assumed he held a copy of the Koran in his hand as part of his efforts to become more culturally aware. One of us had our priorities backwards. Ironically, I had to blow off cultural awareness to support countless short-notice training requirements so everyone could get their "attended ETHAR" check-in-the-box.

Regrettably, the underestimation of IED carnage extended beyond ETHAR training. To simulate an IED during exercise scenarios, we used metal tubes filled with baby powder. When triggered, a carbon dioxide charge created a large white cloud. The simulation worked great for training reaction drills to an IED strike but failed to capture the visceral terror of the real thing. An actual IED didn't just make a white dust cloud; it shredded metal, ripped through flesh and made the world explode into fire and chaos. However, for safety reasons, we didn't have options to simulate being close to real explosions. I didn't know it at the time, but preparing for an IED strike is like training to be in a horrific car accident. Despite the best efforts and training value provided by the powder tubes, they misrepresented reality. The fact some of us emerged from simulated IED strikes smelling like a freshly changed diaper instead of being concussed, if we were still lucky enough to be alive, underscored the stark discrepancy between our training and reality.

Unbeknownst to me, the continual limitations imposed on engineering tasks during the exercise caused significant discontent with my peers. With all the limitations, the infantry began to discount suggestions on manoeuvrability or survivability because it made no sense given the context of the exercise. In some cases, we were ignored or dismissed when dealing with simulated IED strikes. Without an actual explosion that would make the route impassible with a blown-up vehicle and a large crater in the road, it became practically impossible to stop commanders from simply bypassing IED scenes because they had freedom of manoeuvre on the prairies. At the time, I empathized with them because it made sense. Who was I to stop a convoy of vehicles from simply driving around a simulated IED scene that consisted of white mine tape and pickets, and smelt like baby powder? I lacked the experience to interject and correct the misconception, so I went with the flow and "played the game" of going through the motions so we could get our "respond to an IED" check-in-the-box.

Eventually, under-employing engineers reached a boiling point during a hotwash towards the end of our first exercise. In a military context, a reserve plays a crucial role on the battlefield because it provides adaptability. Composed of various assets to fit the situation, it can reinforce weakened positions, exploit vulnerabilities or counter unexpected threats. During the exercise scenarios, engineers became increasingly employed as reserves, not because the situation required our skillsets to be employed in that role but because our unique talents were misunderstood, so we were seen as just another infantry platoon. Major Packer openly expressed frustrations about the marginalization of engineers. One obnoxious outburst concluded with something technical like: "This is bullshit! Engineers are not just reserves!"

While the battle about properly employing engineers ensued, I started winning my battles with administrative protocols. Bret provided some feedback after I filled out a spill report for a 25-litre LAV hydraulic oil leak.

"John, I'm impressed you filled it out. As you know, reporting spills over 20 litres is mandatory. To avoid the paperwork, most folks would have said it was a 19.9 litre spill."

Sitting beside him in the command post, Hollywood smirked.

"Sir, I found your spill report's food and coffee stains the most compelling."

Behind Hollywood hung a large whiteboard, meticulously arranged with individual magnets representing each piece of kit and troop member. The pristine layout couldn't have clashed more with my soiled paperwork. About to leave, Hollywood spoke.

"Hey, sir, I see you read a lot. Brought you a book. Thought you might like it."

Hollywood handed me a well-worn copy of *Semper Fi* by W.E.B. Griffin. It was the first in a series of books known as *The Corps* that told a fictional story about the Marines during World War II and the early years of the Korean War.

"Thanks, Hollywood, much appreciated."

Accepting the book and the reminder to continually improve my administrative skills, I also noted that I would never have an oil spill of more than 19.9 litres.

The first exercise ended with mixed emotions. Despite limitations, we made significant progress bonding with other units, honing sapper skills, and preparing for the next stage of training. However, the restraints on engineering tasks remained a point of frustration, particularly when they marginalized our involvement to the point of being dismissed. As a result, we began to fight for relevancy. We became the default response to form a reserve when irrelevant to an exercise scenario.

Initially, I worried about being continually misemployed. After reflection, I realized the more pernicious issue was being misunderstood. While the tirade about engineering employment in the reserves ensued, I remained quietly confident that it wasn't if our capabilities would be understood or appreciated; it was just a question of when. My intuition told me it would be a different conversation in Afghanistan. That poise stemmed from a seemingly inconsequential briefing I received as a student back at the engineering school from Major Mark Gasparotto and Captain Anthony Robb, two sappers who were Afghanistan veterans from Operation MEDUSA. Freshly returned from Afghanistan, they spoke to the students about the gamut of engineering challenges they faced, one being interactions with other soldiers and engineering advice in the battlespace. Their points lingered in my mind like an unshakeable echo because they spoke calmly and with surety, as if they were teaching us that water flowed downhill. Whether they intended to convey it so bluntly, or potentially I took it out of context, the main takeaway I noted from their brief was: If manoeuvre commanders don't listen to engineer advice, they die first.

# 5

# The Debutant Ball

The next stage of our deployment preparations was a live-fire exercise made up of progressively complex ranges, designed to prepare us for combat scenarios using live ammunition. To replicate the rugged terrain of Afghanistan, mock villages dotted the Wainwright training area. These structures, crafted from sea cans and plywood frames, were arranged in varied layouts. Rows of round straw bales surrounded numerous mock buildings, mimicking the typical walls of Afghan homes. Dispersed around these structures were fortress-like "grape huts" made of stacked hay bails to represent the thick adobe buildings used to dry raisins in Afghanistan. By progressing through the exercise scenarios, we refined soldiering skills, increased inter-operability with other units and became accustomed to operating around the clock with live ammunition.

The first-range serial underwhelmed me. Despite incorporating some simple engineering tasks such as breaching a row of hay bails that simulated a grape field or a plywood wall that replicated a compound door, it felt as if few would notice if the engineers didn't participate. For example, an overzealous infantry section used their LAV to push through a row of hay bales to form a breach lane. This practical solution was difficult to argue against in the simulated scenario, but it was a highly improbable feat with a real adobe wall. In another instance, a soldier leaned against the mock wooden structure, and a portion of the wall fell over. As a result, the infantry and armoured assets moved with relative ease throughout the battlefield without engineering support, so once again we were disproportionately assigned less integral roles like providing flank security or forming a portion of the reserve.

Given the scenario, it was tough to fault the manoeuvre commander. Had I been in their shoes, I likely would have employed engineers similarly since minimizing the coordination between entities resulted in increased speed and violence during the attack. Watching the first couple of scenarios play out from my vehicle, it became apparent that the exercise's main effort rested with combat arms getting their check-in-the-box for live fire and manoeuvre, not for engineers to provide mobility support to the assaults. Fortunately, the ranges did provide some unintended value by giving the sappers time to overcome numerous challenges with the ELAV.

The honeymoon phase with the ELAV faded quickly during the live fire exercises. Initially seen as a brand-new, reliable vehicle to replace some well-worn LAVs, some design limitations emerged. While preparing for another range serial in the staging area, I spoke with Corporal Richer, our subject matter expert championing the ELAV conversion training. A happy-go-lucky sapper and pocketknife aficionado, he possessed an innate mechanical aptitude which made him the perfect ELAV specialist to optimize the new vehicle.

"Sir, frankly, it's a bit of a Frankenstein machine. The blade and mine-clearing package are retrofits pulled off operational stock M113s, and integrating them here has been... a challenge."

Corporal Richer outlined how the ELAV designers drew upon old stock of interchangeable items to save costs or used surplus parts from a national warehouse in Montreal. As a result of the hodgepodge of vehicle components, the sappers had to continually experiment with and tweak them to optimize performance. Corporal Richer gave the front blade a light kick that caused a six-inch knife in a leather case to oscillate on his belt. Pointing to the machine gun on top of the vehicle, he continued.

"The Remote Weapon System is the older model pulled from the RG-31s, so it lacks stabilization."

The stabilization system for armoured vehicles is designed to enhance the accuracy of mounted weapons while the vehicle is in motion. Through gyroscopic stabilizers, sensors, and computers, the system counteracts the effects of uneven terrain, vehicle movement, and weapon recoil so the gunner can maintain precise accuracy while moving. Without this system, the ELAV could only fire accurately when stationary. I found it odd that the latest vehicle incorporated an older weapon system. To highlight another concern, Corporal Richer walked to the back of the vehicle.

"Sir, the hydraulic tool system isn't suited for combat operations. The hydraulic reel mounted on top obstructs arcs of fire. Plus, if a hydraulic line takes a hit, it could spray hot oil into the vehicle. It's a bit like that medieval tactic of pouring burning oil on attackers, except we'd be on the receiving end."

I examined the hydraulic system. The designer could not have put the hydraulic reel in a worse spot for enabling the vehicle to fight. However, if they placed the system inside the vehicle, it would have reduced cargo space. Looking at the vehicle and what we were trying to do, it was as if they designed the system for a different war. Too inexperienced to know for certain, I hoped our vehicle wasn't destined to become a modern version of the Maginot Line.

"Sir, the other issue is the drivetrain," as Corporal Richer knelt to point at the rear axels.

"It's not reinforced for heavy-duty tasks like moving dirt, so we've already had a differential case fail. I'll have to get you one of them spill reports."

Up to that point, we'd been lightly adapting the ELAV because it was verboten to customize vehicles. In most cases, the standard protocol to modify equipment started with administration to get approval from Ottawa. But we didn't have enough time. So, as training progressed, we became more aggressive with clandestine modifications to avoid garnering unwanted attention. The sappers left hydraulic tools in the rear staging areas and removed bustle bins for storing gear to increase arcs of fire. On the back roof of the vehicle, they created a space for a stretcher to support casualty evacuations. Furthermore, we limited digging or moving dirt with the blade to prevent additional damage to the drivetrain. For once, the digging limitations in Wainwright paid a dividend as it minimized the number of times we said, "I know the vehicle has a big blade on the front, but we can't dig with it because it may damage the drivetrain."

Every adjustment became a testament to the sapper's industrious work ethic as they tirelessly trialed ways to optimize the ELAV. Although we made countless vehicle adjustments before completing the proper paperwork, I encouraged Corporal Richer to keep working on the administration behind the scenes to document the changes. I also quickly finalized his oil spill report before commencing the next range serial. I logged the spill to be exactly 19.9 litres to avoid doing a full report. To minimize Hollywood's frustration with the sparsely filled out sheet, I put a yellow sticky note on top that read, "From the missionary's wife. XO." She was a sexually promiscuous character from the book he'd lent me, *Semper Fi*.

Feeling energized by the sappers' ingenuity after witnessing their customization of the ELAV, I pondered ways to make the most of our next range serial. Being assigned flank security during the upcoming scenario, I knew we would have a little freedom of manoeuvre on the edge of the range because everyone would be focusing on the main assault. While preparing our vehicle with food and water, I turned to Wally.

"Hey warrant, how much ammo do we want?"

It was as if he read my mind about the desire to make the most of the upcoming range. Clearly, he had a plan already crafted, and he responded without hesitation.

"Lots! We can conduct emergency training on the weapons systems."

In garrison, we'd been trying to conduct an orientation range on the vehicle but couldn't find time in the packed training schedule. The passive role in the upcoming range serial provided us the chance we sought. While stacking items as tightly as possible in the back of the LAV, Wally justified his thinking.

"In a pinch, every swinging prick needs to be able to fight this vehicle."

I adamantly agreed. It aligned with Major Noe's guidance back at the school that ensured we were fit to fight, and it also mitigated the combat risks that we continually read about in the national newspapers. But as he said it, my mind flashed back to the recent AFES incident and the strict direction to respect qualifications. I became torn between following protocol and ensuring we were combat-ready.

"Warrant, load up with a reasonable amount of ammo. I'll be right back."

As the LAV departed to roll through the ammunition point, I dashed to speak with Major Packer about "emergency training." Little did I know this would be the beginning of a tug-of-war between following procedures and adapting to the needs of the battlefield.

I found Major Packer in the command post and quickly proposed the idea. To my surprise, our "emergency training" concept piqued his interest. Still angry about engineers being relegated to the reserve and frustrated beyond words about the resistance to fuel the AEV because it was seen as a diesel pig rather than a critical mobility asset, he seemed to seek atonement. After a short pause, he cautiously spoke.

"John, proceed, so that our engineers receive more than dog shit training."

His red hair stood on end resembling a rooster's tail as he appeared spent from dealing with issues behind the scenes. He took a moment to look me directly in the eyes.

"But for heaven's sake, be smart about it."

Overwhelmed with joy at receiving permission to conduct emergency training, I dashed back to the staging area. I became speechless when I saw the LAV interior. It was jammed floor to ceiling with ammo; some cases were still bundled in the packaging crates. There was so much ammo that our signaller and air sentry fashioned lazy boy-looking chairs out of the ammunition boxes so they could sit on them while watching their arcs of fire from the rear of the vehicle.

"Hey, Wally. What's with the ammo?"

"Ya, sorry about the crates. Some ammo tech dweeb didn't give us time to uncase. We'll sort it later."

I wondered about his plan, as we had enough ammunition to supply an entire platoon. Similar to an overloaded truck going to the dump during spring cleanup, the weight of the ammo fully compressed the LAV's rear springs, but I didn't have time to ask any follow-on questions.

"Mount up, sir. The Commander is about to issue range orders over the radio."

As soon as I climbed into the turret, the LAV chugged away, blowing black smoke like an overloaded train as we commenced the next range serial. As our engineering sections were attached to platoons throughout the range battle procedure, Wally and I had some agency within the scenario to focus on emergency training.

Once situated in our flank security position on the range, Wally and I concentrated on refreshing our skill sets. After expending the first upload of ammo, we started working as a team to reload the main gun. Loading the 25mm chain-linked ammunition in the cramped turret was a challenge at the best of times. With flexible ammunition trays snaking between the ammo bin and the main gun, the contorting of hands and arms to properly feed the ammunition into the loading mechanism required close coordination. The mountains of extra ammunition in the rear limited the ability of our air sentry and signaller to physically pass up the linked rounds which further exacerbated the reloading challenges. Through some trials and errors, we found a way to make it work.

As the infantry closed with and destroyed the enemy objective, our LAV unleashed incredible volleys of fire as we provided unparalleled flank security to the attack. Zeroing in on a few concrete blocks as targets, we jumped back and forth between them to practice our marksmanship. Our signaller in the back worked overtime with a crowbar, opening countless ammo crates to feed our weapon systems. We fired so many rounds the smell of cordite and hot brass overpowered the whiffs of Wally's cigarillo smoke.

After refreshing our skillsets, one at a time, we cycled our signaller and air sentry sapper into the turret for emergency training. With Wally instructing and supervising, I jumped into the back with the crowbar. With a qualified gunner in the crew compartment conducting one-on-one training, I figured it aligned with Major Packer's direction "to be smart about it."

Peering over the range, I saw the other flank security vehicles sitting idle. Over the relentless thump-thump-thump of our main gun, it felt satisfying to be making the most of what could have been a dull situation. By continuously rotating gunners through the turret, we sustained an unprecedently high rate of suppressing fire on enemy positions long after everyone else had stopped. During one engagement, as we ceaselessly expended a hailstorm of bullets, I heard my call sign on the radio.

"E21A, is that you *still* shooting?"

Knee-deep in wood crates, ammo cans and expended shells, I immediately froze. Expecting a reprimand, I sheepishly answered, "Yes, over."

Wally ordered a ceasefire so we could clearly hear the subsequent radio transmission.

After what seemed like an eternity, the Brigade Commander, Colonel Jonathan Vance, spoke.

"Great suppressing fire. Keep it up. *Chimo!*"

Wally and I exchanged ear-to-ear grins and continued our emergency training with increased vigour. By the end of the first serial, the only thing that precluded us from expending all our rounds was the fact that we jammed every weapon system: the main chain gun, the coaxial, and the pintle mount machine guns.

Back in the staging area, a weapons technician helped us rectify our stoppages. Beyond restoring the weapon systems, he also provided invaluable tips and techniques that helped us adapt for the following range serials. He pointed out common problems such as chain links building up in the ejection ports and brass casing falling into the vehicle and jamming the turret gear. He also examined the main gun round counter and warned us that the barrel required inspection after a couple hundred more rounds. To do the inspection, the vehicle would need to miss a range serial. This requirement would jeopardize the ability to complete our emergency training, so we bent the rules a little to fit the situation. Despite firing another couple thousand rounds over the subsequent serials, we left the barrel inspection to the end of the exercise.

With the weapon systems operational again, we completed preparations for the next range by getting some fresh sappers to conduct emergency training and by loading the vehicle with more ammo. On this occasion, Wally grabbed so much ammunition that we had cases in the exterior turret bins. As we marshalled into formation, I overheard the Expedient Route Opening Capability (EROC) crew on the radio, but I couldn't see their vehicles. The order of march indicated that they should be right in front of us, but instead of their unique vehicles, the Husky and Buffalo, I saw a pickup truck.

EROC was a new capability to the Canadian Armed Forces that focused on rapidly clearing routes from explosive threats to enable safe vehicle movement in combat zones; they were one of Canada's responses to the IED threat in Afghanistan. Composed of specialized teams, they used a combination of mine-resistant vehicles, explosive ordnance disposal equipment, and engineering tools to detect, identify, and neutralize explosive threats. Due to individual training requirements to learn the new vehicles, they missed significant portions of our earlier exercises to attend specific EROC training in other locations. As a result, few of us had ever physically seen a Husky or Buffalo vehicle. As one of my duties would be to advise on EROC capabilities, I looked forward to working with them on exercise scenarios to become aware of their capabilities. Confused why a pickup truck sat in the EROC marshalling spot, I investigated. While walking over, I spotted Corporal Mike Benson, a hard-working country kid and his EROC crew sitting in the truck. He rolled down the window as I began to speak.

"Hey Benson, where are your EROC vehicles?"

Although I'm sure he tried to hide his frustration, he did a terrible job.

"No vehicles. We only have training stock in Canada, but those vehicles are out east."

EROC procurement was so recent that we only had a training fleet in eastern Canada and an operational fleet en route to Afghanistan. The fleet of vehicles to support exercises in Wainwright would arrive sometime after our deployment.

Benson explained that they were required to attend the range to get their check-in-the-box. Being mandated to participate without their equipment didn't bother me, but not being able to see the new vehicles in action did. How could we correctly advise on capabilities without seeing it at work? Worst still, how could we expect the manoeuvre commanders to understand a vehicle they wouldn't see until Afghanistan? We'd already been hamstrung with digging limitations, environmental protocols, and explosive safety templates, and now we couldn't even see one of our best mitigation assets against IEDs. Sensing my frustration about another capability we couldn't showcase, Benson offered some good news.

"At least EOD is here."

During the upcoming scenario, we would face an IED obstacle before conducting an assault. To help us provide mobility on the battlefield in an IED environment, we received a freshly arrived Explosive Ordnance Disposal (EOD) team. Composed of a mixture of folks with diverse backgrounds from across the Canadian Armed Forces, they were the IED experts to render devices safe and to exploit everything from the scene in efforts to attack the IED fabricators. This forthcoming scenario would be our first exposure to them because, like EROC up to that point, they had also been busy conducting individual training at other locations. My conversation with Benson was interrupted by the radio.

"All callsigns, prepare to move."

Wondering how we were expected to train on equipment that didn't even exist on the exercise, I darted back to my vehicle.

Throughout the range preparations, Wally became increasingly agitated about the scenario. As I updated him on the EROC situation, he started to vibrate. He boiled over when I mentioned the consolidation prize of getting to work with EOD.

"Sir, I don't know these EOD guys, but most are prima donnas. They won't understand the tactical situation."

Plumes of cigarillo smoke circled Wally in the turret as the warning continued.

"EOD is going to really slow us down and cause friction."

I didn't fully comprehend Wally's concerns. How slow could they be? However, I respected his technical acumen and experience as I'd never seen the capability in action, so I began considering contingency plans as we started the range.

It didn't take long for Prophet Wally's prediction to come true. Early in the scenario, an infantry section discovered an IED a couple hundred meters from a village's entry point. Exercise staff blocked off all bypass options with white mine tape to simulate a natural choke point, forcing us to deal with the device. A couple dozen armoured vehicles spread out to provide overwatch security as we progressed through the scenario.

The EOD team initially sustained the attack momentum by rolling up quickly to the scene. However, after they parked, the advance ground to a halt. Everyone on the range was charged up and ready to go, like racehorses straining at the gates; however, EOD held them shut. Our assault stalled as they meticulously worked through their routines of testing the robot, prepping the bomb suit, and double-checking critical gear before inspecting the device. These were critical steps to mitigate risks, but every verification consumed time we didn't have. After about thirty minutes of watching the EOD team move as if they were flies stuck to tape, my call sign came over the radio.

"E21A, send SITREP."

Traditionally this meant that we should send a situational report, but in this context, it meant, "Hurry up!"

To assess the situation without broadcasting over the radio for everyone to hear, I drove up to meet with the EOD team.

"Morning, I'm the engineer troop commander. Any time estimate for removing the IED?"

A Navy clearance diver looked at me, oblivious to the tactical urgency of the scenario. Above us, CF-18 jets thundered, but he didn't seem to notice or care. With a dismissive shrug, he provided a non-committal response. He then launched into a lengthy, patronizing monologue about explosives, his team's specialized training, and their meticulous processes. I could barely hear him at times above the deafening fighter jets circling overhead, yet he went on as if he was lecturing a class of captive students rather than conducting an urgent operation. Granted, I didn't know the specifics of his training, but it didn't matter. I just needed a number.

"Timeline?" I interrupted over the noise and his verbal diarrhea.

The EOD commander gave me an exasperated look and then exchanged words with his teammate midway through some yoga stretch. I assumed this was part of his preparation to don the bomb suit.

"A couple of hours for sure, maybe more, depending on what we find," he finally said with the tone of a professor.

"Thanks," I muttered, turning away as he recommenced his soliloquy.

I rushed back to my vehicle to provide an update over the radio. In response, I heard, "Wait out."

In this context, it was another radio procedure euphemism for "I don't like your answer."

EOD operations were relatively new, so the required timelines caught the exercise directing staff by surprise as well. Before long, the radio chirped again.

"E21A, outline the steps you are planning to take here."

After a quick chat with Wally, I responded.

"We would establish a restricted air space over the area in case the use of explosives is required. We'll also continue to maintain the security cordon. If the EOD team needs significant time to exploit the device, we will consider cordon sustainment options."

Another silence ensued.

Ironically, EOD's requirements to handle the device conflicted with the pre-established range timeline. The CF-18s only had limited fuel, so if we didn't proceed quickly, they would return to base without participating in the latter half of the scenario. If this occurred, it would preclude the manoeuvre elements from getting some of their check-in-the-box requirements. However, if we rushed though the IED, we would preclude EOD from getting their check-in-the-box requirements. The situation required an immediate compromise to meet all the training objectives. After fifteen minutes of silence, while the EOD team was still exploiting the device, the exercise staff provided direction over the radio.

"For the scenario, IED cleared. EOD will remain to exploit. Proceed to advance through the breach lane south of the IED site."

As the radio direction came, I looked down range. Sure enough, the exercise training staff removed the mine tape, thus creating a safe lane around the IED. Moments later, we resumed our attack while the EOD team continued their work. The exercise staff decided to conduct portions of the range concurrently, rather than sequentially, so everyone could complete their respective training requirements.

At the time, my inexperience prevented me from seeing the massive training opportunity lost by the subtle decision to remove EOD from the scenario. For all his arrogance and pomp, Mr. Prima Donna was right. Exploiting real devices, if you are lucky enough to find them before they detonate, can take hours. But by simply eliminating the device, we set a dangerous precedent for handling IEDs that grossly ignored reality.

Moreover, by sidelining EOD, we also missed the chance to educate them in an Army context. While EOD teams often train in urban environments where time is more readily available, battlefield situations differ. For example, if cordons remain in place too long, they can become vulnerable to attack when operating in places like Afghanistan. This isn't the case in a North American setting. Furthermore, EOD actions can be observed by adversaries on operations. Consequently, the EOD team could become a future target with secondary and tertiary threats specifically targeting the operators. We didn't know it then, but EOD would also have to adapt to multiple insertion methods, such as a helicopter and via foot, which limited the kit they could carry and, subsequently, their options for dealing with devices. But that was all in the future. For the time being, we needed to draw out the most training value from our current situation.

For many combat arms participants, the live-fire ranges were the debutant ball; the grand performance where infantry, armour, and artillery came together in a symphony of destruction. But for engineers, it often felt as if we were playing an instrument no one wanted to hear. Our contributions—mobility, counter-mobility, and explosive ordnance disposal—didn't fit neatly into a score that prioritized speed and aggression, reminiscent of the Blitzkrieg strategy from World War II. Live-fire scenarios rushed ahead like a conductor ignoring a portion of the orchestra. Without real explosive threats to highlight how the approach was out of tune, misconceptions festered. Consequently, despite three months of collective training and the best efforts of training staff, engineers remained misunderstood.

On the surface, Wainwright's training appeared to be a missed opportunity—engineers underemployed, fighting for relevance in a training system that couldn't fully appreciate our skillsets. But what I didn't realize then was that the fight for relevancy was by far the most valuable training; it forged an adaptability mindset. The true lesson wasn't in the training objectives or scripted scenarios to get the check-in-the-box; it was how we adapted when things didn't go as planned. Whether it was modifying the ELAV on the fly, making the most of flank security assignments, or working around bureaucratic training constraints, we were constantly learning to adapt. The ability to think on our feet, solve problems under pressure, and turn limitations into opportunities wasn't just a useful skill—it was the key to survival. The battlefield didn't care about our plans, qualifications, or check-in-the-box scenarios. It would just throw chaos at us, forcing us to adjust or fail.

In Afghanistan, we would be tested on our ability to adapt from the moment we hit the ground because our adversaries were the true masters of adaptability.

# 6

# Written Prepositions

After getting our check-in-the-box for Wainwright training, the focus shifted to completing a plethora of last-minute items such as individual courses, outstanding briefs, and perennial military paperwork. I'd naively assumed that preparing for war meant focusing on warfighting, but instead, I found myself drowning in a year-end administrative avalanche that intensified the closer we got to deployment. In the process, I learned a hard lesson about army administration. Routine paperwork doesn't stop because you are deploying; it just adds to the already taxing deployment demands. Major Packer summarized the situation best during a squadron meeting.

"We've got to finish all the standard dog shit tasks before deployment."

With a massive wad of chew in his mouth, he momentarily paused to spit in a plastic bottle before continuing.

"John, you must complete personnel file reviews, nail down the tour leave plan, and finish your annual performance reviews."

By the time the meeting concluded, my immense to-do list ballooned to include the requirement to attend Cultural

Awareness training and the Situational Awareness System (SAS) orientation. I also wanted to learn more about EROC before physically seeing the equipment for the first time in Afghanistan. With a little over two months before our deployment, I didn't have a minute to spare.

Exponentially more comfortable operating in the field, I needed to mentally adjust back to garrison duties. As part of the transition, I decided to tackle the most challenging task first; annual performance evaluation reviews, commonly referred to as PERs. As a neophyte to the process, I read the administrative directive on how to write a PER. I learned they are a one-page document comprised of two rating scales and three corresponding text boxes. In addition to providing feedback to subordinates, the documents rolled up through a series of promotional boards, with top-scoring files promoted to the next rank before the process was repeated the following year. At first glance, as I'd never received a written performance evaluation from any employer, I found it intriguing that the military distilled an entire year of work onto one page with just a few sentences and some dots.

Using a get-after-it approach, I wrote my PERs without understanding the nuances or lexicon for promotion boards. With abundant justification from recent Wainwright exercises to back up my rankings, I created my PERs by modifying some examples I scrounged from my peers. Once complete, I added my pristine files to the stack of papers on the Bret's desk and moved on to my next to-do list item.

The Situational Awareness System was one of the first GPS-based systems for armoured vehicles that allowed command posts to track battlefield movement. I'd skipped all SAS-related tasks during the Wainwright exercises because I thought learning how to fight the vehicle was more important than learning how to broadcast the vehicle's location. Plus, I was skeptical of the concept. The system was predominately being pushed by contractors with the biased intention of selling a product. Although the system's benefits sounded great during the sales pitch, I doubted the product's utility.

As part of the SAS orientation process, the contractor fitted a LAV in our unit lines with the system to demonstrate the product. Like other new equipment, the procurement process took time, so Afghanistan deliveries were prioritized over Canadian deliveries. Consequently, we only had a few demonstration kits in Canada to prepare us for the reception of the SAS equipment in Afghanistan. To get our SAS orientation check-in-the-box, Wally and I needed to attend a brief with the contractors inside the LAV. When we arrived, Wally didn't mince words.

"What the hell is this?"

While some grey-haired, ex-military contractor padding his pension outlined the system's benefits, Wally and I stared in disbelief. Mounted in the turret was a thick, reinforced green monitor. It was so robust it looked as if it had been designed to withstand being struck by a Mac truck. Similar to a COVID-19 physical barrier, the screen obstructed the view between the gunner and crew commander. As a result, it grossly impeded physical interaction between the crew and severely impaired the ability to rectify weapon stoppages. It also blocked the ammo bin lid, further hindering the already tricky process of loading the main gun. In an unintended irony, the system designed to help higher headquarters fight armoured vehicle fleets impeded the ability to individually fight the vehicle. Seeing the detrimental layout, I wondered if the SAS designers had ever worked in an armoured vehicle. I didn't have the combat experience to back up my doubts, but the system felt out of place in the context of Afghanistan. With all the canalizing terrain and minimal movement corridors, how hard could it be to keep track of vehicles?

After going through the motions to complete the brief, Wally succinctly summed up his thoughts.

"Sir, SAS is a problem. That screen would be more valuable as a doorstop at my lake lot!"

I was also gobsmacked at the concept, but I knew resisting SAS was futile. Although new to the military, I knew enough to understand it wasn't a matter of if the system would arrive in Afghanistan, but when. Without any options to deny the system installation, I hoped delays in the procurement process would postpone implementation in theatre.

With SAS training complete, next on my list was leave planning. As part of the deployment, each soldier was entitled to a three-week leave block to relieve deployment stresses, known as HLTA (Home Leave Travel Assistance). We could either return home or apply the equivalent cost to travel elsewhere. A much-touted benefit, it granted many soldiers their first opportunity to travel abroad. But in the context of gearing up for combat, I developed nothing but vehement disdain for HLTA.

From the onset, we barely qualified enough soldiers to drive our vehicles and operate our weapon systems. With HLTA, we had to meticulously schedule overlapping leave blocks that wouldn't impact our already skeleton-thin capabilities. Continuity of leadership needed careful planning as well. To do so required another massive Gantt chart that became an administrative quagmire. Growing up in the private industry, I'd never experienced mandatory leave. It seemed entirely out of context to the mission at hand. Imagine a professional sports team scheduling individual vacation blocks for their players throughout the season. It doesn't happen during the season because they have a critical role to fulfill as part of the team. Yet, as a professional military deploying on a combat operation, we were busy de-conflicting vacation blocks for each soldier throughout the tour. Little did I know that, like sports teams, injuries in Afghanistan would impact our roster and become a factor that further stressed our operational capabilities and my detest for HLTA.

Beyond the administrative headaches, HLTA also became the epitome of distraction. Instead of laser focus preparing to deploy to a warzone, some sappers diluted their efforts by finalizing travel plans. Sometimes, we struggled to get soldiers to read post-operational reports or contemporary threat assessments from Afghanistan. But the moment HLTA was mentioned, some became intelligence analysts. Entire evenings were spent pouring over travel brochures, debating the merits of trekking with elephants in Thailand or drinking their way across Europe. Looking back, I'd cancel HLTA during a six-month deployment and find alternative ways to give the troops a reprieve in theatre.

As an interlude between planning leave with mind-numbing spreadsheets and finalizing last-minute training with massive Gantt charts, Wally and I set up an opportunity to connect with Corporal Benson for a rundown on EROC vehicles. After exchanging a few emails, we arranged a briefing in our troop lines. With a couple of photos and a manual in hand, Benson provided us with an overview of the new capability.

"EROC's made up of two rigs, the Husky and the Buffalo. Both are meant to take a hit and keep on tickin'," he said, flipping through some photos as he explained the two vehicles that made up the capability.

The Husky resembled an oversized go-cart. Its V-shaped hull jutted out like a wedge in an engineered design to redirect explosions away from the driver. Climbing into the fuselage felt comparable to stepping inside a narrow, claustrophobic, single-seater airplane. To access the driver seat, you entered through the roof. Underneath the vehicle chassis hung a metal detection panel that resembled a road grader blade turned horizontal. When the driver hears a metal hit from the detection panel on the operator headset, it can be marked with paint for further exploration by dismounts or by the Buffalo.

The Buffalo on the other hand was a massive beast. Incomparable to any other vehicle, it looked like a cross between a small school bus, a monster truck, and a large excavator. Designed to carry counter-IED gear and personnel in highly explosive threat environments, the designers also placed a giant hydraulic arm on the vehicle to physically examine potential devices. Being so large and futuristic looking, the Buffalo was used in the Hollywood movie *Transformers*.

"EROC's straightforward," Benson went on. "The Husky runs point, like a bloodhound sniffin' out IEDs. The Buffalo exploits devices we find."

He pointed to a picture of the Buffalo's exploitation arm and further explained how they employed the large articulating appendage to mechanically inspect devices behind the vehicle's protective glass.

The discussion ensued for about an hour before Benson highlighted some limitations that caught my attention.

"None of these puppies are armed."

It was not ideal, but it was not an insurmountable obstacle, as many logistical vehicles shared the same weakness.

"For patrol speeds, we hunt at no more than 10 miles an hour."

A knot instantly formed in my stomach. EROC would be as slow as a country fair hayride. That pace wouldn't jive with the manoeuvre commanders, and would create a dilemma after our experiences in Wainwright. I wondered how to employ them in an organization that valued speed and aggression. It became a stressful thought as Benson continued.

"We ain't got a clue how it'll work on dirt roads. The detector is designed for flat ground, like paved roads."

Our intelligence reports showed that many Afghanistan roads would be rutted dirt paths. As a result, they could impair the vehicle detection capabilities because the uneven routes would create significant gaps between the panels and the road.

Although far from a panacea against IEDs, the EROC package offered many mitigation measures against our number one threat. As a result of Benson's brief, Wally and I gained a basic understanding of EROCs' capabilities and limitations. I also found it encouraging to know that competent, astute operators like Benson were spearheading the new capability. But it gnawed at me that Afghanistan would be the first time we would witness the equipment working. This approach flew in the face of the standard training progression of crawl, walk, run. For EROC, in an explosively rich environment that had killed and marred hundreds of coalition soldiers, we were going to start by sprinting on roads littered with IEDs.

With many pre-deployment tasks completed, I saw steady progress toward achieving our training plan. This gave me confidence that we were doing a good job. Then, Bret summoned me to his office.

"John, what are these?" shaking a handful of folders at me.

After a quick look, I knew exactly what he held.

"My PERs"

He shook his head in disagreement for a moment before erupting.

"These aren't PERs, these are shit! There isn't enough red ink in NATO to salvage these!"

He chucked the folders against the wall. The Venetian blinds rattled against the window frame while the folders slapped to the floor.

"Listed," he growled, "your soldiers deserve better than this half-assed attempt! Their careers depend on these!"

The Venetian blind gently oscillated in the window frame as he shifted gears.

"Writing effectively is not optional! It is an essential officer skill!"

I'd chosen engineering in school partly to dodge writing. Nobody told me the military would expect me to write.

He paused to look at the hot mess of files on the floor.

"Think of all the trees you just killed! I wouldn't even use your files for fire starter!"

Standing in his office, I grasped the importance of effective writing but couldn't understand the discrepancy in military training. With a commercial trucking license, I couldn't drive a staff car without a military training. Yet, they expected me to write on par with Hemingway without a single military writing course.

After a long silence, I felt the one-way conversation was over and started to pick up the files.

"What are you doing John?"

Halfway through scooping up the scattered folders, I froze at the sound of the Bret's voracious voice.

"Uh…picking up my PERs," I stammered.

His face contorted in disgust at my literary incompetence.

"I told you, those are shit. We don't pick up shit. Get the hell out!"

In slight disbelief about the emphasis placed on writing, I immediately amended my priorities and put PERs at the top. With a long list of outstanding tasks, it was hard to believe that PERs were one of the top priorities before going to war.

In the final weeks before departing, I balanced an endless stream of tasks: last-minute training sessions, leave plans, deployment logistics, and PERs, all while trying to stay abreast of contemporary Afghanistan threats. All thing considered, I felt confident that I'd done everything possible to prepare myself and the troop for the upcoming challenges while also satisfying administrative demands. I had no regrets as I walked into our final squadron meeting in Canada.

The meeting focused on conducting final checks. With so many moving pieces, Hollywood needed to catch and address any last-minute oversights. The briefing ran smoothly, with Hollywood detailing what was completed and what still needed attention. Without intending to, Hollywood's brief highlighted the massive amount of work we completed to prepare a squadron for deployment. We'd overcome numerous training shortfalls, limitations, and last-minute changes due to soldiers quitting or being unable to deploy. Collectively, there was a sense of pride and accomplishment in the room. Then, Major Packer shifted the conversation.

"Gents, most of your PERs are dog shit."

The air in the room turned ominously thick with uncertainty. Was this some sort of dark-humored joke? We had spent months grinding through training, proving we were a competent group, only to be told at the eleventh hour that we sucked at writing? PERs were among the last subjects I thought we'd discuss before deploying to a combat zone as Major Packer continued the rebuke.

"They are a gross injustice to your soldiers!"

The room stirred as we realized this wasn't a joke.

"Hallett, you ended every fourth sentence with a preposition."

Sensing I had no idea what he meant, he told a quick joke to highlight his point.

"A blonde and a brunette meet for the first time in a café.

The brunette goes, 'Where are you from?'

The blonde replies, 'I'm from a place where we don't end sentences in prepositions.'

Slightly taken aback by the prickly response, the brunette rephrased her question.

'Where are you from…bitch?'"

A talented writer, Major Packer's gaze rested on me for a moment to ensure I understood his tip. The room chuckled lightly at my grade three grammar lesson before Major Packer returned to the subject of PERs.

"They're so messed up, you don't have time to fix them. Bret and I must handle them now to meet my deadlines."

His demeanour and tone indicated dread for the additional workload, as some side conversations turned to protests in the room. Still processing my grammar lesson, I took a moment to think.

I recalled reading about the importance of administration in *War as I Knew It* by General Patton. During World War II, when he conducted inspections of fighting units, he closely scrutinized administration in the field. He had discovered a tight correlation between strong administration and stout fighting units. The underlying principle was that how you did one thing is typically how you do everything. I agreed with the observation; however, I couldn't make the connection to administration in the context of war. While operating weapon systems and patrolling IED-laden terrain, who cares if you could write like Hemingway? I wanted competence, dedication, and courage, not the ability to evade dangling modifiers, use potent verbs or avoid ending sentences with a preposition. I thought that writing and soldiering couldn't be more opposite on the warfighting spectrum.

My peers shared this line of thinking with their protests until Bret finally spoke.

"If you don't properly care for your soldiers' administration, who will?"

The room fell silent.

We all knew that without proper PERs, soldiers' careers ended—full stop. During our readiness training, while we focused on developing skill sets to keep us alive, Bret ensured careers remained alive. He was right, and I would champion that lesson later in my career. Sound writing was the blood required to fuel the heart of the military machine. Approvals, orders, and the procurement of equipment all required the ability to write effectively. I was just too immature to know it at the time. Bret concluded his lesson with a hard military reality.

"Sound administration is part of being a professional soldier."

Although I was slightly disappointed that I missed the standard, I did feel relieved to avoid the recursive PER process so I could focus my efforts on staying alive in Afghanistan. Looking around the room, my peers displayed the same relief. It didn't last long, as Major Packer retook control of the meeting.

"To sort out this dog shit, you are all getting an initial counselling."

It was as if he sucked the air out of the room. All the troop commanders and the troop warrant officers in the squadron received an initial counselling for poor writing, an administrative measure that can have career implications. After receiving numerous accolades for being the best warfighting battlegroup from the brigade commander, countless generals, and even the Chief of Defense staff, we were capping our deployment preparations with this?

The troop warrants immediately protested; to them, it was a kick in the nuts just before deploying. Still learning about the ceaseless forms in the military, I'd never heard of an initial counselling. I had no concept about the process or the career consequences that could stem from the document. Although our writing sucked, it seemed equally unacceptable to issue administrative measures just before deploying to a war.

As I sat there, I thought war was about physical risks, not paper risks due to bureaucracy. Yet, in the military, paperwork was its own form of warfare. The fight for promotions, resources, and even respect often came down to words on a page. Despite all our work up to that point, we departed Canada with a failing grade. Defeated by an enemy we never trained for: the English language.

# 7

# You're Not in Kansas Anymore

Just travelling to Afghanistan was a mission unto itself. After several commercial flights between Edmonton and Dubai, a C-117 Globemaster flew us on the final leg to Kandahar Airfield. It was the world's busiest single-runway airport at the time, as the flight lines buzzed around the clock with military helicopters, jets, and transport aircraft. The scene resembled a large airshow, except for all the visible aircraft munitions and countless soldiers walking between hangers. The sudden increase in temperature debarking the plane squeezed the air from our lungs. The thick scent of jet fuel and fine powder dust permeated the air as we stepped onto the tarmac. In the background, four A-10 Warthogs burdened with bombs laboriously rose with the sun as they departed on their morning mission.

The initial brief welcomed us to Kandahar International Airfield, known as just KAF. A small community that had recently ballooned in size comparable to a gold rush town, it was a mixture of tents, sea cans, and rapidly erected infrastructure. Despite the quick expansion, the urban planners still managed to integrate many small-town creature comforts like a bazaar and a Tim Hortons. The briefing was delivered by a sergeant who looked as if he single-handedly kept the KAF Tim Hortons in business. On a map, he showed us the location of our transient quarters and the mess hall options. He concluded the brief by outlining the agenda for the next three days to complete our training. After months of preparation, this would be our final check-in-the-box before we began Afghanistan operations.

Exiting the briefing tent gave us the first reality check that Afghanistan was a different world. The distinctive sound of jet engines filled the air as the four A-10 Warthogs who took off upon our arrival returned to KAF. With their wings bare from the initial load of bombs, they descended light as a feather to the tarmac. Something, or more likely someone, had received an explosive wake-up call.

Those three days in KAF were a grueling, not stop blur of activity. We received our final kit issue of encrypted radios, night-vision goggles, infrared lasers, and strobes to augment some of our previously issued items, such as rifles, Kevlar plates, and tactical vests. In designated parking lots, vehicle transfers occurred while crews did last-minute checks and received informal debriefs from departing soldiers. Service personnel had vastly different experiences during their tour depending on if they had stayed in KAF or worked "outside the wire," a common phrase to denote soldiers who left the security permitter of KAF.

An intelligence officer delivered one of the last orientation briefs that provided an update on the war and the contemporary threat. Long story short, there had been a slight lull in the fighting over the winter. However, they anticipated the perennial summer "fighting season" would begin again soon. Thankfully, the threat brief hammered on IEDs for what felt like an eternity, driving home the silent danger lurking on every road and path. By far, IEDs remained the deadliest threat to soldiers in Afghanistan. Hearing so much emphasis placed on explosives threats was validating as it addressed my biggest concerns. National headlines regularly included casualty reports stemming from IEDs. Yet, some folks still lived in another world and worried more about how they would finalize leave plans without sufficient Wi-Fi access. In the smoke pit on our final night at KAF, a soldier about to rotate out gave us a raw, unfiltered truth.

"I thought we belaboured IED training in Canada."

He paused for a moment. Resembling a dying man who only had one more sentence to speak, he made sure we heard his last point.

"They are beyond horrific. They either kill you or put you on edge all the time that you might be killed by one."

The chilling caution aligned with my biggest fear: underestimating IEDs. The last "IED" our battlegroup experienced consisted of exploding baby powder from a metal tube.

The following morning, I departed for Sperwan Ghar in a convoy of armoured vehicles. Located approximately two hours west of KAF, the journey was surreal. The smells transitioned between burning garbage, dust, and unfamiliar spices to open sandy deserts as we navigated the roads. Before long, we arrived in Kandahar City. The streets were a chaotic ballet of honking horns and darting scooters, weaving through overloaded jingle trucks painted like carnival floats on acid. The bazaars exploded with vibrant colours and the scent of roasting meat, diesel fumes, and trash, all battling for dominance in the air. I saw one boy, barefoot, kicking a makeshift soccer ball against the metal façade of a shop wall. Children darted out from narrow doorways; their eyes were sharp and eager to see the military convoy as we rumbled past. Even amongst all the chaos, our green armoured vehicles stuck out like a sore thumb.

As the buildings faded to the desert, my headset chirped as the convoy commander reported a route checkpoint.

"Leaving Kandahar City now, out."

The radio transmission signalled a transition to the infamous IED-laden routes I'd read about. The hum of the diesel engines picked up as we gained speed. The desert heat filled the air. In the distance, parallelling the highway as far as the eye could see, stretched sun-baked villages made of adobe huts. Bustling around the villages was a mix of inhabitants, herds of sheep and goats, and small packs of dogs. The landscape looked comparable to a scene ripped straight from the Bible. Camels moved lazily in the distance, herders guiding them through a land that had likely changed little since the days of Paul the Apostle. It felt as if he could walk out of one of the villages at any moment. Thoughts of what we would do if we hit an IED circulated in my head as postcard-like scenery passed overtop of the LAV gun barrel. I found it hard to believe that such a beautiful landscape concealed so many deadly threats.

After a two-hour voyage, we arrived at Sperwan Ghar. Set atop a giant dirt pimple, the outpost created an imposing silhouette on the horizon as it looked over the desert plains and scattered verdant patches of farmland below. Previous rotations had developed an outpost approximately halfway up the hill. On one edge of the camp stood an old concrete building. Allegedly built as a school, it had been repurposed to form a headquarters and a place to billet troops. To control the dust, truckloads of gravel were spread throughout the camp. Vehicles parked around the edges of a large gravel parking lot so the center could remain free for a helicopter landing zone (HLZ). A high wall of Hesco bastion enclosed the base itself. Far from the comforts of KAF, the only creature comforts were fresh food and showers. Besides poker nights, you couldn't spend money in Sperwan Ghar if you tried.

Upon arrival, Wally took off to recce the camp. Before long, he returned with a list of improvements.

"Sir, the front gate is a hot mess. I'm gonna lay some gravel down to prevent it becoming a mud pit every time it rains."

I concurred that the front gate needed some attention and not just the infrastructure. Beyond lacking a robust chicane entrance, when we arrived, I swore I saw three Afghanistan National Army soldiers holding hands with no rifles in sight.

"See that sandbag observation post?"

Wally pointed to a structure overwatching the eastern exclusion zone.

"It's barely holding up. A fart will knock it over, so we'll get some Hesco and sort that out."

To be environmentally friendly, or maybe it was the only type available, someone constructed the observation post out of biodegradable sandbags. They can be excellent in temporary applications; however, they are not suitable for more permanent structures. The hot sun and arid weather had deteriorated them, making them look as if they had made out with a weed-wacker. With gaping holes and sandbag material strands blowing in the breeze, the observation post slowly deflated as sand spewed out or blew away in the wind.

"The engineering stores are all over Hell's half acre. I'll get Corporal Richer to round them up, and we'll get a Beaver Lumber going."

Unbeknownst to me, Wally envisioned a lumber yard like you see at Home Depot, which he affectionally dubbed Beaver Lumber. Our predecessors had done an excellent job procuring various engineering stores such as wire, pickets, and copious amounts of wood. We just needed to take stock and get them into a controlled area to prevent random soldiers from completing self-help projects that could waste or destroy critical material. I recalled a soldier in Wainwright who needed a small board to hang a map in the headquarters. Instead of asking for some off-cut materials that were out of sight but readily available, he grabbed a full sheet of plywood, used a quarter of it, and tossed the rest. Quality wood was in short supply and tough to purchase in Afghanistan, so we couldn't afford waste.

Controlling supplies was also crucial to ensure quality standards of engineering projects. For example, previous rotations had problems with locally procured wood because the suboptimal quality created structural problems. Long story short, local wooden beams were inferior to Canadian grade lumber and broke under minimal loads. Consequently, to be certain that structural designs aligned with Canadian standards, we imported a lot of lumber and other engineering stores such as electrical and plumbing components directly from Canada to avoid using questionable quality supplies.

While the troops settled in and tackled some of the camp improvement projects, Wally and I got to work learning about the area of operations. After receiving some handover points from the outgoing leadership, we had a good idea of their accomplishments so we could build upon their successes. Mid-discussion in our quarters, a room off the back of the old concrete school, we heard a knock on the plywood door.

"Howdy. Name's Doug. I'm a 'merican dog contractor. I hear tell you lads are the new engineers."

In the door stood a slightly pop-bellied, dark-haired six-foot man with a goatee sparsely surrounded by other facial hair.

"My dog's name is Tex. We do explosive detection. Lookin' to get outside the wire. I'm tired of just sniffin convoys comin' into camp."

With the troops focusing on camp improvements to help the battlegroup live safely and comfortably, Wally and I immediately saw the potential for an explosive dog team to help us move on the battlefield.

"How 'bout a little demo? I'll set something up. You'll be impressed, guaranteed."

Keen to potentially have a new tool in our arsenal and further mitigate explosive threats, Wally and I went to see what Tex could do. Sure enough, the dog was exceptional. Doug hid a few training bags filled with explosive traces in several spots around the HLZ. Tex quickly found each one. He also found explosives hidden amongst petroleum products in the mechanic lines and the kitchen garbage bins during a second demonstration. It was impressive. Then Doug brought up the catch.

"Look, to keep his nose working like a charm, he's gotta have A/C."

A tall order for patrols. Wally and I shared a doubtful glance as Doug continued.

"Tex is also a bit irascible."

He paused momentarily, looking both ways as if he was about to commit a crime. Hesitant to elaborate further, Doug went on in a softer tone.

"Uh, he's a bit racist. Don't know why, just gets grumpy around dark skin folks."

I appreciated Doug's upfront honesty; however, it created some real challenges. We were in Afghanistan, a completely different culture. To add to the cultural complexities, we now had a dog handler peddling us the services of a racist explosive detection dog. Reluctant but still intrigued because of the lethal IED threat, I provided a non-committal response.

"Thanks for the show-and-tell, Doug. We've just arrived, so let us get oriented. Uh, we'll be in touch."

With significant progress on camp improvements and Beaver Lumber starting to look comparable to a hardware store wood yard, Wally and I shifted focus on being fit to fight. Having only fired a few zeroing rounds while passing through KAF, I figured we needed a troop range to refresh some weapons-handling skills.

In discussions with my peers, some of the most common stoppages with the C7 rifle stemmed from the magazine not correctly feeding the round into the chamber. I'd heard an apocryphal story that the lowest compliant bidder manufactured the magazine springs – a good possibility given government procurement processes. Further exacerbating the problem, some of the issued magazines could have been loaded for months while they sat idle in a weapon vault. If this were the case, the springs would have lost their compression force.

Veteran soldiers told us they disassembled their magazines to stretch and subsequently renew the compression force of their springs to ensure they functioned properly. To further mitigate spring-related stoppages, some of them only put twenty-eight versus the total thirty-round capacity into the magazine. By limiting compression, they further eased stresses. As it was hard to ensure troops stretched their magazine springs, I figured the best way to maintain them was to host regular ranges. One, it would keep our weapons handling skills fresh, and two, it would provide an easy opportunity for the troops to empty their magazines so they could be maintained.

Luckily, behind Sperwan Ghar, immediately adjacent to the garbage pit, was an austere range. A quick check-in with the command post granted us permission to proceed; the camp sergeant major just asked us to light the garbage pit on fire after we finished shooting. The range played out just as I imagined. The troops had a ball while expending copious amounts of ammunition refreshing their skills. There were even a few stoppages due to magazine issues, further justifying the range practice and the requirement to regularly conduct them.

Once the range was complete, Wally and I commenced the garbage burn. Before the range, Wally had grabbed a couple of trip flares and diesel cans to assist. After fixing a magnesium-based trip flare to an old forklift pallet, we dowsed the refuse mixture of cardboard, plastic, and wood with forty-plus litres of diesel fuel. With a quick pull of the trip flare line, WOOF. Black smoke billowed in the air. Resembling schoolboy pyromaniacs, we shared a giggle as the fire grew in the large garbage pit.

While observing the fire from our John Deere Gator, we took a moment to reflect on the first couple of weeks in theatre. We were happy about how the troops had acclimatized to the Afghan environment and were equally delighted to add value around the camp. We'd already received numerous accolades for the engineering improvements to the observation posts and main gate. Throughout the entire process, engineering limitations were conspicuously absent. None of our improvements required any building permits, environmental clearances or administration approvals. For instance, we'd just spilt 40 litres of diesel fuel to start a bonfire without more than a verbal order from the camp headquarters because if we didn't burn the garbage, it would blow all over the surrounding countryside. Daily SITREP administration with Hollywood also got simpler. During one tranquil day when there was not much to report beyond routine progress on camp projects, I put a line in my report that the troop morale was high because the missionary's wife arrived. The jest commenced some colourful commentary with Hollywood.

"Ah, she'll never change, sir! Big Chi, Little Mo! Stay safe out there. You know how I worry."

Smoking a cigarillo with Wally while massive clouds of smoke continued to rise, it became apparent that Afghanistan was different. The new agency, a blend of freedom, empowerment, and responsibility to do what made sense versus what the policy said was refreshing. For the first time in months, I felt we finally had enough liberty from rules and regulations to do our job as combat engineers. It was if we had just finished going through metamorphosis from being a caterpillar in training to a butterfly in theatre.

As we were enjoying the flames, another scene began to unfold. Sperwan Ghar also billeted a small unit of Afghanistan National Army (ANA) soldiers. Seeing the billowing smoke from the fire, the ANA rushed in like it was a Black Friday sale, frantically yanking the discarded pallets from the flames. No matter how broken the pallet, they worked swiftly to collect them. I later learned via the interpreter that the ANA soldiers pulled the pallets apart to reuse the nails and cook with the lumber. They often recovered items from our trash, such as these, and took them home to help support their families. In a sparse country, they didn't waste a thing. Witnessing the resolve to save the precious wood and nails we classified as garbage was humbling. Unfortunately, it wouldn't take long before Afghanistan humbled us again.

March 16th, to be exact. In our sleeping quarters, beside our wooden bunk beds, sat a six-foot plastic table with a computer that we used as a desk for daily administration. On top of the desk sat a wooden shelf that contained a combat radio equipped with an audio speaker. Wally possessed an insatiable thirst for information, so we always had the radio speaker on low to hear every radio transmission. While going through our morning rituals, an urgent situation brought the radio to life.

"Contact, wait-out."

A few troop members gravitated to the radio speaker. Details were thin while the situation developed.

"IED strike."

Another few minutes of silence ensued.

"One casualty."

The tone of his voice indicated a heightened sense of urgency and unease. We were no longer in the training environment where mock casualties revived at the end of the scenario; this was real.

"Nine-liner to follow."

The soldier on the radio knew his drills. We waited with bated breath while listening to the nine-liner transmissions to finalize a medical evaluation helicopter. Time stood still as short, crisp communication occurred between the outpost and the higher headquarters, relaying information no one wanted to hear. Somewhere along the process of evacuating the casualty to KAF, we heard the dreaded three-letter acronym.

"VSA, over," meaning vital signs absent.

Soon after, a communication lockdown broke soldiers off from their loved ones. This essential protocol ensured that the families of the fallen would receive the devastating news from an official notification team in Canada, not through an unofficial call or message from a grieving friend in the field. Over the next few hours, we learned that the first casualty of our deployment was Sergeant Jason James Boyes, a section commander from the Princess Patricia's Canadian Light Infantry. Reading the tactical exploitation team report, we learned that the IED strike occurred during a foot patrol in a spot habitually used to survey the surrounding area. Within only a couple weeks of our arrival, the Taliban had already noticed this proclivity and attacked it. In Afghanistan, engineers could finally work without restrictions; unfortunately, it also meant contending with an unrestricted enemy. We would have to avoid setting patterns while being constantly observed by an adversary searching for patterns to target. The high-stakes chess match had begun.

# 8

# Playing With Fire

While coping with our first casualty, we prepared for our maiden operation. Until then, we'd only conducted simple presence patrols around Sperwan Ghar to get acquainted with the environment and hone our patrolling skills. From how much ammunition and explosives to carry, to the amount of water needed, to communication plans with the help of embedded interpreters, we learned a great deal about operating in Afghanistan. Tactically though, the patrols didn't amount to much. That would change on Operation TOORA AAZADI.

It always intrigued me to know who came up with such obscure names. They must have been the top candidate on the cultural awareness training. Immediately after failing to pronounce the operation's name, the troops would stop trying and just give it a nickname that made practical sense. In this case, we called it "Fosters" because the mission aimed to re-open Route Fosters.

Located in the Horn of Panjwai, this route traversed highly contested terrain. Previous battlegroup rotations built multiple outposts along the route to establish a foothold. Spaced roughly three kilometres apart, these austere outposts were made of Hesco, lumber, and sea cans. In efforts to choke out resupply to these locations, the Taliban laced Route Fosters with IEDs. By denying the only road connecting all the outposts, the Taliban's siege-type strategy aimed to starve us out of the area. To show our resolve, counter the Taliban's move and ease the logistical supply chain, our first operational mission was to re-open Route Fosters.

Hearing rumours around the camp about all the potential explosive devices on the upcoming mission, Doug the dog handler walked by to remind us of his services.

"Heard y'all going out to find a ton o' bombs. Tex and I are still rarin' to rock when you are."

We already had enough problems, so I politely took a raincheck on the offer.

My main concern was the rag-tag state of our mine detectors. Since our arrival, I'd been trying to get them replaced. Held together with duct tape from the previous rotation of sappers, they looked more like a toddler's homemade contraption of plastic and tape than a precise instrument to find a pin-sized piece of metal in a land mine. After submitting multiple requests for replacements, nobody in the supply chain could help. Having recently watched the HBO series *Band Of Brothers,* I remember being shocked to learn about all the logistical challenges that paratroopers overcame because they didn't have proper gear or sufficient equipment during their European operations. Yet here we were, preparing for our first operation with the same challenges over sixty years later. Desperate for proper equipment before being sent to search for IEDs, at the last moment, Hollywood worked his magic and scraped together a solution. He pulled some strings with our coalition partners back in KAF and sent us brand-new mine detectors the day before our operation. I thanked him on the phone from our command post that night, but he just responded with his affectionate customization of the engineer's mantra.

"Big Chi, little Mo, Sir. Stay safe out there."

The concept of our task was simple enough, but the execution was complex. Fosters was a single-lane dirt road lined by grape fields, adobe houses, and irrigation canals, so establishing the correct order of march was crucial. Without passing lanes, changing the order of march would be as awkward as two obese strangers trying to pass each other in the aisle of a crowded airplane. After much debate, the two EROC vehicles would lead the single file column, followed by some armoured assets with plows and rollers. As they advanced, the AEVs would scrape the top four inches of the road, and the freshly scraped road would be inspected by two dismounted engineers with our new mine detectors. EOD, an armoured resistant jeep for security, my LAV for communications, the armoured recovery vehicle and the ambulance would follow the dismounts. To provide security and flush potential triggermen, an inverted V of dismounted infantry would flank the leading elements of the convoy in the surrounding grape fields.

The morning of the operation started as usual. *Aaalllllaaaahhhuu Akbar* echoed from the mosque minaret loudspeaker, signalling the morning call for prayer. In the distance, I could hear the hollow rattle of bells from a small flock of goats. Soon, the sun rays painted the horizon and highlighted the copious number of vehicles pre-staged in Sperwan Ghar. The convoy was a motley mix of over fifty vehicles, including tanks and logistical trucks carrying sea cans.

Our driver, Corporal Aaron MacMullin, was renowned for making a strong cup of coffee. Built comparable to Conan the Barbarian, it wasn't uncommon to see the French press half full of coffee grinds before he would add a splash of water and pulverize the mixture. The coffee-like sludge would be so thick that Wally nicknamed it a "Mac attack." From the turret of our vehicle, we could see shepherds herding their sheep through the labyrinth of routes that cut through the surrounding grape fields and adobe compounds. While enjoying the last of our Mac attack, we departed Sperwan Ghar on our three-day mission to clear twelve kilometres of Route Fosters.

After a couple of hours slowly advancing up the route, the engineering net crackled to life.

"Potential IED find by Husky. Buffalo advancing to investigate."

We had a dedicated radio frequency for engineers to communicate with each other, ensuring privacy for tactical or technical-level discussions. As my vehicle contained multiple radios, one of my main responsibilities was to filter engineering-specific information and relay only critical items on the battlegroup's all-informed net. I promptly provided an update to the convoy commander.

"Contact, IED. EROC team proceeding to exploit."

I shared a big grin and fist pump with Wally as he spoke over the intercom.

"Sir, buy a lottery ticket. Horseshoes just fell out of our arse."

Finding a device before it exploded was lucky on several fronts. Most importantly, it minimized casualties and damaged equipment. However, it also provided valuable insights from a forensic perspective. Similar to a crime scene from a serial killer, collected evidence could help link devices together so we could target the IED-making network. However, gathering evidence took time, which, in this context, exposed the entire convoy to an attack. While EOD fought the bombmaker, I commenced a battle with the patrol commander regarding timelines. Major Micheal Lane's expectations to sustain a rapid advance stemmed from the unrealistic precedence established in training scenarios.

"E21A, send SITREP, over."

Accustomed to the Wainwright IED timeline of a couple of hours or the magical removal of devices on exercises because EOD procedures took too long, the infantry became impatient. Torn between EOD requirements and infantry desires, I needed to strike a balance fast. As EOD had a bomb in their face, I figured they deserved a bit of space. In the moment, I decided to fabricate a best-guess update.

"Uhhh, EOD starting to approach the device."

With a cigarillo hanging out of his mouth, Wally gave me a where-did-that-come-from look.

Since exploitation took time, we just had to wait and provide security while EOD worked. Thirty minutes later, the patrol commander was back on the radio.

"E21A, send SITREP, over."

The dismounted security element started to resemble dehydrated raisins as they boiled in the grape fields. By now, the sun had risen and produced searing heat. The midday temperature swelled to over 35 degrees Celsius In some cases, if you left your rifle in the direct sun, you could inflict a light burn picking it up. Exacerbating the fatigue, the soldiers were traversing the rugged terrain of grape fields, mud walls, and irrigation ditches with full combat loads of gear. At the time,

I cared less about targeting the IED network and all about the sappers charged with clearing the way. My mind raced for ways to buy them more time as I knew I had to set the tone early for the remainder of the operation. After a long pause, I provided a feeble best-guess update.

"Uh, EOD still exploiting the device."

This vanilla radio exchange continued for the next hour as Major Lane's tone became increasingly irritated. Even I started to think it was taking too long, but how could I tell someone to hurry up when they had a makeshift bomb in their face? We were no longer dealing with metal tubes that discharged baby powder if you messed up. Heaven forbid pressure from me to get on with it would result in an accident. After about two hours, I was about to push EOD to pick up the pace when they provided an update. The Husky had discovered an IED, and they used the Buffalo arm to help exploit it. The device was made of a forty-litre plastic jug full of homemade explosives, an artillery round, and a detonation cord, but they didn't discover an initiation set.

By withholding the initiation set, the Taliban could activate the device at a time of their choosing. This allowed them to leave the main charge buried dormant for extended periods while they waited for a target of opportunity as it only took a few minutes to arm such a device by burying the initiation set just below the surface of the road. This proved to be an effective technique to mitigate collateral damage against innocent civilians while awaiting a coalition vehicle to target.

I provided a detailed update on the all-informed net to justify the exceptionally long halt. Since nobody had any questions, I concluded the event.

"Device exploited, continuing the advance."

Soldiers for the security elements staggered upright from various positions in the surrounding grape fields. After being baked in the hot sun for a couple of hours, we recommenced our snail-pace advance. Just before sunset, we finally arrived at Haji, the first outpost on our route, about three kilometres from our starting point. The convoy leaguered in the area around Haji while the infantry began a "patrol matrix" along the portion of the route we had just cleared. The ping-pong-type patrol consisted of three vehicles driving back and forth between Haji and our starting point to sustain a presence on the road. The logic behind this was that the route couldn't be reseeded with IEDs if we sustained a presence. Throughout the night, the droning hum of diesel engines rose and faded every thirty minutes as the patrol resembled something like kids driving round and round on a large go-cart track.

Day Two of operations began early to avoid the intense Afghan heat. Right after the morning stand-to—a military drill ensuring readiness for potential attacks—we resumed clearing Route Fosters. While it was never explicitly stated, I felt an omnipresent pressure to quicken the pace. The eagerness to make up time was palpable as we had only advanced a quarter of the way to our destination. I could only imagine the stress of the soldiers in the leading elements, knowing their job was to find bombs deliberately placed to kill them. That was enough on its own. They didn't need additional pressure to speed up or cut corners. As I pondered ways to help buy time, the radio came alive.

"Dismounts found IED with mine detector. EOD called forward."

Wally and I looked at each other in disbelief. Two finds in two days? We really needed to buy a lottery ticket. I reported the update on the all-informed net and began to wait.

And wait.

And wait.

In the distance, a farmer worked his shovel with an effortless rhythm, the blade slicing through the earth like a hot knife through butter. While watching his proficiency, I began to think about our IED training. They taught us that it took approximately forty-five minutes to place an IED. Therefore, you must check the route every forty-five minutes or less to mitigate the risk. I always wondered how they came up with this number. Did they interview a bombmaker? The timeline seemed exceptionally long in an agrarian-based country filled with citizens who probably learned how to use a shovel not long after they could walk. As I watched the farmer work the shovel like a maestro, something felt wrong. My ruminations ceased with another call on the radio.

"E21A, send SITREP."

The tone indicated we needed to hurry up. I'm confident I would have received some profanity-laced motivation if not for the all-informed net. Frustrated by the incessant pressure to push sappers to rush their drills, I looked at Wally, who didn't hesitate to speak his mind.

"Three days for this route? I don't think so."

I lacked the experience to know for sure; however, as Wally continued, my gut screamed that our operational time estimate was delusional.

"We found a bomb. What's the rush?"

The sappers didn't want to bake in the sun anymore than anyone else, so I new they were moving as fast as they could. They didn't need pressure from me to hurry up. But based on the previous day and the desired operational schedule, my intuition told me we would receive many more requests for SITREPs. Therefore, to buy EOD time and placate the patrol commander, I elbowed Wally.

"Give me your best impression of an EOD operator."

Thinking I needed a laugh, he went off, never missing a chance to poke fun at the prima donnas. With the enthusiasm of a Shakespearean actor, he tossed out terminology such as "positive action," "exposing the device," "need the robot," "doing a manual approach," and "rendering safe as part of the act." I jotted down all the technical terms on the cardboard sleeve from my military ration. I figured since almost nobody knew what EOD did I could buy time with technical bullshit so they couldn't ask questions. With an all-informed radio, folks were cautious about asking questions that might make them look foolish. Reviewing my shopping list of terms, I just picked one and got on the radio.

"EOD needs the robot, over."

I didn't even know if they had a robot, but it didn't matter. In this situation, we had three choices: bypass, blow the device in place, or let EOD exploit. While exploit remained the chosen course of action, it didn't matter if EOD was using a robot, yoga stretching to put on a bomb suit, or delivering a monologue about their own awesomeness. They were working, doing their best, and needed time to do their procedures while dealing with a life-and-death situation.

Years earlier, I had a boss who used to say, "John, if you are not adding value, get out of the way of someone who is." Sitting relatively safe in my LAV while the sappers did the work, the only value I could add was making time. So, I made a radio log on another cardboard lunch box with all the terms Wally spouted off during his Oscar-winning performance. To further buy time, I figured pushing updates versus waiting for requests would be better. Every twenty minutes, I rotated through phrases. Similar to ordering a meal at a restaurant, I just picked a word off my technical jargon menu and formulated a SITREP.

"EOD exposing the device."

Twenty minutes later.

"EOD rendering device safe."

Twenty minutes later.

"EOD taking positive action."

Anything to proactively show likely progress without hassling the EOD operators. I would only reach out on the engineer net every hour to get an update and adjust my radio log accordingly. After about three hours, we learned the IED consisted of a PMN anti-personnel mine covered by a washbasin, a plastic jug full of homemade explosives, as well as a command wire. This was an interesting, more complex find as the dual initiation meant the device could be triggered by someone watching at a distance or by the victim. The washbasin was a crude way of preventing a dismounted soldier from triggering the device. As the weight of a soldier wouldn't crush the washbasin, it protected the PMN mine from being initiated. This rudimentary technique allowed the insurgents to specifically target vehicles as their weight would crush the wash basin. While the anti-personnel mine itself wouldn't damage an armoured vehicle, it would initiate the plastic jug of explosives buried beneath the mine, which absolutely would.

I quickly provided another detailed update to show the long wait in the scorching sun wasn't in vain. Again there were no questions, and soon the security element could be seen awkwardly rising like newborn calves as they regained their legs.

"Continuing the advance. E21A, out."

About an hour later, after we were just starting to build momentum, a radio call stopped our progress.

"Buffalo found IED. EOD called forward."

Utter disbelief. Another find, pre-detonation. Wally and I were ecstatic as the sappers continued putting on a route-clearing clinic. It was tough to say from only radio communications, but I didn't feel that other elements in the convoy shared our ecstasy as it would mean sitting for another couple of hours in the boiling Afghan sun. With a routine established, I grabbed Wally's cardboard lunch box and copied my radio log from the last find. I then recommenced providing updates every twenty minutes over the radio using the exact same timeline as the previous find. After another three hours, we learned the IED once again consisted of a PMN mine and a plastic jug of homemade explosives, so I concluded the device exploitation with my standard update.

"IED exploited, continuing the advance. E21A out."

Long past the peak of the afternoon sun, Wally and I began to think about the evening. Having only advanced a few hundred meters during the day, the patrol was in a precarious position. If we didn't make the next outpost before sunset, we would be like sitting ducks for an attack throughout the night. While contemplating contingency plans, the radio chirped.

"Dismount found an IED, EOD called forward."

Holy crap. Another pre-detonation find? This discovery vindicated my guilt for taking so much poetic license with radio updates. How could you argue with three finds?

By now, everyone knew the drill. Only this time, plans for the evening filled the all-informed net while we waited. Luckily, we had an EOD team that knew the tactical situation. Understanding that staying the night on Route Fosters was riskier than not exploiting the IED, they blew it in place as the sun set on the horizon. Immediately after transmitting the SITREP, Major Lane provided evening direction.

"All call signs, return to Haji for the night."

Since we had only advanced about a kilometre, the order mainly applied to the route clearance elements, as the back half of the convoy was still parked in Haji. They never moved all day.

Back in Haji, we reset while the ping-pong patrol continued along the route we had already cleared. Day Two of the three-day operation was complete. From an engineering perspective, it was an outstanding success. Three pre-detonation finds in a single day. It couldn't get much better. However, from a patrol perspective, we were way behind schedule.

Unfortunately, the weather caused additional delays the following morning. A dust storm arrived, creating low visibility, which grounded medical evacuation helicopters. After a short leadership meeting with Major Lane, he decided to hold firm for the day. Although a great decision from a safety perspective, the storm yielded the Taliban time and concealment. As they were undoubtedly watching and knew our axis of advance, they would have twenty-four hours to plant IEDs as their forces weren't grounded by the storm. In fact, the tempest gave them idyllic cover for their clandestine acts. During the meeting, I also expressed my concerns about the ping-pong patrol. Moving as a complete packet up the road made more sense than trying to keep the cleared portion open. As we'd already found multiple IEDs, I thought the situation had changed, and we should revisit our plan. We couldn't ping-pong into perpetuity. We'd have to stop at some point, so why not now? However, the mission was to clear the route, not simply move along as a convoy. Despite pleading my case, the ping-pong patrols continued.

Even though it was the right call, I hated staying put for a day. But what really started to eat at me was the belief that the ping-pong patrols effectively mitigated IEDs. Maybe they never used a shovel as I had, growing up in the construction industry, so they didn't question the forty-five-minute timeline to bury an IED. But after two days on Route Fosters, I saw the ping-pong patrol as a specious concept.

To make the most of the layover, Wally and I closed with the engineers to see if we could do anything to improve the clearance process. Behind our vehicle in a semi-circle, while chewing tobacco and chain-smoking cigarettes, the sapper shared a chuckle about my overly technical reports on the radio; they also expressed their gratitude for not being continuously hassled for updates. During the conversations, I gained a deeper appreciation of the pressures being placed on the sappers as Corporal Richer recounted his IED find.

"First, the mine detector squeaked when I found the electrical wire. That led to prodding the ground until my bayonet sank into the road."

As he told the story, he spun the large knife in his hand.

"When I popped the dirt," he said, demonstrating with the bayonet, "I saw a bright orange det cord on a yellow canister."

The story was interrupted by the ping-pong patrol. Three LAVs pulled into Haji, conducted a tight turn on a well-worn track and left as quickly as they came. A light dust hung in the air as the sound of their diesel engines faded. Corporal Richer continued.

"When I found the wire, I did the number one thing you're not supposed to do. I lightly pulled on it to find out its direction."

Everyone's arses puckered as we cringed at his confession. It was analogous to saying you covered your hand with bacon and waved it in front of a starving alligator.

"Then I called back to the security vehicle to check the bushes to my left, as that was where the wire lead. From the gunner's thermal imagery, no one was there."

Astonished by his admirable grace under fire, I'm not sure how many folks could retain their composure inches from an IED within full view of the firing point, or if Corporal Richer will ever look at a bush the same way again.

Our string of luck continued that night as the ping-pong patrol hit an IED. The strike did minimum damage to the LAV because it was likely just an anti-personnel PMN mine. After a quick exploitation in the dark, no explosive jugs or other munitions were found. As the radio reported the location, my heart stopped. The strike occurred in the exact same location as our first IED find, the one without an initiation set. Unbeknownst to the Taliban initiation placement guy, we removed the main charge earlier. It's tough to say, but it is reasonable to conclude that a rookie bomb maker placed the initiation set in the spot as instructed, assuming it would detonate the main charge buried underneath. Only by sheer luck had we removed the main charge earlier in our operation.

My fear was coming to fruition. Like moths to a flame, the Taliban were starting to gravitate back to Route Fosters, and they were bringing their IED equipment with them. We got lucky again, as the outcome could have been drastically different if the main charge had been present. In the Canadian Military Engineer's prayer, there is a line, "May our charges never fail." I prayed for IED charges to continue to fail as the ping-pong patrols felt like we were playing with fire. I started to wonder when we would get burnt.

# 9

# Deer Hunting

It took twenty-four hours for the dust storm to pass, so we resumed our operation early the next day. With the morning call to prayer echoing in the background and the smell of diesel engines filling the air, the dismounted security elements deployed along the edges of Route Fosters. Once set, the radio nets came alive to signal the recommencement of the route clearance mission. One by one, we watched the clearance vehicles roll out of Haji with their antenna masts flopping back and forth like a metronome.

Standing in the turret of our LAV, Wally and I savoured our morning Mac attack coffee in the peaceful Afghan dawn. In between sips of the tonic, Wally gave our muscle-building driver, Corporal MacMullin, a hard time about shrinking because he was missing gym workouts while on operation.

"Hey Mac, you muscle shirts won't fit anymore."

I chuckled at the jest as Mac formulated a response.

"Hey warrant, I don't..."

KABOOM.

A hellacious explosion shattered the morning peace as if we'd been hit by a giant invisible sledgehammer. The leaves on the tree fluttered violently, and dust rose a few inches off the adobe walls as a massive shock wave whooshed through us. At the scene, less than fifty metres away, dirt and shrapnel shot everywhere as a small mushroom cloud rose above the grape fields. Just outside the dust cloud, flying in a large arc, a vehicle tire flipped end-over-end. It looked exactly like a coin toss to start a football game, except it was a couple hundred-pound tire and rim sailing twenty metres in the air. The mine detonation trailer of the Husky had struck an IED, sending one of the tires directly over one of the security elements before it thumped into the field.

For the first time, the majority of the deployed soldiers, myself included, experienced the ferocious power of an IED. Until that point, they had been academic, hypothetical situations with simulated explosions from small metal tubes releasing a cloud of baby powder. With our first real explosion, everyone could finally see the tangibility of the combat engineering trade on display. We had a counter-mobility problem and needed mobility support to recover a disabled vehicle, remediate a blast hole and triage a potential casualty in an explosive threat environment; all of this was required immediately after experiencing the visceral blast wave of the explosion. Without saying a word, the sappers responded.

The blast also shattered the tension between me and the incessant pressure to remove IEDs at breakneck speed. Even as the morning sun started to bake the security elements, the tone on the radio instantly changed from "Hurry up" to "We are happy to roast in the sun while you do your job." Not once did we hear "E21A, send SITREP," as we confirmed the driver was okay, repaired the route with the AEV, and helped recover the Husky trailer back to the outpost.

That IED detonation marked a watershed event and hurled us headfirst into a new raw world with different rules. The game board flipped. There were no more check-in-the-box activities to meet the standard, scenarios requiring you to play the game, or exercise staff that could remove challenges because they took too long to solve. We now faced a primal, unrelenting reality that it was "game-on." The enemy had just rung the bell for round one, and we were officially in the fight. That blast called the combat engineers up from the reserve, and we never returned.

While recovering the Husky trailer, a heavily weighted towable unit designed to trigger devices by applying significant pressure to the road, a farmer and a small herd of goats walked by Haji. I couldn't confirm my suspicion; however, the locals seemed to know to stay away that morning until after the blast. With an increased pattern of life, military jargon that denotes daily routines, movements and behaviours of the local populace, it hinted that the imminent threat had passed. Similar to a loudspeaker saying "all clear" during a school fire drill, the habitual activity around the outpost resumed shortly after the blast.

With the Husky trailer recovered and stashed within the exclusion zone of Haji and the road repaired, we did a final check on the engineer technical net. Since the Husky trailer was damaged beyond repair for the operation, we lost a small piece of our IED clearing capabilities. After confirming we were ready to recommence without a trailer, I jumped on the all-informed net.

"Husky continuing the clearance."

About an hour after having a trailer explosively removed from his vehicle, the Husky operator, Corporal Cody Cameron, displayed remarkable grit and dedication to duty by returning to work. Affectionately known as Wolfman because chest hair often protruded from his collar, I can only imagine every hair on his body stood on end as he continued to spearhead the advance.

While awaiting our turn to move, the EOD team advised that the strike likely resulted from a reseeded IED. In most places, the surface of Route Fosters resembled concrete because the dirt road had been compacted from hundreds, if not thousands, of years of traffic. This made digging into the road exceptionally tough. Consequently, the soft dirt of previous IED sites was highly desirable because the softer ground facilitated quicker and easier emplacements.

Eventually our vehicle drove over the remediated blast scene from the Husky strike. While inspecting the site with my own eyes, it became immediately apparent that the forty-five-minute timeline to place an IED was a gross misnomer. We were playing with fire that required a significant paradigm shift. Watching our tires sink into the soft, lush dirt, I estimated that I could place an IED in under ten minutes with a dilapidated shovel in soil that fresh. With our patrols still ping-ponging back and forth along the cleared route to our rear, I realized our risk mitigation plan was specious. We were exposing the patrol to risk, not mitigating it.

I wrestled with my thoughts about the ping-pong patrol as the column advanced at a stop-and-go pace. Our movement resembled a traffic jam on a congested highway as the dismounted engineers meticulously inspected the road. While stationary at one point during the slow advance, a sturdy Afghan man in his late forties skirted our vehicle. He wore a faded, earth-toned robe layered with a worn vest and a dusty turban crowned his head. Years of hard labour showed on his calloused hands. I smiled and waved at him like two passing strangers on a country road back in Canada. He saw me but didn't acknowledge me. His demeanour showed hesitancy as if he feared reprisal for being associated with us.

Beside me, Wally was full of energy. Having consumed a couple of Mac attacks that morning before starting, he needed an activity.

"Sir, I'm going for a walk."

He disconnected his headset from the radio, climbed out of the turret and dismounted from the vehicle. Curious about where he would walk, I watched as he climbed onto the Armoured Recover Vehicle (ARV) immediately behind us in the order of march. A juggernaut of military vehicles, the ARV is like a tow truck for tanks. Equipped with a crane, winch and a welder to help repair vehicles, the ARV also has a robust blade up front to stabilize the vehicle frame during recovery operations. The blade could also be used to remove debris or create paths. This is precisely what Wally had in mind. Moments later, the ARV roared to life and knocked over a few feet of adobe wall immediately adjacent to the road. After his short stroll, Wally returned to the turret and gave me an update.

"Had a Vulcan mind meld with the ARV crew. Just created a bypass lane in case we need to recover vehicles."

One of Wally's favorite expressions, a Vulcan mind meld is a Star Teck pop culture reference about communicating telepathically.

I momentarily froze at the sight of the flattened wall. In Canada, the heritage status of infrastructure begins when it is 50 years old. Demolishing or changing the façade of heritage buildings required a tome of paperwork. Yet, over the last five minutes, we'd destroyed a wall predating the Christian calendar. Undoubtedly, we should have filled out a piece of administration. I debated seeking permission to continue; however, I feared the answer. Some staff officer who didn't understand the threat would provide a well-intentioned "no" and unintentionally pass on a bunch of risks to the route clearance operation. Then I recalled a maxim my father taught me years earlier: don't ask the question if you fear the answer.

I leaned over to Wally to ensure I understood the details of his telepathic conversation.

"What else do you have in mind?"

Without hesitation, Wally outlined his plan.

"We need to strip this place of all combat indicators and create passing lanes in this congested mess. Nothing fancy, just enough to let vehicles jockey."

Wally's logic made perfect sense. In removing the wall, we destroyed aiming marks for detonating devices or reference points for IED emplacement. In anticipation of another IED strike, proactively creating passing lanes on the single route expedited the ability of convoy assets to respond to an incident, potentially saving lives. Wally paused to take a drag on his cigarillo before continuing.

"We also need to be able to slap together a quick HLZ."

Preparing for a medical evacuation in advance would also significantly accelerate response times to injuries. Institutionalized from exercises and training, I caught myself looking for someone to confirm our actions with before I realized we were alone. No dig permits, environmental clearances, or exercise directing staff were monitoring for the standard. The risk assessment and subsequent decisions came down to us evaluating the situation.

I fully concurred with Wally's plan based on all the explosive devices we had already found and the inherent risk of the operation, however I didn't mention anything about our actions on the radio. I figured it would be easier to beg forgiveness than ask permission, and I didn't want any regrets about responding to an IED strike. Playfully, I leaned over to Wally.

"So, we're saying the ARV is making some wide turns?"

"Exactly," Wally said with a wink and a nod.

As we slowly advanced, Wally would routinely turn around and make arm gestures to the ARV. Resembling the ground crew at an airport, full-arm gesticulations from Wally guided the ARV crew to remove IED aiming points, create bypass lanes, and build access points to flat fields in the event we needed to land a helicopter. While the ARV continued to "make wide turns" as we advanced, I continued to monitor the clearance package's progress while enjoying the last of my Mac attack. Our progress halted again when the radio cracked.

"Dismounts found IED. EOD called forward."

By this time, we were like a well-oiled machine. Everyone knew the drill. While waiting for EOD to do their work, the Afghan man with the faded earth-tone robe returned from his errand. I smiled and waved. Once again, he saw me, but there was no response. The morning continued to pass as the sun's rays increased in intensity. Having consumed my Mac attack, I took a moment to relieve myself in front of the LAV and stretch my legs before returning to the turret. After providing another best-guess update on the radio, the Afghan man walked by again. I smiled and waved. This time, he stopped. He made a small, almost imperceptible explosion gesture with his hands and then pointed in front of our vehicle. I nudged Wally so he could witness the conversation. I repeated the sign language back and made a confirming gesture that the explosion was in front of the vehicle. The Afghan man made a single head nod and proceeded to walk away, as befriending the coalition troops in any fashion could mean a lethal reprisal from the Taliban. I immediately gave well-enunciated directions to the driver on the vehicle intercom.

"Mac. Back up."

Once removed as far as possible from the potential IED, I provided a SITREP on the radio.

"Found another potential IED. EROC and EOD will investigate once they finish with their current IED."

Absolute insanity. I dreamed about finding one IED, and now we potentially found two at the same time. Around mid-morning, we received an update on the first IED that I relayed on the radio.

"IED consisted of a Chinese rocket and a radio-controlled device. Found just within the blind spot of the Haji observation mast."

Some outposts had Coyote reconnaissance vehicles with a ten-metre surveillance mast. On top of the mast rested high-power optics, like a telescope for long-range vision. The combination of technology and height improved our observation capabilities around the outpost. In this situation, the enemy completely negated our technological advantage by placing the IED just a few inches inside a blind spot. Although our adversaries' tactics were simple, they were surprisingly effective. Coalition forces had all sorts of fancy optics to observe the battlespace. Despite this advantage, by carefully studying our capabilities and actions, the Taliban's devious resourcefulness found simple ways to move unobserved and attack our blind spots.

There is a saying in warfare when an inferiorly equipped force combats a more technically advanced adversary: you have all the watches, but we have all the time. I used to think it just referred to time and that the enemy could outwait us to win. However, while pondering events on our operation, I realized a deeper meaning. The watches also represented our technology. We had the upper hand in every aspect, yet we were still going toe-to-toe with the Taliban. Just like they didn't need watches to tell time, they didn't need technology to compete with us. By taking the time to watch, they negated our sophisticated optics and superior vehicles by simply placing rudimentary homemade bombs in our blind spots. With makeshift explosive devices costing less than a hundred dollars, they could destroy vehicles worth millions of dollars. It felt as if we were a professional sports team with all the coaches, trainers, gear, and nutritionists; however, on game day, we were grinding it out with a poorly resourced high school team because they played with a different strategy, mindset, and motivation.

There was some intricate vehicle maneuvering and choreographing to get the Buffalo back to the site of our potential device. Since it had been ahead of us in the order of march, it couldn't use the numerous hastily created passing lanes behind us. Watching large vehicles struggle to pass on a narrow dirt road—and the time it took—I was reassured that our decision to create bypass lanes as we moved was the right one. It ensured we could respond as quickly as possible to any medical emergencies.

Once on site of the potential IED, the Buffalo's exploration arm went to work, eventually spearing a yellow jug filled with homemade explosives.

"IED found. EOD requires more time to exploit," relayed over the radio nets.

The EOD operator, Master Corporal Marty Gratrix, updated the engineering net. A ruggedly handsome farm kid from Alberta, he possessed a natural, likeably charm. Beneath his hearty sense of humour was a quick mind with a knack for solving problems. Since the plastic jug of explosives stuck to the Buffalo arm, a hook-and-line kit was required. This tool allows technicians to manipulate or move suspicious devices from a safe distance. During the removal of the yellow jug, Gratrix's crafty intuition said there had to be more to the bomb, so he requested additional time to exploit the scene.

As Gratrix followed up on his hunch, the gravity of the situation hit me. Our vehicle had been parked for almost two hours immediately in front of an IED. All the clearance vehicles and dismounted engineers had missed it. We were so close I urinated on it. Only by the grace of a local did we find it. I'd heard about the power of a simple smile, but I never thought one would lead me to find a bomb that could have had my name on it. Over the next ninety minutes, I went up and down my list of pre-established updates on the radio to buy Gratrix time. Finally, we received the plan, which I passed over the radio.

"Confirm command wire IED. Large cooking cauldron full of homemade explosives found. Have taken a sample of the homemade explosives, going to blow the device in situ."

By grabbing some of the explosive mixture, further forensics to help target the IED network could occur in a laboratory. Technically known as ANFO (Ammonium Nitrate Fuel Oil), it is a widely used homemade explosive composed of ammonium nitrate, a standard fertilizer, and fuel oil such as diesel. Being relatively easy to produce and effective, it is commonly used in mining, construction, and by insurgents to fabricate IEDs.

The radio nets buzzed with activities as we prepared to detonate an unknown amount of explosives still buried in the road.

KABOOM!

Dust and debris once again filled the air around the convoy as a shock wave passed through, reminding everyone of an IED's latent power. As soon as the all-clear signal was given, we patched the crater in the road and continued our advance. Towards the end of the day, we arrived at Zangabad, the second outpost on our route clearance mission. Although exhausted from the hot sun and the stresses of the environment, we had a few tasks to complete before going to sleep.

As the shadows grew longer, the primary item that required attention was the Buffalo exploitation arm. If a device detonated during exploitation, the end of the arm is designed to shear off to minimize damage. The problem with this design is that the arm would bend where it was designed to shear while digging into a hard surface. Working closely with the ARV crew and their welder, EROC reinforced the Buffalo arm by fusing six-foot pickets to it so it would withstand the harsh demands of the operation. Like plowing over walls earlier that day, I'm sure we pushed the limits of some policy by modifying a vehicle without permission. Still, it made the most sense after a quick risk assessment, so we proceeded. After furtively completing the unsanctioned modifications, everyone endeavoured to get as much sleep as possible, while the evening ping-pong patrol kept the route open throughout the night.

The following day, we'd developed a rhythm and were advancing towards the next outpost with minimal chatter on the radio. We made steady progress throughout the morning and into the afternoon. After a long halt, Wally called our driver, Mac, via the vehicle intercom.

"Hey Mac, how you making out?"

"Just rocking out with my cock out, warrant."

We all laughed at his sarcastic tone, which indicated he was bored out of his mind.

"Hey Mac, it's not a cock, it's a penis."

Surprised by the sudden political correctness of the warrant, Mac replied.

"That's a…"

BOOM.

The mud huts and surrounding earth walls muffled the explosion and attenuated the blast wave; however, a distinctive mushroom cloud rose into the air. After a minute of silence, EROC came on the radio.

"Buffalo hit an IED. Need MEDEVAC for one casualty."

The explosion completely removed the front tire and axle from the driver's side of the vehicle. Wally immediately started gesticulating like a marionette puppet to the ARV crew, who formed another vehicle bypass lane and an access point to the adjacent field. His Vulcan mind meld with the ARV crew kept him off the radio so I could use it to help quarterback the evacuation. Over the next thirty minutes, the training from Wainwright kicked in as medics responded to the scene. The infantry secured the site and aided the casualty movement to the helicopter that touched down in the field adjacent to Route Fosters. The speed and efficiency of our response to the strike stemmed from our pre-established passing lanes, fully validating our decision to create them along the way. Once the casualty was evacuated, the resemblance with our Wainwright training ended.

Responses on the radio started to pass more and more through our LAV. The patrol commander was dismounted with the flank security using a small radio. Although lighter, it didn't have the bandwidth of a larger radio, resulting in our LAV being used as a rebroadcasting station. This was a significant change from Wainwright, where we were so uninvolved we had time to conduct emergency weapon training concurrent to the critical ranges.

The other distinctive difference from training was the aftermath of an IED explosion that required physical attention before we could proceed. In this case, the enemy buried the IED immediately adjacent to a steel reinforced concrete culvert. Using this approach, they caused us to miss the metal IED components with our detection systems because we assumed the metallic signature came from the concrete rebar in the buried culvert. As a result of the detonation, in front of our convoy sat a twenty-four metric ton Buffalo without a front end. Exacerbating the situation, the Buffalo was resting at a thirty-degree angle because the front end had fallen into the large crater left by the blast. Only the sheer ingenuity of the EROC engineers and the ARV crew allowed the recovery process to occur.

Being a relatively tall vehicle, over four meters, the Buffalo became very unstable during the recovery pull back to Zangabad. Lacking adequate tow points to connect recovery cables, the ARV crew did their best to latch onto the vehicle's frame. Progress was steady for about half a kilometre before the Buffalo flipped onto its side. Based on the threat of being attacked during the recovery operation, time was of the essence, so we didn't care if we caused further damage to the vehicle. Consequently to avoid becoming sitting ducks, the ARV commenced to drag the Buffalo. In the process, the hull of the Buffalo started to plow a forty-centimetre-deep rut into the road, similar to an old-fashioned farm implement. But even that didn't phase the herculean power of the ARV's diesel engine.

The gearheads marvelled at the tractor-pull-type scenario. From our LAV, I too was drawn to watch and revel before commenting on the vehicle intercom.

"What a display of horsepower. I'd..."

KABOOM.

Another explosion drowned out the earth-jarring hum of the diesel engine.

Once again, the patrol launched into IED strike reaction drills. After the dust settled, I summarized a flurry of communications on the engineering networks.

"Buffalo hit an IED during the recovery process. Sustained one casualty, nine-liner to follow."

Physically, we had not moved since the last blast, so we rinsed and repeated the process with another casualty. Master Corporal Jake Wilkinson from the ARV crew sustained numerous face lacerations from the explosion that would eventually result in the loss of an eye. As many made the mistake of thinking the route was clear, we were not all under armour during the recovery. By sheer luck, we only sustained one casualty. Somehow, an overzealous bomb maker buried the IED too deep for detection by our route clearance package. We only applied sufficient pressure deep enough to detonate the device by plowing into the road during the vehicle recovery. Once Jake was evacuated, we jockeyed personnel to cover off patrol duties. Fortunately, we had sufficient redundancy nested within the operation to allow us to continue the operation.

The struggle to open Route Fosters continued for the next couple of days. The daily routine consisted of finds, small strikes, and exploitation of devices. Eventually, we arrived at Talukan, approximately nine kilometres from our start point. Going over the statistics with Wally, I seriously questioned our ability to sustain an operation like this. What was supposed to be a three or four-day operation had lasted over ten days. During that time, we'd encountered twelve IEDs - six finds pre-detonation and six finds by detonation. The IED strikes resulted in multiple casualties, with two requiring evacuation and four disabled vehicles. These busted vehicles started to form small boneyards in the outpost exclusions zones. In many respects, the tiny rows of damaged vehicles resembled a pick-your-part auto wrecker. Accounting for breakdowns, IED finds, and the subsequent exploitation, IED strikes, recovery operations, route remediations, and casualty evacuations, on average, we cleared just over one kilometre of road per day. Shocked by the statistics, I looked at Wally.

"We can't sustain this. We need to change our approach."

He silently agreed; however, he was fighting another paradigm shift. The nightly ping-pong patrol didn't always use vehicle lights so they could remain tactical. "Blackout drive," a military term for driving without headlights, is a great strategy when the threat is armed forces with machine guns and rockets trying to ambush you. In our new environment laced with IEDs, the axiomatic procedure deserved a second thought. Seemingly counterintuitive, white light helped illuminate combat indicators such as freshly disturbed dirt on the road. These potentially life-saving clues were masked while driving without headlights. Even though we had air assets such as drones with thermal imaging that could detect the temperature difference in the road caused by freshly disturbed earth, we were underutilizing a primary sense on the ground.

Sitting in the command post of Talukan, I had a rare opportunity to talk with a couple platoon commanders from Bravo Company. Captain Rob Clarke, an infantry platoon commander with a genetics degree, regaled us with the challenges of completing PERs while in a combat outpost. These places were so austere that soldiers pissed in a funnel that drained through the wall. To defecate, they used sanitary bags that were later burned in the garbage pit that sustained a smouldering fire around the clock. Revelling in our shared commiseration about PERs, I turned to Rob.

"In your PERs, did you put works well without taking a shower?"

At this point in the operations, we all stunk to high heaven.

"John, I like to use…"

KABOOM.

With the sun setting, another IED strike occurred just east of the outpost. Exhausted from the last few days of fighting ghosts, an on-edge group jumped back into action to respond to the strike. Wasting no time, Captain Clarke and his crew exited the command post and drove off without their helmets and flak vests. At the scene, the blast had hit underneath the driver's compartment of a LAV, which violently jarred the driver and subsequently caused a fatal head wound. Later that night, we learned that the strike had killed Private Terry John Street. The recovery team also noted that the IED blast hole was significantly smaller than previous sites. This indicated a hasty, shallow burial, which meant the device was likely seeded in the road during one of the gaps in the ping-pong patrol. Deeper burials tended to result in larger craters. Even more chilling, it was placed at a ninety-degree turn in the road, just inside the Talukan mast blind spot.

Shortly after our thirteenth incident, the order was given to withdraw. After dropping as many logistical supplies as possible at each outpost, we proceeded to snake our way back up the route we had just cleared. Behind the last vehicle, no further ping-pong patrols ensued, thus wholly giving up any attempt to retain the route.

I remained on edge while returning to Sperwan Ghar, unshaven in days and edgy from the volatile explosions that sporadically rocked our world. One moment, we were smoking and joking with each other in the vehicle, the next, we were responding to a life-and-death situation. It became a weird oscillation between diametrically opposed worlds.

Trying to piece it all together, I couldn't help but notice the similarities between fighting the Taliban and deer hunting. Growing up, my uncle Walter showed me how to hunt deer by looking for patterns and concealing my movements. He also showed me how to find choke points that funnelled deer and how to obscure my presence from their senses. During the earlier stages of his tutelage, he also showed me one of his favourite spots that habitually yielded many kills over the years. The exact same process happened on Route Fosters. The Taliban identified our patterns, they found ways to conceal their movements from our observation, and they looked for choke points in the road to attack us. Like my uncle passing on his favourite hunting spots to me, undoubtedly, the senior Taliban passed on their favourite attack locations to their junior members as part of their grooming process to make fighters, as demonstrated by the reseeding of IEDs in previous spots. As I wondered whether planting an IED was a rite of passage for them, similar to harvesting a first deer is for young hunters, a chilling realization struck me. The only difference between hunting deer and fighting the Taliban was that in Afghanistan, we were the deer.

# 10

# Venus Flytrap

Sperwan Ghar hummed with activity as we reconstituted from the Route Fosters operation. As the troops reorganized their vehicles and auxiliary gear, the kit was strewn everywhere in the hot sun. In the engineering common area, after shaving and showering, troops exchanged stories of their exploits while chain-smoking. One sapper after another swapped war stories between drags of their cigarettes about their first exposure to an IED or contact from enemy fire. The golden thread throughout the tales: engineers were finally understood and appreciated. While cleaning weapons, I overheard many of the sappers recount the requests for support they received.

"Hey, Chimo, can you have a look first?"

This became a regular question from patrol members traversing chokepoints in dangerous terrain.

"Hey, Chimo, what do you think about this?"

This became another common request for engineers to inspect a dispersed piece of earth or a random piece of garbage that might be hiding an IED. This meticulous attention to detail showed a metamorphic shift from training, where the infantry never sought a second opinion about disturbed earth or random trash.

But by far, the most noteworthy stories came from Gratrix. Using a basic digital camera with some movie recording capabilities, he showed Wally and me pictures of the exploited IEDs.

"Check this out. This is where I cut the detonator off the det cord, and we collected the command wire."

We squinted to see the small photo on the Canon camera. Gratrix's finger traced across the screen until he switched to the next image.

"This is from the firing point."

We strained our eyes to see the photo on the dust-scratched screen. Gratrix embodied his trade. His passion as an EOD operator exuded from his pores as he switched to the video setting on his camera. The screen came alive with a homemade video depicting the IED discovered in front of our LAV. In the short video, Gratrix showed his work to unearth the main charge; he highlighted how the bombmaker created the device and the tactical placement. The footage was detailed, but based on the context in which it was made, it struck me as too detailed.

"Holy smokes, how much time did you spend making videos?"

Gratrix gave an awkward chuckle and stopped talking. While I'd been fabricating best-guess situational reports to buy EOD time, I envisioned EOD sweating bullets in a bomb suit while we baked in the sun providing them security. From the videos, it looked as if we were protecting a film crew making a documentary series about IED placement with Gratrix acting like the next Steven Spielberg. Sensing my discontent with the videos, Gratrix elaborated.

"Sir, this is why the videos are important…"

Gratrix went on to explain that the degree of IED sophistication depended on the available resources and the bombmaker's skill. By exploiting devices, patterns could be identified to help target the bombmaker. Detailed photos and videos helped the exploitation team see things that might have been missed on the ground. His well-articulated explanation made perfect sense. Taking time to make videos seemed so out of place in a warzone, and I could only imagine the reaction I would have received to a truthful SITREP.

"EOD is just taking some time to make a home video of the scene. We'll be on route when Gratrix gets the right cut."

We laughed at the thought as he proudly showed us the remainder of his material. Written by Gratrix, filmed by Gratrix, and narrated by Gratrix, it looked as if he moonlighted as a videographer. As he went through his scrapbook of photos and videos, I could see Gratrix was right. Lots of details could be harvested from the digital records. Moreover, the snapshots were exceptionally educational. I learned more about IEDs in the sixty-minute discussion with him than the previous six months in training. Gratrix's detailed explanation of the diverse devices and the differing tactical emplacement showed a resourceful enemy prototyping tactics against our patterns. It resembled studying a film about the sports team you were about to play. Gratrix kept the conversation light, but examining photos of IEDs designed to kill you felt eerie.

Now that we were back online from the operation, daily SITREPs and post-operational reports were expected by a plethora of staff officers in KAF. After our exploits, they were keen on learning the details. While hammering out a report in our makeshift office, Wally broke my chain of thought by busting in and showing his mischievous side.

"Hey sir, how much cash you got? I want to get a donkey."

Under a tight deadline to finish my report, I didn't think about the random request.

"Uh, two hundred bucks. Cash is under the book on my bunk."

He grabbed the cash and left just as quickly as he came. With the troops watching TV in the common area just outside our quarters, the relative peace and quiet gave me time to submit my post-operational report. The report contained photos of blown-up vehicles drooling every imaginable petroleum product onto the ground. As I hit submit, I worried about some staff officers requesting spill reports. Hopefully, they would assume the spill was only 19.9 litre.

I was finishing up our daily SITREP when Wally barged in again.

"Hey, request a leather couch on our daily SITREP."

Drawing upon his passion for home décor, he added, "I'd like a second one to complement the one we already have."

During the countless hours we spent together in the turret over the last two weeks, I'd listened to Wally's plans to develop our common area with a large wooden deck, a shed, and a pond. Based on his desire to build a small oasis to facilitate troop gatherings, I didn't question the couch request. He also mentioned wanting a donkey to boost morale and foster unit cohesion around the camp. At the time, I didn't think he was serious. I was wrong. As I wasn't sure if anyone read my daily SITREPs, I thought a surefire way to check was to request a merlot-coloured leather couch and state we were buying a donkey.

After a couple day's reprieve, we were back to work. As our Route Fosters operation fell short of the fourth and final outpost, Mushan, our next mission was a resupply run to the last location. The plan saw us driving up the Arghandab River to avoid Route Fosters. This would allow us to parallel it a few hundred metres to the north. The wide riverbed offered multiple route options, significantly mitigating the IED threat because there were fewer canalizing choke points. After some technical discussions with armoured assets, we decided to use the same style clearance package with a slightly tweaked order of march. Due to the uneven terrain, tanks with rollers and plows would take the point while the AEV would plow the top four inches of the riverbed. This scrape would help uncover IEDs and create a drivable lane for the wheeled vehicles that would follow. Everything flowed seamlessly until I received a call from Hollywood.

"Sir, got a project for you. It's uh… a little different."

Knowing Hollywood's meticulous attention to planning details and common-sense approach, his voice made it clear something was up.

"To control dust in Zangabad, you're going to create a helicopter landing pad out of Hesco."

The phone went silent. The concept of trying to control dust in Afghanistan was like trying to cage a fart. For an instant, I thought he was joking, potentially as a rebuttal to our request for a merlot-coloured couch. However, he provided additional details.

"A sea can full of Hesco and rebar to make staples is inbound to your location."

I started to push back on the concept; however, Hollywood ended the conversation.

"Sir, sea can is inbound. Hollywood, out."

While being busy on operations, we'd missed many KAF-based undertakings. During our absence, somebody came up with a *really good idea*. As Major Packer was on the road, I couldn't even reach him for additional details. As the convoy for Mushan was leaving in the morning, we didn't have much time to formulate a plan. After a quick discussion with Wally, we decided to leave one engineering section in Zangabad on the way to Mushan. We would then pick them up on the way back. I then briefed the plan to Sergeant Bob Jones, the engineering section commander we would leave behind to build the HLZ pad. A tall, middle-aged man who was one of our reservists, his high intellect created a penchant to overanalyse situations. On one occasion, we discussed the sheer strength of construction nails while building a small shed. Sergeant Jones didn't take long to review and comment on the HLZ pad.

"Where is the rest of the plan?"

He held the paper plan in his hand as he started to point out some concerns.

"This is analogous to a crossword puzzle with half the clues missing," he concluded.

After a quick glance, the plan did appear to be thin, but it was an order, and we needed to get after it.

"Sergeant, I agree it is a bizarre concept. Just try. If it doesn't work, stop."

I had a disparaging view of the entire concept. Even if the HLZ plan was complete, any relief from the dust would have been ephemeral at best. Realizing I had no further information, Sergeant Jones left and began questioning his peers like a treasure hunter, searching for clues to ensure the HLZ project was built correctly. In hindsight, I should have advocated for more clarity on the opaque initiative.

The next seventy-two hours were a blur of activity. The logistical resupply up the river, commonly known as a "river run," went as planned. Similar to the Route Fosters clearance, we dropped off supplies to each outpost. The enemy took potshots at us along the way, but nothing serious. Once back in Sperwan Ghar, I finally got to catch up with a frustrated Sergeant Jones.

"Sir, nobody in the outpost knew we were coming to build a HLZ pad."

I wrongfully assumed the project sponsor in KAF passed on details to the outpost. Due to this oversight, I added another additional friction to an already arduous task as Sergeant Jones continued.

"We also didn't spend much time outside the protective walls of the outpost due to the threat of being shot by insurgents."

Listening to Sergeant Jones describe the situation, it became clear that the project risk to the sappers was even greater than I anticipated.

"Eventually we were able to start construction, but we couldn't bend the rebar into staples, and we still have questions about where to place the fasteners."

While reviewing the initial design, I noticed the plan required rebar bent into large U-shaped staples. Once the Hesco was spread out flat, these U-shaped staples would pin the HLZ pad flat against the earth. I wrongfully assumed that these staples would have been prefabricated. Transforming a dumb idea into an inane one was the expectation that we could fabricate rebar staples in a desolate combat outpost without tools. The place was so austere that troops defecated in bags. I empathized with Sergeant Jones' frustration as I wondered what clown had created this circus act. On the bright side, Sergeant Jones took some time to thoroughly recce the situation so he could make suggestions to meet the HLZ pad intent. Although we submitted the recce report for consideration, frustrations about the project and the lack of a clear plan lingered.

As Wally tried to calm the frustrations of Sergeant Jones, I started the gruelling process of writing my post-operation report.

About a week later while typing away at my computer, I heard on the radio speaker that Major Packer was en route to our location. I found it strange that his visit would be so impromptu. However, it would give me an excellent opportunity to connect about the HLZ pad. Much to my surprise, Major Packer's visit wouldn't last long.

At the time, Canadian military convoys required at least three vehicles to move on the road. Major Packer's and the artillery officer commanding's respective vehicles created the required three-vehicle packet to allow the Battlegroup Commander freedom of movement. On many trips, they filled the role of a chauffeured escort service. Not having a moment to waste before he needed to escort the Battlegroup Commander to his next appointment, Major Packer hustled into our makeshift office wearing full fighting order.

"Hey, John, I heard the HLZ pad is a mess. But listen, we gotta get it done."

My head snapped back in disbelief. What did he mean we had to continue with ill-conceived plan?

"Let me know what you need, John. Hell, if you want me to call in a witch doctor to bless the dust, I'll make it happen."

I expressed my concerns about the lack of details in the design and how it wasn't required since we already landed helicopters in the area without dust concerns. Based on Sergeant Jones' recce, the troops suggested buying water pumps to spray the landing area to control dust. Despite my best efforts, Major Packer remained resolute. I got the feeling it wasn't because he thought it was a good idea, but someone with a much bigger epaulet told him to make it so. Realizing resistance was futile, I stressed that we needed prefabricated staples. He took note in his field message pad before changing the subject.

"As for Sergeant Jones, he's fired. We're here to pick him up."

I snapped my head back as if the words had physically struck me. Fired?

"Long story short, he wrote an insubordinate email that broke every rule in the book. I can't trust him."

On a tight leash to escort the Battlegroup Commander to the next rendezvous, the conversation abruptly concluded. Just before Major Packer walked out the door, he stopped and turned.

"The next river run is in two weeks. Try to finish the HLZ pad on the next run."

"Roger, sir."

With the dust of Major Packer's convoy fading in the distance, Wally and I looked at each other in disbelief. What just happened? A fired section commander, and we still needed to finish the most ill-conceived project ever. Wally and I chatted for a few minutes and then spoke with the engineering section about the firing of Sergeant Jones. It wasn't a shock as they were already more conversant about the content of the email than me. We then explained that the second in command, Master Corporal Scotty Noonan, would fill the section commander duties. Known for his slapstick, sarcastic sense of humour, Scotty's charisma kept everyone around him in high spirits. Being the kind of guy who'd give you his shirt off his back, the section adapted quickly to the change in leadership.

That evening, Wally and I chatted late into the night on the lone merlot-coloured couch long after the troops retired from a boisterous poker game. We war-gamed how to reset the HLZ pad project and how to restart with a new section commander. Ultimately, we had a sound plan, which Wally summed up succinctly.

"I'll get Scotty up to speed. You do your officer thing and look into this HLZ farce."

Over the following week, I tried to get a copy of the infamous email without any luck. Through conversations with headquarters staff, I learned that, allegedly, the insubordinate correspondence stemmed from the HLZ pad fiasco, and the wording went along the lines of "I won't take responsibility for the death of troops due to your decisions." I also learned the HLZ pad idea stemmed from a Falkland War concept to increase the bearing capacity of the soil. If that was the case, why did anyone think it would control dust? We even linked Scotty up with some engineering experts in KAF. During the conversation, the design expert pointed out that we may need to dust off the matt as part of our maintenance routine.

During his back brief to Wally and me, Scotty succinctly summed up the absurdity of the concept:

"Sir, that's like trying to sweep dirt off a t-shirt."

The entire situation stunk. I couldn't stand up for Sergeant Jones based on his actions, however, I didn't like how his message was overlooked: the HLZ pad design lacked details. After exhausting efforts behind the scenes to find the missing clues to the design, Sergeant Jones finally reached out to headquarters in a last-ditch effort to get answers to his questions. He desperately wanted to confirm the plan because he didn't want to build the design incorrectly and subsequently risk helicopters and their crews when they landed on the pad. Granted, his email had a poor tone, and he deserved initial counselling for writing too, but what about the message? How could the tone drown out the content in a warzone where phrases about killing people isn't hyperbole? In the end, what troubled me the most wasn't the tone of the conversations but the direction. All tell, no ask. We already tried to complete the project, and we identified numerous shortfalls to the idea beyond highlighting that the project was unnecessary in the first place. We also physically knew the area as well as the kinetic threats of bullets and IEDs. To placate the project sponsor, we even offered alternative solutions that might work based on our knowledge of the ground. But it all fell on deaf ears.

Approximately two weeks later, we rinsed and repeated another river run. We dropped off Scotty and crew on the way by Zangabad with a crap ton of prefabricated staples. The remainder of us continued to Talukan to improve the fortifications of the outpost and build a bunker. We received daily updates from Scotty and crew by monitoring the radio. They had to overcome a few challenges unravelling the Hesco, and the staples could only be pounded in during the mid-day heat, or they would break. It was something about the metallurgy being changed during the staple prefabrication processes with a blow torch. Apart from a few potshots throughout and one volley of fire towards the end, the project went as smoothly as could be expected. After two days of hard work, Scotty and the crew were ready to be extracted the following day.

Relieved that nobody was hurt, I prepared for our return trip to Sperwan Ghar the following day where we would pick up Scotty and crew en route. While sending my evening SITREP on the radio, Hollywood mentioned an additional task.

"Chinook helicopter inbound for Zangabad tomorrow at 1000 hours."

I stopped writing on my field message pad. I turned to look at Wally, sitting like a starfish in the back of the LAV, blowing smoke rings with a cigarillo while enjoying a Mac attack. He perked up to hear the subsequent transmission over the LAV radio speaker from Hollywood.

"Get photos."

Jiminy Crickets. Who is behind this project? We mortals were driving zig-zag patterns through a riverbed to avoid IEDs, and this demigod could arrange for an airlift in a few hours. We could only get a confirmed airlift once we had a casualty, not to avoid one in the first place. I found the situation so absurd that I could only reply with a half-assed remark.

"Roger that. The missionary's wife and I will get front-row seats."

"Big Chi, little Mo, Hollywood out."

Hearing the unspoken words behind Hollywood's tone, I knew he wanted photos to help highlight the project's dysfunction.

The following morning, after moving to Zangabad, I greeted Scotty to congratulate him on a job well done. During our conversation, I learned the firefights had been a little more dire than reported on the radio and that they had been lucky not to sustain a casualty. He then pointed out yet another design oversight.

"Hey sir, what's the plan when a mortar hits?"

Great point. As the HLZ pad already looked as if it should be recorded in the *Guinness Book of World Records* as the world's largest Venus flytrap, I could only imagine the rat nest of wire a mortar would create if it hit the pad. If that happened, a helicopter might not be able to land. Oh boy, I could already envision the jabs. The Chimos made a HLZ pad that was so bad it precluded helicopters from landing. It had all the makings of a terrible joke.

I climbed into one of the outpost security towers with my Canon camera to get some photos. At the top stood two ANA soldiers charged with manning a PKM machine gun. On the floor around the Hesco walls were dozens of cans that looked like grossly oversized sardine tins, Russian ammunition canisters for the belt-fed machine gun. The small five-foot-nothing soldiers were clad in old, mismatched U.S. military fatigues that were five sizes too big. Large bulges of cloth popped out at their bellies due to their belts cinching the oversized pants to their waistline.

Without an interpreter, I struggled to communicate with the ANA soldiers. Bored from inactivity, they seemed content to have a visitor break up the monotony. After taking a few still photos of the HLZ pad, I even rehearsed a video to be just like Gratrix. While waiting for the helicopter to arrive, I enjoyed the warmth of the morning sun as it crept higher into the clear sky. From the elevated position, I could easily see out over the surrounding fields that contained the odd farmer tilling the soil. In the background, the generator's diesel engine hummed. Besides the acrid stench of the ANA soldiers, waiting for a helicopter under a clear blue sky was a pleasant reprieve from the hectic operational tempo.

At 1000 hours, right on cue, the distinctive thump-thump of the Chinook's rotors echoed across the valley resembling distant thunder. Two Kiowa gunships zipped ahead, slicing through the sky as the armed escort. From my perch in the watchtower, I had a front-row seat to the premiere. With my camera, I started to film the final approach of the Chinook. Ominous Armageddon-looking dust clouds whirled in immense concentric circles as it swooped in over the surrounding trees and touched down. Nanoseconds later, a *Guinness Book of World Records* sized dust ball engulfed the outpost and surrounding area.

As I was putting my camera away to prevent it from getting filled with dust, machine gun bullets and the distinct whistle of RPGs, a Russian-developed shoulder-fired rocket designed as an anti-armour weapon but equally deadly against soft targets, filled the air. Even the Taliban wanted to see the maiden landing on the Hesco pad. In response to the fusillade, the sentries returned fire. The PKM machine gun roared beside my head, drowning out every other sound as it spat out round after round. Grimacing under the noise while the Chinook helicopter continued to kick up a plumes of dust, one of the ANA soldiers dropped to the ground and started flopping like a fish out of water. Thinking he was hit, I began to pat him down in search of a wound, but it only made it worse when I touched his legs.

"Hooootttttt ammmmmmmooooooo!" he screamed.

"What?" Through the dust, I saw sheer pain in his eyes as I shouted back at him.

"Where are you hit?"

As soon as I said it, I knew it was useless. His head and body vibrated so fast we couldn't communicate even if we spoke the same language. I frantically checked for wounds. As he continued to flop uncontrollably on the floor, copper-coloured casing poured out of the machine gun beside us as the barrel glowed a crimson red. Not seeing any reasons for the violent convulsions but feeling the stinging heat of the casing as they hit my hands, I figured it out. In very slow English, I yelled.

"HOT AMMO?"

His eyes bulged. He gave a goofy smile with his face covered in saliva, snot, and dirt.

"Yasha!"

When the PKM started firing, the hot casings had gone straight down his baggy pants. The large loops caused by his belt created perfect chutes to flow hot shells down onto his bare legs. Relieved that he was okay, I heard an abrupt clunk. The machine gun stopped. The gunner looked down.

"Noooo Ammmmoooo!"

I turned to the oversized sardine cans that required a can opener to access. Then I saw one tied to the machine gun tripod. On a piece of string, swinging like the pendulum of a grandfather clock, was the cheapest Colemen can opener you could buy, one of the ones designed for a key chain to help cook the odd can of beans when you are camping. I was beyond pissed. Inhaling piles of dust while RPGs streaked by similar to little jets, an ANA soldier with first-degree burns from his genitals to his ankles vibrated beside me in a bath of hot shell casings, now we were out of ammunition in a firefight. The HLZ pad will control the dust, my ass. I started opening ammunition tins at lightning speed so we could get back into the fight. I moved so fast that we completed a trifecta of Guinness World Records: most enormous flytrap, most immense dust cloud, and fastest opening of a Russian ammunition tin. But the bullets weren't required.

As quickly as the fighting started, it stopped. A few minutes after landing, the Chinook took off as if nothing happened. Likewise, the camp activity returned to normal. Just another short firefight in the Horn of Panjwai. No different than a brief thunderstorm interrupting a summer picnic. After helping reset the observation post, I bid farewell to my ANA comrades. Before leaving, I took one last photo of the HLZ pad. Due to the Chinook idling on the pad for so long, it was already starting to resemble a famished Venus flytrap, just waiting to eat the next helicopter.

Back in Sperwan Ghar, I proudly submitted my photos and video. No response. During the next few days, nobody mentioned the HLZ pad except our infantry brothers in Zangabad. Concerned that the design was unstable and would impede helicopters landing, they unilaterally decided to push it into a ditch with the outpost backhoe. Nobody said a word even after I highlighted this point in my daily report to KAF. It was as if the operation never happened. The only person who commented on my video besides Wally was Gratrix. After laughing that a massive dust cloud blocked my video of a dust mitigation device, he suggested I needed to provide more dialogue next time for a heightened emotional connection to the audience.

After all that effort, we had created nothing more than a mound of smashed Hesco the size of a three-car garage on the edge of the Zangabad exclusion zone. I wanted to tell them I told you so. However, I stopped short because it wasn't required. That derelict pile provided a metaphoric fulcrum for a shift. The KAF project sponsors knew they had screwed up. They also knew that we knew they screwed up. From then on, the tone of the conversation changed from a "tell" to an "ask."

From then on, they listened to the sappers on the ground.

# 11

# Adjustments

I once heard a general officer say that life can be divided into three buckets: what you can control, what you can influence, and what you can neither control nor influence. He implored us to focus on the first two buckets. As we learned a lot during our initial months in Panjwai, this analogy resonated with me more deeply as we made adjustments.

At Sperwan Ghar, we had a lot of control over the fortification and improvement projects. Immediately after resetting from an operation, we recommenced projects to fortify or improve our position. Projects such as bunker reinforcements, observation post modifications or electrical distribution network upgrades with a technician. In addition, we also tackled some of Wally's nesting ideas to create a Zen Garden. It didn't take long before we had a massive wooden deck, a small pond with a water feature, and our second leather couch installed in front of the television. The sappers created a cozy area for relaxation and entertainment that pulled them out of the isolation of their bunks.

In hindsight, the sappers got a little too creative. Somehow we acquired a square, glass fish tank. As part of the Zen

Garden, some sappers created a little habitat for insects inside the aquarium. Then one day, action in the fish tank intensified. While completing projects around camp, the troops would encounter deadly bugs like scorpions or black widow spiders. Instead of killing or tossing them aside, they began to place them inside the aquarium. Territorial battles inevitably ensued with the addition of too many insects in the tank. As a result, the "Thunderdome" staged countless minibeast contests. As insects fought to the death similar to ancient gladiators, the Thunderdome became the mini-Colosseum of Sperwan Ghar for several months of our tour.

While some troops played Guitar Hero on the Xbox, I christened the new couch with Scotty as he recharged from HLZ pad debacle. During our conversation, I commented on the ludicrous supply system.

"We can get a merlot leather couch delivered in under two weeks, yet we can't get mine detectors or water pumps to hose down the HLZ."

With an easygoing smile, Scotty summarized the problem.

"That's just how the nutty army rolls."

I sighed; he wasn't wrong. Someone somewhere prioritized a couch over mine detectors or water pumps in the labyrinth of military logistics.

We also tightly controlled the sleeping and eating routine. Every morning in camp, we consistently rose early and started working. I always found it easier for the troops to respond to an unforecasted requirement when they were already conscious versus starting from a deep sleep. This approach also allowed us to miss the mid-day heat with a short nap in our relatively cooler barracks. Sometimes, naps were in short supply as the Red Bull energy drink became a craze. Eventually, Wally had to ration it to one can per man per day, as some troops were drinking it like water to stay hydrated. Through the daily grind, morale remained high between comfortable quarters, a steady routine, and the Zen Garden in our common area. When I thought morale couldn't improve, a visitor named Hughes brought it to a new level.

Late one afternoon, Wally affably strolled by the troop area leading a miniature brown donkey on a corrugated rope. With a small band of groupies in tow snapping photos, he glanced over and quipped as if nothing unusual was happening.

"Hey sir, just taking the newest troop for a walk."

Behind him, one sapper after another cracked jokes.

"Nice ass, warrant."

"I'm jealous of your ass."

"Careful, that ass kicks!"

By nightfall, the troops named him Hughes after a sapper who bailed before the deployment. They also established a stable in an L-shape portion of the Hesco wall behind our barracks by scrounging some concertina razor wire and six-foot pickets. They even hung a tarp to provide some shade. Everything looked good, except they placed the animal pen very close to the quarters of the company commander and sergeant major. Slightly concerned about the proximity, I had a more pressing worry.

"Hey Wally," I asked, suddenly realizing we hadn't actually planned for donkey nutrition. "What's this thing going to eat?"

With a big grin, Wally took a long drag on his cigarillo and said, "Just wait."

In the distance, I heard the low put-put of our John Deere Gator. As it pulled to a rickety halt, my jaw hit the dirt. Marijuana plants overtook some sections of the Sperwan Ghar exclusion zone. Some were so big they looked like trees. As part of the exclusion zone clearance task, the troops cut down pot plants and loaded them into the gator. To feed Hughes that night, they piled plants so high on the gator it looked as if six families used the same car to go shopping for Christmas trees. The troops howled with laughter as the band of merry men began unloading Christmas-tree-sized bundles of pot plants into Hughes' pen.

"Enjoy, buddy," one of them said as he patted the donkey affectionately.

Another piped up. "Hughes is gonna have a hell of a night."

Besides a few erratic ee-aws, I thought Hughes had a peaceful first night in his new abode.

The camp sergeant major, Master Warrant Officer Gorden Cavanagh, strolled briskly into our area the next morning. By the jump in his stride, I thought we would get scolded for Hughes's Tourette syndrome-like ee-aws outbursts from the night before. Cavanagh was tall and fit for his age, and he commanded attention with his stentorian voice. He came right up to Wally and me.

"Morning Chimos, you need some sandbags filled?"

I exchanged a quick look with Wally from across the table.

"Uh, no, sergeant major, we're good."

Missing the rhetorical question, he continued as if I didn't respond.

"I've got a glue bag ready to fill sandbags."

Like a tic, he called malingers a 'glue bag.' He went on to explain that he caught one of the soldiers attached to the unit without their ballistics plates on patrol—a dangerous ploy to try and save weight. Instead of a charge parade, filling sandbags became the remedial measure. Just out of earshot stood a diminutive soldier with a shovel.

"Uh, we could use a few sandbags to help pen in the donkey," I said, grasping for a make-work project.

"Thanks sir. Fifty sandbags coming right up." He departed with the guilty party to create a military-grade fortification to protect Hughes' weed stash.

We also closely oversaw discipline within the engineer troop, but it never became a problem. Besides a negligent discharge that punctured the back of our new couch with a bullet, we didn't have any issues. On the contrary, filling sandbags became a running joke between us and the camp sergeant major as he busted troops for various infractions such as running a speakeasy, tardiness, or slovenly deportment.

Another area in which we retained some control was how we completed administration, and it hit a turning point after a nonchalant comment from Wally. He had just returned with a few sappers from giving Hughes a revitalizing skin detox with the camp pressure washer. After regaling me with Hughes' insatiable appetite for kitchen scraps and bushels of marijuana, he noticed that I was buried in paperwork.

"I see you're feeding the beast," before quickly departing to let me work.

I don't know why, but "feeding the beast" struck a chord. Since the HLZ pad disaster, I'd been pondering options to prevent a similar reoccurrence. The answer was to feed the beast. Up to that point, I'd been miserly with information to KAF staff officers because it distracted me from tangible work on the front line. Although true, how could I expect them to have any idea about the lay of the land if I didn't provide sufficient information to give them the whole picture? They wanted to add value but couldn't telepathically communicate like Wally's Vulcan mind meld.

Moreover, many staff officers never had the opportunity to leave the confines of Kandahar Airfield, so they lacked context. Sitting there, I realized that most of the time my poorly written reports were all they had to make sense of the situation on the ground. This made them exceptionally valuable. KAF personnel actually did read them, as demonstrated by our new couch arriving in under two weeks. And if their actions were, in my opinion, sub-standard, that only reflected the quality of the information I provided to them. With uproarious laughter penetrating the walls, because Hughes was munching cannabis at an unprecedented rate on our new deck, I realized why it became incumbent upon me to push KAF as much information as I could. They were no different than Hughes. If you didn't feed them, they got cantankerous and ornery and became at risk of making misinformed decisions such as building an HLZ pad to control dust. If I didn't provide them sufficient subsistence, it was my fault, and I became the ass.

From that point forward, I unbegrudgingly submitted abundant information about our tasks, the situation on the ground and our assessment. Several times, I went overboard pushing information. On one occasion, we submitted a photo of Hughes carrying a radio, tactical vest, and a weapon. What started as a good-natured joke created a mountain of security concerns, piles of emails, and phone calls. Some folks in KAF, and all the way back in Ottawa, missed the gag and expressed grave concerns about the donkey running away in a firefight loaded with sensitive equipment. In a twisted way, these overreactions helped me gauge the hunger for information at the headquarters. By judging how staff officers responded to random injects of information, such as a missionary's wife visit or a donkey on patrol, I could get a feel for when we provided enough information for them to stay adequately suffonsified.

For other adjustments, we could only apply influence. As dismounted patrols became more popular in response to the IED threat, we could recommend routes, orders of march, and patrol composition. But the final decisions about patrol matters rested with the respective commander. Similarly, we could only influence mounted patrol compositions and timings. We tried to help consolidate multiple patrols into one as much as possible to minimize movement around the battlespace. But still, even with this economization, I found it peculiar that we moved so much in an IED-rich environment. On multiple occasions, we conducted patrols just to shuffle soldiers to and from HLTA travel or to seek signatures on paper copies of PERs; this seemed absurd considering the risks. I always treated movement around the Horn of Panjwai like driving on icy roads in Canadian winters. If travel wasn't required, you should stay home.

During one of those patrols, Major Packer formalized my initial counselling for crappy writing. For various reasons, the official paperwork took a couple of months to catch up after the verbal warning I had received back in Canada. As he handed me the document, I know he recognized how dumb it appeared. But he didn't have to explain much; he was right, and I deserved it. After all the gunfights and explosions, I considered myself a lucky man for only having an administrative scar. Yet, as I signed the document, the military's infatuation with writing stirred something in me. While being counselled for spelling, grammar, and sentence structure, I wondered who corrected people for content. The orders for the HLZ pad were brilliantly written, but they never should have been issued. On a similar note, Sergeant Jones' email wasn't just a flawed piece of writing; it contained a stark warning about the HLZ pad, which was entirely ignored because of poor tone. The inveterate preference for good writing with weak content over poor tone writing with good content remained a riddle I never understood.

In addition to sappers, Doug and Tex became our responsibility simply because the engineers owned the contract. One afternoon, Wally and I received a one-way conversation from Sergeant Major Cavanagh.

"Hey Chimos. Sort out that dog-handling glue bag!"

It turns out Doug took exception to a small detachment of American Military Police. They also had a dog and allegedly didn't clean up after it. Long story short, Doug unilaterally decided to teach the Military Police about cleanliness by putting a plastic bag of unclaimed dog feces on the front step of their building. While Wally educated Doug on camp etiquette in his quarters, he discovered what looked like a human skull in Doug's room.

When questioned about it, Doug responded, "Found her by the front gate. Gonna take her back home."

On the edge of the Sperwan Ghar hill was an old graveyard where some bones had become exhumed with the passage of time. Wally unequivocally laid out the law regarding expectations, respect and civility surrounding dog poop, and human remains. He also instructed Doug to return the skull, which he did immediately. As Wally told me the story, I realized why our predecessors left Doug on gate duty to sniff out trucks while other dog teams conducted operations.

The constant ebb and flow of adjustments continued as the days passed. About a third of the way through the deployment, I departed on HLTA and left Wally at the helm. My whirlwind three-week leave passed in a flash. Once back in Sperwan Ghar, Wally brought me up to speed.

"Man, glad you're back, sir."

He had lost ten pounds in my absence.

"I've been busy," he said while smoking dart after dart (having run out of cigarillos.)

He recounted a tiff with a patrol commander in my absence. One evening, a rapidly installed culvert was too small for a wadi crossing. After half the convoy crossed and formed a leaguer on the far side of the wadi, water started to overflow and flood the crossing site. On his own volition and to conduct his job of providing mobility support, Wally left the leaguer so he could prevent flood water from destroying the crossing site. Wally quickly resolved the situation, but not before the water turned the crossing site into a muddy mess. Consequently, many vehicles couldn't cross the wadi without assistance. Only by individually towing them throughout the night under the guidance of Wally could they finally reach the leaguer.

"Sir, the crossing site looked like the opening scene of the movie ET."

A pop culture reference where trucks and police shine white lights everywhere during a night-time search.

"We'd still be there if I didn't engage."

Despite Wally's actions preventing a portion of the convoy from being bogged down in Afghanistan mud, departing the leaguer and using white light to save the crossing site brought no end of wrath from the patrol commander.

Another friction point between a patrol commander and Wally occurred when he used the Buffalo as a section vehicle. This approach provided the same capabilities and offered better force protection to the soldiers since the Buffalo was designed to protect against IEDs. For some reason, this concept encountered significant resistance, so much so that it required Major Packer's intervention. While fighting some of his own battles to integrate into the battlegroup, Major Packer came up big in this situation. He fought for influence and control to protect the sappers. Not only did it solidify Wally as the acting troop commander, but his recommendation also proved prophetic. The Buffalo struck a large IED on the subsequent operation, which lifted the vehicle up into the air and dropped it like a sack of potatoes. Based on the size of the blast, it is reasonable to conclude that it would have breached the hull of a LAV or ELAV; breached hulls usually meant critical casualties. If not for the protection provided by Buffalo because of the vehicle swap, the sappers may not have walked away. From that point forward, no one questioned Wally's engineering advice.

Hearing the trials and tribulations of Wally during my leave aggravated me. Having to endure comments of "You're not in charge" or "I'm going to shove your flashlight up your arsehole so you look like a jack-o-lantern" while dealing with some complex situations wasn't right. While balancing all the challenges of two jobs in my absence, in addition to the stresses of Afghanistan, he had enough on his plate without having to contend with the hubris of egos and personality rifts. It shouldn't have taken a vehicle blowing up to have folks realize Wally was an asset and adapt their plans based on his engineering advice. The professionalism and performance demonstrated during my leave contributed to Wally receiving the Meritorious Service Medal post-tour.

Unfortunately, as we adjusted our tactics, techniques, and procedures, so did our adversaries. Sitting on our red couch in the troop sanctuary, I caught up with Sapper Daniel Stegmeier. Twenty-two years old, he was passionate about hockey and golf. In excellent physical shape and full of testosterone, he joined the military to gain experience; one of his most recent patrols gave him a lifetime worth.

The aim was to search a suspected IED factory used to assemble components of explosive devices. During the approach to the objective, Stegmeier noticed children playing games, laughing, and exploring. The patrol spent the morning setting up a perimeter to watch the suspected compound before searching the IED factory early in the afternoon. After uncovering numerous components for making makeshift bombs, the patrol paused outside the compound beside a mud wall. After a few minutes, two locals approached. Stegmeier took a breath; his expression darkened as he recounted a horrifying turn of events.

"It was one of the ten-year-old kids I saw playing earlier and an old man."

He took a long pull on his cigarette as he continued.

"Two ANA soldiers were dispatched to search them."

Stegmeier had the attention of everyone within earshot, as we'd all heard rumours about the surreal experience.

"Just as the ANA soldiers started searching the kid, the old man ran and hid behind a tree."

In the background, we could hear vehicles marshalling in the Sperwan Ghar parking lot as they prepared for a convoy move.

"Then, BOOM," said Stegmeier as he made an explosive motion with his arms. A chill shot up my spine as Stegmeier took a slow breath.

"The child exploded from a suicide bomb strapped to his chest."

I felt a surge of emotions as Stegmeier described the subsequent injuries and evacuation of casualties. My stomach knotted. Who were these sub-human, vile souls that would employ unspeakable savagery by weaponizing a kid? As children tended to approach patrols seeking a pen by making a writing motion on their hand, troops had become habituated to their presence as an indication of safety. On countless occasions, I dropped my guard because kids were in proximity. But comparable to the Trojan horse tactic, the Taliban found a way to slip in undetected and attack. While battling the daily grind in Panjwai, I didn't give much thought about the strategic picture of why Canada was in Afghanistan; after hearing about a barbaric geriatric making a suicide bomb out of a child so they could attack a patrol, I knew one reason we were involved was to eradicate evil.

Adding to the traumatic events, Stegmeier assisted with casualty treatment and the post-blast investigation. One of the surviving ANA soldiers walked out of blast cloud covered head to toe in blood. Stegmeier described how he proceeded to lay him down and apply first aid along with a tourniquet to stanch the bleeding from a golf ball size hole in his leg. Confusion continued to ensue as sappers attempted to communicate with wounded ANA soldiers via an interpreter. To evacuate the casualties, a Blackhawk helicopter touched down amidst the adobe buildings, its rotors clearing the walls by mere feet. The pilot's precision was nothing short of insane, risking everything to evacuate the wounded.

With leaves and branches scattered everywhere from the explosion, several sappers documented the scene while uncovering pieces of the child and scraps of clothing—a leg leaning against the wall, the scalp in the alleyway. Being exceptionally close to my grandfather, he was the best man at my wedding; it sickened me to hear about this innocent boy. I understood the concept of a martyr, but a kid? To this day, none of us understand why this happened to a child who, only a few hours earlier, was playing games, laughing and exploring.

Later that day, Wally and I caught up with Sapper Ryan Murphy, who had recently returned from two hellacious back-to-back operations. Murphy was the quintessential fit solider, a former alpine ski racer who aspired to be a combat diver because he loved the water. He joined the military in response to the 9/11 attacks and quickly wound up in Afghanistan. On his most recent patrol, while working with a reconnaissance element, Murphy's section experienced a well-coordinated ambush. Decisively engaged on two sides, the agile enemy moved to flank them as RPGs crumbled walls and machine gun fire rattled their positions. The rounds were so close that they could feel the dirt splatters rain down on their bare knuckles as the bullets embedded into the surrounding adobe walls. The patrol returned fire with everything they had while calling for air and artillery support to break contact from the assault. Listening to him recount the story, it became clear that this enemy element was not composed of fighters laced up on a cocktail of drugs like some of our previous engagements where their actions were discombobulated and uncoordinated. This group had faculty. They were hostile and organized — comparable to a pack of wolves pouncing on their prey.

The ambush sparked many conversations around the camp because of the sheer intensity. Several multi-tour soldiers commented that it had been one of the most concentrated engagements they had ever experienced. While sitting at the troop table in our common area, Wally and I listened attentively to Murphy as he switched gears to his second story.

Due to the HLTA schedule and casualties, we lacked enough sappers to support operations — I'd estimate we were at seventy percent manning by this point. People like Murphy floated between several sections to augment numbers and overcome these shortfalls. His ability to quickly adapt into other sections was an asset, but it also placed him on back-to-back operations. While HLTA offered a brief respite from the line for some, it could put a burden on those who remained. In some cases, it resulted in some sappers having to participate in consecutive operations to backfill critical positions gapped because of other's leave. Just before the ambush patrol, Murphy participated in another operation that received a short notice task to search a compound. If Murphy was a cat with nine lives, he used half of them in that compound.

Murphy started his story by saying, "Miraculously, nobody was killed."

While working with a reconnaissance platoon and an ANA platoon, they received short-notice orders to search a compound that harboured a high-ranking Taliban leader. If intelligence reports were correct, the compound could be booby-trapped if he wasn't home. The patrol commander explained the risks and expressed concerns to the headquarters about quickly searching a booby-trapped compound in attempts to stop the task. However, he received directions to proceed. To make matters worse, no one informed the patrol commander that special forces had already searched the compound twice. Unbeknownst to the ground force, they would be the third group to inspect the compound.

Due to engineers being spread so thinly across the battlespace, the highest-ranking engineer providing mobility support to the search was a Master Corporal acting as a section commander. Although I had confidence in junior leaders to step up, I thought we needed a better reason to place them in incredibly demanding, life-and-death situations than to support our HLTA leave plan.

I'd like to think I could have influenced the situation with some radio procedures. A trick I'd use to smoke out staff officer ideas versus a Commander's direction was to ask for a restricted airspace over the objective. This request is a standard procedure to prevent aircraft or helicopters from flying through an area that could become enveloped in an explosion. If it was an assertive yes, I knew a Commander was behind the order because they diverted assets around the battlespace to facilitate the task. However, several times, the radio response to my restricted airspace request flushed out a staff officer idea.

"Uh, wait out…. Uh, never mind."

I wished someone had posed a similar question that may have caught a well-intentioned staff officer overstepping their lanes. Someone could also have provided the time estimate.

"No problem. We will start the compound search. I estimate it will take the rest of the day."

It may sound flippant, but it's not. EOD averaged three-plus hours per IED. In this case, the task was to search a compound potentially replete with IEDs.

It's tough to say, but a question or comment like that may have ended the story. Unfortunately, Murphy continued his recapitulation.

"We felt the enemy combatant threat was greatest, so we planned to clear the compound first. But somebody wanted it done *macht schnell.*"

While Murphy described their room clearances, he emphasized the pressure the section felt to clear the compound quickly—an unrealistic, impossible demand. Asking someone to clear a potential bobby-trapped compound quickly is comparable to asking someone to cook a turkey dinner in thirty seconds. Only instead of just a disappointing meal with guests potentially contracting salmonella poisoning, rushing a search of an IED laden compound could entail a catastrophe where soldiers are killed.

Unable to influence the decision, the sappers focused on what they could control and admirably entered the compound first to minimize the exposure of others to potential devices. They spearheaded forward with unwavering courage, making swift, life-or-death decisions in a harrowing situation where information was scarce and uncertainty reigned. Follow-on elements entered the compound once the sappers established a foothold inside the structure.

"That's when the first explosion went off. We were rocked to the ground. For thirty seconds, debris fell from the sky. We couldn't see anything."

Wally and I sat wide-eyed at Murphy's description of the blast. By sheer luck, everyone survived with only a couple of concussions. Murphy described the ensuing confusion as they checked fellow section members, Sapper Carignan and Sapper Odegard, for injuries.

"I found blood on Odegard's left leg. Upon further investigation, I realized it came from a dead bird he sat on."

With no casualties, the sappers took a moment to reconsolidate. With a damaged mine detector from the blast, they were in the process of zap-strapping the head back onto the handle when a second explosion rocked the compound.

"It felt like I got hit by a truck. Ears ringing, everything went black."

I continued to listen with rapt attention as Murphy recounted events after the second blast in the compound. Running on pure adrenaline, everyone sought to escape. Debating which way to go to avoid another attack, a sniper caught the group's eye by waving his rifle over the lip of a wall. He then proceeded to show them another egress route. Murphy recalled his thoughts while exiting through a small hole that led to a grape field.

"In the rear of the compound was a beautiful courtyard with grass and the nicest building. It was like regular North American-style construction. Complete with windows and everything."

Once outside, everyone regrouped and waited for EOD to exploit the scene. After waiting three hours for their arrival, Murphy and crew returned to the compound to help with the exploitation. In the process, they discovered four IEDs daisy chained together. Odegard had been sitting on one while recovering from the first blast. During the process, EOD discovered why the daisy chain didn't detonate. The first explosion severed the detonation cable; this meant that the electrical charge from two car batteries located in the firing point six hundred meters away couldn't fully initiate the lethal trap.

By this point, Murphy started sketching a picture of the situation to show the compound's layout. In total, there were thirteen mortars across the four linked locations that didn't detonate. Based on the hand-sized pieces of shrapnel that rained down as far as three hundred metres away, the first blast was likely a dozen artillery shells. Murphy explained EOD's assessment while pointing at specific locations on his drawing.

"EOD showed us how they hid the command wire under the door's steel frame."

The installers could cache the wire's metallic signature by burying the wire deep and using the visible metal infrastructure to mask it. Without a trained or suspecting eye, searches would assume any hit from the mine detector stemmed from the metal door frame, leaving the wire undiscovered.

"EOD also figured that the trigger man detonated the trap backwards by mistake."

The intended nature of the sophisticated trap became even more hideous and exposed the dichotomy of our systems that were designed to be safeguards. From training, we were biased to standardize operating procedures to improve efficiency, address safety protocols, and enhance interoperability. But by creating standards to protect us, we inadvertently caused a deadly vulnerability – patterns. An unintended soft spot that our adversaries attacked.

Murphy showed one device in the compound centred in the perfect location for a casualty collection point. The Taliban knew from previous observations that we tended to collect casualties in a perceived safe area for triage before evacuation. This IED layout attacked that pattern by placing a monster-sized bomb in our anticipated casualty collection point. The only reason the IEDs detonated out of sync with the troop movement in the compound was because the triggerman crossed his wires between the two devices at the firing point. This error caused the casualty collection point to detonate first instead of the compound device co-located with the sappers clearing rooms. As troops scattered from the first blast inside the compound, they miraculously avoided the lethal impact of the second blast. This confluence of errors and a lot of luck resulted in a near miss versus a catastrophic kill of everyone in the compound.

In similar situations, special forces executed compound searches of other high-value target compounds with precision via a deliberate operation, not a half section of sappers with a couple of mine detectors because they happened to be in the area. Hindsight is twenty-twenty, but if the engineers had not been spread so thin on the ground, I'd like to think we could have collaboratively come up with something better to influence and control the situation. On another compound search, which achieved nowhere near the notoriety of this one, I sent up an estimated timeline of eight-plus hours to complete the search. In short order, we were instructed to forget about it. I've always wondered how things would've played out if we'd given an eight-hour-plus estimate to clear the daisy chain compound.

As Murphy concluded the story, I couldn't help but feel as if we were duped. The order to go quickly and search a high Taliban leader's house didn't make sense. It was wrong on so many levels. How did we get this sudden intelligence, and why was there a rush? We could have flipped the script on the phrase: You have all the watches, but we have all the time. In this case, our adversaries had the watches with their complex traps, but we had all the time. We could have planned a deliberate search or assault, or maybe just dropped a massive bomb on the place when the high-value target was home. Yet, for some reason, we ceded our advantage right back to the enemy. Was this a command decision, or did an overzealous staff officer using a Tim's coffee as a spittoon for a mouthful of dip make the call? I couldn't prove anything, but my inclination said the compound search was a setup right from the intelligence gathering. It was a tactic comparable to tales from World War II, where false orders and marked maps were planted on the bodies of casualties in conspicuous places so the enemy would undoubtedly retrieve them.

As the troops slept that night, I reflected on the recent events while sitting on the tailgate of a John Deere Gator. The general's advice seemed simple. Life can be divided into three buckets: what you can control, what you can influence, and what you can neither control nor influence. But instead of saying focus on the first two, he should have said vehemently fight to retain control and influence over the first two buckets. Insidious drift occurs if you don't fight as items shift from control to influence to no control or influence. Like the law of entropy – if you do nothing, things inevitably slide into disorder.

Our training habituated us to control and influence situations by establishing processes and procedures. Unfortunately, this penchant established patterns. Consequently, the Taliban attacked these tendencies. They exploited our trust of children. They attacked our clearance patterns and targeted our casualty collection points. In addition to fighting us physically, they continually fought for control and influence to impose us into the general's third bucket. They forced a tyranny of entropy upon us, and in the process, they weaponized all three of the general's buckets.

# 12

# Short Patrol

The orders were simple, clear and concise. We were to conduct a presence patrol just north of the Arghandab River near Sia Choy, accompanied by ANA soldiers. In turn, they brought with them Canadian soldiers from the Observer Mentoring and Liaison Team (OMLT), who were responsible for moulding the ANA into a cohesive fighting entity. The patrol objective was to clear two villages suspected of harbouring IED production facilities and explosive caches. In the process of maneuvering, we would also generate enemy chatter on their radios. Coalition forces could potentially identify hot spots for future strikes by listening in and triangulating the radio broadcasts via intelligence assets. Located approximately three kilometres northwest of Sperwan Ghar, everyone thought it would be a quick stroll. However, after the recent bedlam caused by the quick search of the high-ranking Taliban compound, all the talk of a short patrol should have been a harbinger of the chaos waiting to unfold.

I asked Wally about his thoughts on including Doug and Tex. Eager to try them on patrol, we had debated the pros and cons for weeks. Pro: Tex was an explosive detection dog and could save lives, and his handler was motivated to come. Cons: Tex's temperament to bite every ANA soldier in sight and Doug's untested grace under fire. Overall, the chemistry seemed off, however, based on the IED threat, an explosive detection dog could be a lifesaving asset. As we'd ruminated about using Doug outside the camp for weeks, this short patrol provided an excellent opportunity to beta-test the concept. After weighing the pros and cons, we decided to give the team a try.

"I'll get 'em ready," said Wally as he hopped up to speak with Doug.

Over the previous few weeks, we'd become proficient on dismounted patrols. We'd honed the gear we carried, how we supported maneuver elements, and vastly improved our physical fitness by carrying heavy packs in the hot sun. To best support dismounted operations, we found that four sappers per platoon hit the sweet spot. This ratio allowed us to carry sufficient engineering gear and created the versatility to split into two pairs if required. In addition to munitions, water, and food, the groupings of four sappers could share the load of engineering kit like mine detectors, explosives, hook-and-line kits, and maybe a set of bolt cutters. Wally and I also split up some sapper kit, only on a much smaller scale compared to a standard section load. Besides the amount of equipment, the distinctive difference between a section load and what we carried were communication tools. Wally carried the Iridium Satphone as a backup method to contact our headquarters in a pinch, and I lugged a PRC-117F Falcon radio.

Weighing twelve pounds, the radio filled half of my backpack. A non-standard issued item, the 117F was a special radio we somehow procured through the supply chain. I hated lugging it around on patrols. However, it provided us unparalleled situational awareness and connectivity when Wally and I moved independently around the patrol to help influence mobility tasks. In many instances, the 117F transmitted in locations where lighter and smaller radios became ineffective. Having witnessed some communication challenges from small radios without enough bandwidth on previous operations, I wanted the best odds to communicate. All the multi-million-dollar assets used to support our patrol, like assault aircraft, gunship helicopters, and artillery, were useless if we couldn't talk to them.

With the most unergonomic headset, which could have been labelled "one size fits no one," I clipped it to my helmet strap with the volume cranked. This allowed soldiers in very close proximity to also hear the radio chatter. Loaded with radio crypto for every station in the battlespace and equipped with a handheld device to change frequencies, I could easily switch between channels with the push of a button. Similar to a teenager who ceaselessly changes the car radio station searching for their favourite song, we could switch between frequencies to tune into the action: higher command, flanking platoons, or helicopter nets as they passed over. As troops came into contact, we could switch to their respective net to listen in. Starved for female interaction, Scotty always enjoyed dialling in to call-sign Banshee, a female Kiowa gunship helicopter pilot.

"Sir, her voice is just fantastic!"

It did provide for some surreal moments as we'd listened to her sultry voice on the radio confirm a target seconds before her Kiowa gunship swooped down and unloaded a lethal barrage.

In addition to being heavy, the 117F tended to overheat and stop working. This quirk became an increasing challenge as daytime temperatures often climbed over 40°C. To counteract this, we surrounded the radio with eight to ten frozen water bottles at the beginning of each patrol. Unfortunately, the ice added another ten-plus pounds to the arduous weight of my helmet, rifle, ammunition, and tactical vest with plates. To this day, I'm still surprised we didn't rip the straps off more backpacks due to the heavy loads we carried. To mitigate the mid-day heat, we often departed pre-dawn and returned before noon. This was the scheduled departure and return time for our presence patrol in Sia Choy.

Long before dawn broke or calls to prayer echoed across the landscape, we linked up with Doug and Tex on the morning of the patrol at the camp front gate. Sitting tall and proud, Tex's tongue hung out of his mouth while Doug held his leash.

"Ol' Tex and I are ready to get this show on the road. Let's get some."

Doug's appearance caught me off guard as he looked less like a man preparing for a combat patrol and more like someone heading to shoot gophers on a Sunday afternoon in Saskatchewan. His outfit consisted of a floppy hat, a short-sleeved shirt, a tanned-coloured tactical vest with a few magazines for his rifle, and a small daypack to carry water and his lunch. I couldn't knock him on his outfit; we did tell him to pack for a short patrol. As the troops filed by, Tex suddenly broke the rhythmic crunch of boots on gravel.

"Grrr-rufff! Ruff!"

Tex yanked aggressively on this leash as he savagely snapped at an ANA soldier. His notably darker skin roused Tex's bias. With some sign language, I suggested the ANA soldier keep his distance. In return, his gesture implied that he would shoot the dog if there were any follow-on problems. I don't know if he was serious; however, he had the means in his hands. For the first time in months, under the cover of darkness, Doug and his racist dog Tex left the confines of Sperwan Ghar.

It didn't take long before we began crossing the Arghandab River. Seeing the mix of Canadian and ANA soldier fatigues in patrol formation across the riverbed, I became keen to work with the OMLT. Over the last couple of weeks, their morning melees with the Taliban became a bit of a reveille in our command post. Wally and I routinely listened in on the radio traffic as they battled insurgents and called in air assets or indirect fires. Watching the OMLT spread out on the far side riverbank, they appeared to be a well-organized and trained force. We came under contact just as we started establishing a foothold on the north bank: nothing major, just some potshots and a few bursts of machine gun fire. But to Doug, this was it. He moved to the wall beside a couple of other soldiers. While they provided a slow cyclical rate of fire, Doug started hammering out rounds. Somehow, he emptied the entire magazine before I caught up to him.

"Doug, calm down! Let the infantry deal with this."

Undeterred or too stressed to listen, Doug remained partially petrified. While crouching behind the wall, I, too, became partially petrified about getting eaten by Tex as his leash dangled loosely beside him. His mouth was so close to my face that I could smell his breakfast. Instead of picking up Tex's leash, Doug reloaded.

"Time to lock and load. We're about to start getting some!"

The fighting stopped as soon as it started, typical for a shoot-and-scoot attack. As the patrol resumed the advance, Doug remained on edge. A few minutes later, another few staccato machine-gun bursts broke the peaceful morning as RPGs whistled like bottle rocket fireworks. This time, Doug went full *Rambo*. He sprinted to a mud wall and braced himself. He then started spraying a field on full automatic with the rifle stretched out over his head while he crouched behind the wall. A large rainbow-like arch of brass casings flew out of the rifle's ejection port. This time, he dumped two magazines before I reached him.

"Doug, calm down!"

One of the secondary aims of the patrol was to help provoke adversary radio chatter. If the intelligence community couldn't pick up any chatter from the enemy radios, no doubt they picked up the clamoring of Doug's rifle as expended casings surrounded him.

"Sir, we're about to get some!" he huffed as he reloaded his rifle with one of his last magazines.

"Doug, if you run out of ammo, the only person who will get it is you. Calm down."

I know some psychological blocks prevent people from calming down when you order them to; however, I didn't know what else to say. For all the worry about Tex reacting negatively to the heat or eating an ANA soldier because of his skin colour, Doug became the biggest concern, and it was my fault. I never read his contract terms. However, I'm confident we breached every safe working environment clause by taking Doug to Sia Choy, a volatile place without *any* laws. The only people in the area were miscreants and armed Taliban.

Moreover, Doug didn't have any training to be in this situation. He only trained enough to get to a camp outpost, not fight while staging out of an outpost. Although Afghanistan posed inherent risks, I amped them up to an unacceptable level by bringing a contractor on a dismounted patrol tasked to search IED facilities and to create enemy radio chatter. My well-intentioned notion of integrating an explosive detection team into a combat patrol was naïve and dangerous. Seeing his trigger-happy ways, I felt lucky we didn't cause a fratricide incident.

Squatting behind a mud wall while Doug caught his breath, Tex remained oblivious to the recent events. He sat erect, ears perked with his tongue wagging as if we were hanging out in the park on a peaceful Sunday morning playing fetch. During the tactical pause, Doug and I exchanged a few looks as we both realized he should be in camp, not crouched behind a dirt wall in Sia Choy. Tacitly, we acknowledged my error in judgment and allowed my mistake to educate both of us. With some sage advice from Wally, we formulated a plan to leave the gunfighting to the infantry so Doug could focus on getting back to Sperwan Ghar.

We snaked through the adobe structures on well-trodden paths for the next two hours. The scorching sun beat down relentlessly as we guzzled bottle after bottle of water to stay hydrated. The long sleeves of my fatigues turned pasty with sweat, becoming a tinge of white from all the salt I was perspiring. The air was thick with the scent of sunbaked earth, mixed with faint traces of dust. The odd gunfight erupted, and we responded with withering gunfire of our own. After one engagement, I was fascinated to hear the OMLT mentor confirm that we shot an insurgent.

"See here, lung shot."

He pointed to bubbly blood on the ground. He tracked the enemy just like I'd been taught to track deer when hunting them. The patrol interpreter translated the lesson to a few ANA soldiers, and one of them asked a question through the interpreter.

"How do you know if you hit one with artillery?"

Without missing a beat, the OMLT mentor responded.

"You see pieces of their clothes in the trees."

At one point, we stopped to allow the ANA to search some ignoble-looking individuals along the path's edge. Fatigued from lugging a heavy pack, I took the chance to slump to the ground to relieve the load on my body. The hasty search was interrupted by a deafening, "Brrrrt."

A short machine gun burst erupted. By the piercing sound, I knew it was close as dirt splattered around my head and the faint aroma of gunpowder immediately filled the air. The patrol scattered to the surrounding walls in slight confusion, trying to track the source of the bullets as an ANA soldier slumped to the ground beside me.

The cry "Medic! Medic!" went down the line.

As the medics responded, the patrol commander discovered the source. A fellow ANA soldier accidentally squeezed the trigger of his rifle and shot the guy beside me in the upper femur. The injured soldier was so young he looked as if he hadn't hit puberty. Seeing the grotesque grimace and the wounded area, I knew the situation was dire as the medic growled in frustration.

"You can't tourniquet a sphincter."

Listening to the radio, I knew a medical evacuation helicopter was inbound, but the HLZ was a few hundred meters to the south. Ready to help form a stretcher party, an OMLT member rolled up on a bike he hijacked from the bordering area.

"Put him on here," he ordered with a distinctive confidence that indicated this wasn't his first time evacuating a casualty on a stolen bicycle. In amazement, I watched the most efficient casualty evacuation as a crew of three soldiers draped the ANA casualty over the bike and pushed him down the path toward the HLZ. Although it took a bit of balancing to steady the load, rolling the casualty was significantly easier than lifting; having suffered the gruelling physical demands of a stretcher party, using a bicycle was ingenious.

We recommenced the patrol once the casualty evacuation was complete and eventually meandered back to the riverbed. With the noon sun in the sky, the plan was to eat, rest, and hydrate for a few minutes before searching the second village. During lunch at an abandoned, partially constructed school facility, I sat beside Major Mark Campbell, one of the OMLT commanders. We chatted about trivial matters while choking down an insipid military ration, enjoying the break. During the conversation, I noticed he had a distinctive rifle scope on his weapon. A Trijicon designed with an integral, red-tinted tactical level comparable to a carpenter bubble level. I found it strange that a non-standard scope was on a military weapon—a new level of chutzpah. I'd modified some military kit without permission. However, I never considered getting a non-issued rifle scope for my sacrosanct weapon. I wanted to ask him about it when the radio blared.

"Contact, wait out!"

The voice was Captain Rob Clarke, one of my peers in the rifle company. His platoon was patrolling north of our position. They initially set out to conduct a key leader engagement. What should have been peaceful talks with village elders and leaders over a cup of chai had boiled into a fray. They had an engagement alright, but it didn't involve smiles and handshakes. Instead, they exchanged volumes of lead as several firefights broke out that culminated in the latest scrap.

"One casualty, gunshot wound. Nine-liner to follow."

I could hear the firefight in the distance. On the scene, Master Corporal Brent Gallant valiantly dashed through heavy enemy machine gun fire to treat the casualty. His gallantry would eventually be acknowledged with a Medal of Military Valour. As we listened intently to the radio, it became apparent that the platoon struggled to break contact with the enemy. They called in artillery, but the enemy was too close. We quickly mobilized from the river's edge and pushed north to help the platoon break contact.

We took a shortcut across a large water-filled wadi to get into position as quickly as possible. About three feet wide, it had a steep bank on both sides. By the smell and appearance, I knew it doubled as a sewer. As the wadi flowed slowly, we jumped over one by one. Each man helped the next man secure their footing on the far side before proceeding. I turned around to help Doug, who had Tex by the leash. Tex leaped effortlessly but caught Doug off balance. In an instant, Doug went head over heels into the drink. Up to his chest in the putrid stream of raw sewage, I helped extract him by giving him a hard tug onto the far bank. His hat floated gently down the wadi while Tex sat high on the bank. Another unlucky break on Doug's maiden patrol.

"Doug, you alright?"

He looked at me in disbelief and nodded. Ordinarily verbose, he simply said, "Yah."

We didn't have much time, as we blocked the main wadi crossing point, and the radio remained alive with contact updates.

"Doug, we need to move out."

A couple of minutes later, we arrived at a T-intersection. Lined by adobe walls on all sides, a couple of large mature trees sheltered the junction. The senior leadership of the OMLT gathered quickly in the intersection to discuss the plan. Captain Clarke's platoon was a couple of hundred metres to the north. To help break contact, we would form a blocking position at the intersection for Captain Clarke's platoon to withdraw through with their litter casualty. Based on the heavy fighting and terrain, the only option for an HLZ was to our south. Like a football huddle, everyone broke to form the blocking position.

The next moment has replayed in my mind countless times over the years. The textbook firing position was directly in front of me, just on the other side of a small ditch. With a large tree casting shade over the spot, I could see a waist-high mud wall on the edge of a field with clear arcs of fire. The wall even had a distinctive notch, perfect for resting your rifle while observing the open field. Back in Canada, it would have been an ideal spot to wait for an unsuspecting deer to pop out of the wood line. As a hunter, I instinctively gravitated to the spot but stopped at the narrow ditch for some reason. Little did I know, I was the unsuspecting deer as someone was trying to outwit me. For a split second, I considered hopping the ditch. Whether because I was tired, scared about blowing out my reconstructed knee while landing with the weight of my backpack on uneven ground, or through divine intervention from my guardian angel, or just plain luck, I distinctively remember saying to myself, "screw it."

Instead of jumping the ditch, I turned to the left to find an alternate position. After taking a couple steps, I paused to survey the options. One moment, I stood; the next, I was tossed to the ground in a cloud of dust and debris. Someone triggered an IED, planted in the textbook firing position, and I never heard a sound.

# 13

# War of Inches

It took a moment to get oriented. At the time, I didn't know an IED had just detonated. Further contributing to the confusion was my momentary loss of hearing. I'd read about auditory exclusion, a phenomenon where a person temporarily loses hearing ability. It can occur during high-stress or life-threatening situations as part of a body's fight-or-flight response. Until that moment, I'd never experienced it. Along with the dust and debris, the figurative fog of war descended.

I didn't know why I was prostrate on the ground or why fragmented leaves flickered down from the sky. Despite the turmoil, I instinctively knew that whatever happened was close. I could feel a faint earthy coolness on my neck. I would later learn the cool feeling came from the blast crater. Cool dirt from the bottom of the hole untouched by the sun gave a brief cooling sensation comparable to walking into a basement cellar on a hot summer day.

As I rose to my knees to face the path, hails of bullets started clipping the trees and pockmarked the surrounding walls. Farther up the path, I saw the flash of an RPG as it thundered into a compound. As bullets sliced through the trees above, fragmented green leaves continued to flutter downward and blanket the ground. Looking around, the situation started to crystallize. Immediately in front of me, multiple casualties lay strewn on the path. ANA and Canadian soldiers took up firing positions along the surrounding adobe walls. Some were kneeling behind cover, while others returned fire from their shoulder. Although only a few feet away, I couldn't see the IED epicentre from the textbook firing position that set off the ambush. Still lacking information, the fog of war started to lift. I knew enough to get on the radio as everything had gone to hell.

"Contact, mass casualty. Wait out."

In that instant, training kicked in and guided our next moves. It seemed as if everything we'd learned culminated in that moment. My mind zeroed in on the threat: win the firefight, or we'd all be dead, and nothing else would matter. I could tell the rounds were close, making crack and snap noises versus swish and whiz sounds typical of pop shots. I went to engage with my weapon, but the infantry was already returning volleys of fire. Going through the priorities of effort in my head, I shifted my focus to the casualties.

In front of me was Warrant Officer Chuck Cote, an OMLT mentor. He was one of the toughest soldiers I worked with, and he played an instrumental role in helping soldiers evacuate from the daisy-chain IED compound a couple of weeks earlier. Throughout the tour, he became known for his frequent run-ins with IEDs – this was his fourth incident. On his hands and knees, he advanced slowly like a caterpillar, making a slow searching motion with one outstretched hand. He called out in a strained voice.

"Where's my rifle?"

Blinded at the time due to shrapnel and dirt in his eyes, he padded the ground with deliberate taps in a circular motion before shuffling forward a few inches to repeat the process. Concussed, lacking equilibrium, he struggled to continue. I tried to direct him from the fray, but it was pointless. He was on a one-way mission: to find his rifle.

"Where's my rifle?"

On the ground to my left rested a rifle - one with an integral, red-tinted tactical-level rifle scope. It was Major Campbell's. But where was Major Campbell? I paused to think. I figured Cote just needed a rifle, not necessarily *his* rifle. He probably couldn't have used one in his state, but that didn't matter. I knew he was a first-class soldier, and he would search until he found a rifle. To avoid him potentially crawling into harm's way, I picked up Major Campbell's rifle and lied to him.

"Here's your rifle."

Having gained a lot of respect for him during the couple of times we worked together before the incident, I felt momentarily guilty for lying to him. But at the moment, I didn't know what else to do. Even in the mayhem, he became noticeably relieved about being reunited with a rifle. It made me think about stories I'd read about forest firefighters who clung on fatally to all their heavy gear when ditching it may have allowed them to outrun the fire and ultimately save their lives. Years of training taught us to care for our kit at all costs.

Calmed by the familiarity of a rifle, I directed Cote towards the casualty collection point that began to form on the main path. I started to guide him but had to stop. Beside me on the edge of the T-intersection path laid an incapacitated interpreter.

He had been beside me when the IED blew. Laying on his back, his face was a canvas of lacerations. It looked as if one eye hung out of its socket like a grotesque Halloween masque with an eyeball on a slinky spring. His face was so dusty and scraped up I couldn't tell which eye. I instinctively pulled him underneath a tree for cover to get him out of the way. The ad hoc casualty collection point continued to grow.

Leaves continued to fall peacefully from the trees as bullets split leaves and tossed branches down from above our heads. It felt as if we were lying underneath a bag of microwave popcorn. With the OMLT mentors directing the firefight, we couldn't move until we triaged the casualties. My mind cycled between winning the firefight, treating casualties, and evacuating the scene as I searched for a way to add value. Then I saw two soldiers drag a casualty by his exposed femurs to the casualty collection point. With both legs blown off around the knees, they looked similar to half-eaten chicken wings. Immediately, I recognized the face as of Major Campbell.

Once they stopped pulling him, in a stressed but perceptible voice, I heard him ask, "Do you have something for the pain?"

I didn't hear the medics respond as they started screaming orders to first aid responders who helped like Sapper Matthew Brown.

"Hold here!"

Moving like octopuses, they feverously used their mouth, arms, armpits, and laps to patch-up Major Campbell.

"More gauze!"

Another soldier rifled through a medical bag, pulling out packet after packet of medical supplies.

"Tourniquet!"

The sterile white packages juxtaposed starkly against the sun-baked dirt and blood.

"Bandages!"

It looked as if a newspaper stand blew over as the innards of countless pristine white medical packets fluttered on the ground. Throughout the response, the medic operated on autopilot from years of training. After each action, he yelled out the medical updates required for the nine-liner. Scanning the entire situation, I noticed nobody was compiling the medical information needed for an evacuation request. So, I pulled out my field message pad and started writing.

The entire chain of events up to this point unfolded in just a few minutes—from the blast to assembling the evacuation request. Before the patrol, I came prepared with three blank nine-liners ready. I needed six. Collocated within earshot of the medic, I started compiling nine liners and passing them over the radio.

"Nine liner one, grid…"

After completing the process, I rolled right into the next.

"Nine liner two…"

This process continued until I reached nine-liner six. For some casualties, updates ensued as more medical details became known as part of the MIST report: Mechanism of Injury, Injuries Found, Signs and Symptoms, and Treatment. Via the medic's words, I finally pieced together what just happened.

"Casualty one, IED strike, double leg amputation, losing consciousness, tourniquets applied."

These brutal updates continued for the other casualties as well: concussed, unconscious, and lacerations. Years later, I would learn that some of the shrapnel in the wounded came from Major Campbell's lower legs, which had been blasted into bone fragments. To this day, the casualties from the blast continue to remove pieces of the IED – and of him – from their bodies. With so many medical terms flying around, it sounded similar to a game of charades, with the clue being a horrific car accident.

For an instant, I couldn't believe it. Even in a firefight during a mass casualty situation, I couldn't get away from completing administration. Adding even more to the confusion, two soldiers at the casualty collection point had the same last name. While deciphering casualty information, I became agitated by leaves falling onto my message pad while writing. They blocked the movement of my pen and made my notes harder to read over the radio. Like trying to catch someone playing a childhood prank, I paused to see who broke my concentration in such a dire situation. That's when I realized an intense, unrelenting firefight still ensued. Being so immersed in accurately compiling medical notes, I didn't notice the tree above me resembling a deflated scarecrow. The pulverized leaves and splintered branches landed on my notes as they fell. The accumulation of shot-up foliage blanketed the ground to the point it looked and smelled like fresh mulch.

The medic who yelled out the medical details was Sergeant Martin Côté. Post-tour, he would be awarded a Medal of Military Valour. His citation succinctly sums up the actions at the casualty collection point.

*On June 2, 2008, insurgents ambushed a joint Canadian-Afghan patrol in the Zhari district of Afghanistan. As the patrol moved to seek cover, they triggered an improvised explosive device that seriously injured four members. Shaking off the effects of a severe concussion and oblivious to the ongoing attack, Sergeant Côté triaged the casualties, passed vital information to headquarters and began life-saving treatment. With the patrol unable to effectively break contact, he continued to expose himself to intense enemy fire to treat injuries and encourage wounded personnel during the prolonged fighting withdrawal.*

Concluding our preparations for the prolonged fighting withdrawal mentioned in the citation, Captain Clarke's platoon withdrew through our location. Some sappers had started to clear hasty safe lanes and mark them with foot powder to help facilitate the link-up. As he burrowed down the path, I saw why Captain Clarke's nickname was "crooked helmet." Like me, he monitored a myriad of radio networks. To do this, multiple radio headsets were tied underneath his helmet strap so that his helmet never sat straight on his head. As the platoon pushed through with a litter casualty, every soldier with a free hand became part of a stretcher party for our casualties. The blocking force initially sent to help had become the force in need.

At this point, Major Campbell was in excruciating pain as the first responders applied painful tourniquets to each leg to stanch the bleeding. On a scale of one to ten, it looked like a thirty. To help offset the pain, he chewed on a fentanyl stick as a medical trick to block pain signals to the brain. The once relatively robust stick resembled a toothpick as he feverishly gnawed it down to a nub. After exhausting every medical technique to stop bleeding, the medic issued Rescue Flow, a product designed to expand the remaining blood in your body. With the tourniquets set and a cocktail of drugs administered to combat the injuries and offset the pain, we were ready to evacuate Major Cambell.

The situation became even more precarious as they elevated Major Campbell on the stretcher. We carried a canvas foldable stretcher that slides into a backpack as part of the standard patrol kit. For a double amputee, the foldable stretcher became a nightmare. Designed for a full-bodied soldier, it became an atrocious situation because Major Campbell didn't have full legs. Consequently, each lifting point became a different height due to the uneven load. I winced as the stretcher, bearing a 200-pound load, pressed into the stumps of his thighs while it lumbered down the path.

The discombobulated scene produced a flashback. It looked exactly like a barrack box of boots on a makeshift stretcher. A wide-eyed, grinning apparition of Major Eric Noe beating his chest flashed before me.

*What's your casualty evacuation plan, Hallett?*

In that instant, I realized he was almost dead on, and I was mistaken for doubting him in training. The situation played out like the horrific scenarios he had dreamed up in training, only worse.

With Captain Clarke's platoon securing an HLZ to the south and our casualties on the move to be medically evacuated, my attention shifted to withdrawing. It was time to move on from our unanticipated fifteen-minute stop in Sia Choy. For the first time since the blast, I saw Wally. He'd also been thrown by the explosion but still managed to shepherd Doug to safety, assist with the firefight, and help provide critical medical treatment to the casualties.

"Hey sir…, need… smoke."

Need smoke? Confused, I paused. Granted, it was a stressful situation, but I thought, let's get out of here, and then you can have a smoke. I realized the misunderstanding when he pulled out his GPS to read a grid.

"Call in smoke to help us extract."

I immediately knew the grid was close after calling in all the nine-liners. Listening to the radio chatter that day, I knew the guns had been called multiple times but could not always engage because the enemy was too close. But that was with high explosive rounds; we wanted the smoke to cover our movement to the HLZ. I started to debate and do math in my head to calculate distances but gave up. I stopped vacillating about whether it was too close and called in the fire mission. I focused on providing accurate information so the artillery crew could calculate safety distances. As troops withdrew in pairs by leapfrogging, one member would give cover while the other would bound to a new position to provide cover, we waited for artillery support as the blistering enemy engagement persisted. Though the rate of fire diminished from the initial onslaught, the place still crawled with cunning combatants brandishing an armoury of weapons. Comparable to sharks who smelled blood in the water, they were in hot pursuit to add to their score. As the majority of troops had departed the scene, I started to fire at some muzzle flashes in a nearby grape hut when my radio chirped.

"Shot, over."

With the announcement, my adrenaline surged.

"Hey Wally! Smoke!"

He gave me a confused look. Now he thought I wanted a smoke. Then we heard two crisp booms like a bass drum — doon! doon! In the distance, a pair of M777 howitzers fired their opening salvo. Based on the geometry of the guns, the target and our position, the rounds would fly directly over our heads. A couple of seconds later, a whistle grew overhead that culminated with a loud bang. The artillery round fuse dispensed smoke canisters mid-air so they could rain down in a dispersed fashion over the target. Using the opening rounds as a reference, I made a slight adjustment on the radio to bring the rounds even closer before concluding the transmission.

"Fire for effect," signalling the guns to fire a barrage of rounds.

Moments later, the radio confirmed our request.

"Fire for effect."

*Doon! Doon!* Echoed again in the distance. A couple of seconds later, more smoke rained down on the target. But we didn't account for the artillery round that delivered the smoke canisters. When the smoke canisters discharge mid-air, the artillery round that provides the canisters falls short. Like well-casing cutoffs, the solid metal pipe the size of a two-litre Coke bottle became a lethal projectile as it plunked through our position. One clipped the top of a mud wall before embedding into the field, while another casing slammed into the dirt a little way up the path. Over the tinging sound created by the metal rounds hitting hard earth, Wally turned to me, eyes wide, "That was close!"

I barked back, "You said you wanted close!"

Despite the carnage, we exchanged a boyhood smirk, resembling two mad scientists witnessing their concocted experiment play out differently than planned. The *doon, doon* echoed again, and without saying a word, we knew it was time to go. Being the last to leave the scene, we did one last scan to ensure nobody was left behind. Through a cacophony of machine gun fire, distance artillery shots, smoke canister bursts, and metallic ringing noises as artillery rounds bounced off adobe walls, we withdrew. My last recollection of Sia Choy was an artillery smoke round ricocheting off the path we'd just left before flying over a wall.

Adrenaline surging, it didn't take us long to catch up with the stretcher parties. Working in unison as they shuffled along the path, each successive step became a struggle. A physically fit group composed of some muscle heads and gifted athletes, I could tell they were dog-tired from the physical exertion. Switching off to share the burden of the load, the stretcher party pushed through the pain, misery, and exhaustion toward the HLZ. Caught in the midday heat of 40 degrees Celsius, our short out-and-back patrol just crossed the nine-hour mark. A stickler for staying hydrated, I couldn't recall the last time I drank water and assumed we were all at risk of dehydration in the boiling sun.

Captain Clarke and Warrant Officer Pickhard established HLZ with the sparse remnant of the platoon members not carrying casualties. The radio channels buzzed with chatter as helicopters and artillery fire were coordinated to support the casualty evacuation. Over the maelstrom of activity, I heard the thumping of Blackhawk helicopters escorted by Kiowa gunships. Over the tour, I'd had countless frustrations with KAF-based personnel as they often lived in a different world which resulted in weird expectations. They made up for everything by sending a casualty evacuation helicopter and not a medical evacuation helicopter, a subtle but crucial distinction. Under the Geneva Convention, a medical evacuation helicopter is designated to transport the wounded only. It must be clearly marked with a red cross and is protected from attack while being used to support medical operations. The Taliban didn't get the memo, but we followed the rule. On the contrary, a casualty evacuation helicopter is not protected from attack, but it can resupply fighting troops with food, ammunition, water, and evacuate casualties.

Still under contact, the casualty evacuation helicopters came in fast. We ran to the anticipated landing spot to speed up the process as the chopper made the final approach. Just before the bird touched down, the loadmaster sunk his boot into a saran-wrapped pallet of water, jettisoning it all over the ground; a resupply that wouldn't have been possible with a medical evacuation helicopter. The downwash from the blades pushed the lush grass aside as the turbine exhaust and heat filled the air. While up to our knees in water bottles, we loaded the casualties.

Initially thinking the loadmaster kicked out too much water, the bottles vanished. That water became a lifeline for the remaining members of the patrol. I knew we were dehydrated but didn't know the extent. As the sound of the choppers faded over the horizon, the patrol took a minute to reconstitute before continuing the return march to Sperwan Ghar. Checking myself over, I saw that my clothes were dry from the sun evaporating the moisture from my body. Typically drenched with sweat, my combats were a pasty white and felt like sandpaper. While doing a quick survey, I noticed that other patrol members were also conspicuously dry, which was odd considering the recent physical exertion. I pounded several water bottles and pulled out additional water from my pack. My radio-cooling ice bottles were warm to the touch.

There are a lot of five-dollar words to describe combat: counter insurgency, guerrilla warfare, differing ideologies. Guzzling water to rehydrate with blistered hands, I didn't need much more than five letter words to define the experience. In combat, you go to hell to fight demons, an evil foe fueled by hate. It is raw, loud, life and death. Sadly, many troops fight demons long after they leave. For my quick trip to hell, I'm glad I had a radio to help us home.

Wally and I reconnected with Doug and Tex shortly after commencing the three-kilometre hike back to Sperwan Ghar. It didn't take long before my radio headset lit up with activity as the heat zapped our remaining strength with each successive step. By concentrating on the casualty evacuation, many never thought about or underestimated the gruelling march required to get back to Sperwan Ghar. All the dialogue on the radio could be summed up in a simple transmission.

"Heat casualties."

The enemy contact stopped after the helicopters departed. Consequently, the adrenaline high many operated on through the last ninety minutes crashed. We were in a world of hurt and needed help. The beleaguered patrol moved similar to zombies, attempting to look like soldiers as we crossed the Arghandab River. To mitigate heat casualties, ANA transport trucks were dispatched from Sperwan Ghar to meet us on the river's edge. ANA and Canadian soldiers started piling in the back. Even Doug and Tex jumped into the truck for a ride home. Oddly, Doug never asked to go on another patrol.

With a shearing headache from the heat, my mind raced with contingency plans if one of the soft-skinned trucks hit an IED. On unclear paths near Route Fosters, after experiencing contact all day, one wrong or unlucky move could result in devastating consequences. But what else could we do? Troops started dropping like flies from heat exhaustion, which can quickly become a life-threatening emergency. As the minutes passed, we continually lost the ability to control and influence the situation. With no viable alternatives, we had to pick the best of two bad options and use soft-skin trucks to transport casualties. Walking up the road to Sperwan Ghar, Wally and I kept our distance from folks in case another event transpired.

With the front gate clearly in sight, grief overcame some of the ANA soldiers. Through a thousand-yard stare, their ashen faces and puffy eyes filled with tears—some from the events of the day, others for the unknown status of their comrades. They feared the worst. Under an indigo blue sky, with nothing left in the tank, we resembled the retreat from Stalingrad in our mixture of camouflage fatigues. Walking into camp, rocks hurt my feet through my boots as we collapsed in our troop lines. We'd cheated death and returned to our protective bastion. Although we met the patrol aim of creating chatter, we paid a tremendous cost. Hours later, we learned that the first soldier shot by the negligent discharge was critically wounded but would live. Likewise, we received a similar update for the interpreter who blew up beside me. Major Campbell died on the operating table in KAF, which required the surgeon to use a defibrillator to revive him; he also had a life-threatening complication with a blood clot in Germany while being repatriated to Canada. Years after the fact, Major Campbell told me about the strike.

"I felt heat from a yellow and orange blast before I landed on my back. I went to sit up, but only the stubs of my legs came up because my centre of gravity changed. That's when I knew I was hit badly." He went on to described unsuspected injuries from the IED, like the wounds he received when the kinetic energy of the blast caused his belly fat to be violently pinched between his belt and ballistic plates.

Major Campbell also brought up a point that had always bothered him – was the device victim operated our command-wired? Although the official report stated that the device was victim-operated, he had reasons to doubt it. In discussions with his sergeant major, who coordinated return fire with lethal precision, he stated that the platoon directed a couple of rockets into a grape hut believed to be housing a trigger man for a command-wire. Since Major Campbell was visibly a leader, carrying a map and communicating on the radio, this could explain why they waited a bit to specifically target him and why the ambush followed immediately after the strike. We will never know for certain. Clausewitz's fog of war doesn't just cloud the present – it also lingers over the past, leaving questions unanswered. Due to world-class medical treatment and an unshakeable will to live, Major Campbell survives to this day and has become a steadfast advocate for veterans.

The Sia Choy patrol provided a lot of full-circle events. The multiple nine-liners, the discombobulated stretcher, and the casualty evacuation gut drive to reach the HLZ. I recalled Major Noe's trick of walking past the habitual ruck march stopping point that one morning. I, too, got caught up in the casualty evacuation and overlooked the fortitude required to overcome the mentally draining death march back to Sperwan Ghar. Pushing past the HLZ reminded me that it isn't over until it's over; we had to stay ready to fight. A combination of stubborn will and luck allowed me to walk home; in a way, the 117F radio uniquely saved me. If not for the extra weight, I may have jumped that ditched in Sia Choy and triggered the IED, and if I hadn't consumed the extra frozen water bottles used to cool the radio, I, too, would have been a heat casualty.

In the end, the biggest full-circle revolution came from Sergeant Six Inches. I finally understood why he kicked my arse unmercifully to instill good habits: especially the habit of paying attention to little details. It finally all made perfect sense. Little details are a big detail. We flirted with life and death throughout the day, with the difference between them coming down to little details. If the muzzle of the negligently discharged rifle was six inches to the left, it would have discharged into my face. If the interpreter had been six inches to one side, the shrapnel that critically wounded him could have killed me. And if that ditch had been just six inches narrower, I could have initiated the IED myself. The cumulative delays from the countless small details snowballed throughout the day, ultimately threatening the entire patrol when we ran out of water. Although we travelled thousands of miles to fight in Afghanistan, in the end, the war came down to inches.

# 14

# Contractors

Comparable to a never-ending apprenticeship, Afghanistan continually showed us how quickly risks can compound out of control and that she didn't play fair. The dust had hardly settled from Sia Choy before we experienced our next casualty. The day following our return, insurgent gunfire killed Captain Richard Leary during an intense skirmish while on patrol. As gut-wrenching as losses such as these were, mentally, we all knew combat-related casualties were plausible considering our mission and environment. However, Afghanistan provided implausible and unanticipated risks as well. Only a few days later, Captain Jonathan Snyder drowned after falling into a twenty-meter-deep well, a *kariz,* while on a night patrol. Many wells in our area were two-by-two-metre square columns that went straight down. As some lacked markings, they could be death traps when concealed by darkness. On another occasion, we repatriated a soldier who broke his leg after a tree fell on it. I'd mentally prepared for kinetic-related casualties from IEDs and combat, but I never thought we'd be dealing with a drowning incident or tree-falling injuries in the Afghan desert.

As the casualties and repatriations for personal reasons started to accumulate, plus the ongoing HLTA absentees, we began to get noticeably thinner on the ground. Our effective strength continued to decline despite the replacements sent from the operational reserve in Canada. To help offset this, we started to employ more innovative strategies with contractors around camp; the more work they performed inside-the-wire, the more soldiers we had available for outside-the-wire operations. Although contractors had been present all along, only out of necessity did we start to fully capitalize on their capabilities.

Sperwan Ghar's logistics received the most overt contract support, such as maintaining portable toilets and sanitation stations at the kitchen. I found these hand-washing stations repulsive. Even though they had cute little sinks that smelt like citrus soap, they contained a vague, unsettling undertone of filth. I always felt dirty in Afghanistan, even after showering and donning freshly laundered clothes. So, washing my hands in an area splashed with questionable looking suds triggered my gag reflex. It may sound gross to an outsider, but my intuition said to stay away, and in the context of a warzone, I leaned heavily on my instincts. Therefore, to avoid exposing myself to the perceived bacteria, I'd use hand sanitizer when available and just feigned washing my hands while going through the meal line. Then, one day, our Kitchen Officer, responsible for the establishment's health, safety, and cleanliness, stopped me.

"Sir, you need to wash your hands!"

A top-notch manager who ran a tight ship, he caught me red-handed, making cleansing-like gestures at the hand-washing station. I stood speechless. Potentially exhausted from a hard day or aware of my habitual hand-washing charade, he addressed me in the most patronizing tone.

"Sir, you need to clean your hands, or you'll get sick."

After all the recent gunfights and IEDs, the least of my concerns was getting sick from dirty hands. Besides, I always thought a little bacteria never hurt anybody.

"Just as if you were a kid, sir," he said as he proceeded to provide a physical demonstration.

*"Wash, wash, wash your hands*

*Make them nice and clean,*

*Scrub the fronts, scrub the backs,*

*And fingers in between."*

I just stood there listening to the children's rhyme sung to the tune of "Row, Row, Row Your Boat," as a grown man belted out the song like a Karaoke performance. Beside me putrid-looking fluid drooled down the side of the hand-washing station, forming a small bubbly puddle on the ground. Unconvinced that my hands became cleaner after the process, I wondered why I was the only one who found the wash station a disgusting cesspool. I knew arguing was futile, so I silently acquiesced to the lecture so I could eat, but I remained defiant. I simply upped my hand-washing act and avoided the kitchen officer's prying eyes.

Around the same time as my hand-washing lesson, a contractor named Ali arrived at Sperwan Ghar. A small Afghan man about the same age as me, he recently received a contract to support engineering tasks. Although he had a lot of experience building roads and dams from working with American and

Russian contractors over the years, I remained apprehensive of his utility based on my experience with the ANA. Since many members of their ranks came from poor, undereducated backgrounds and joined the army out of necessity for a job, they tended to complete tasks perfunctory due to an unmotivated desultory work ethic. I assumed the same disparaging epithets applied to Ali and his contracting company.

To test Ali's skills, we started with an easy project. We employed him and his small crew to place gravel on top of the Hesco bastion wall surrounding the camp. By putting a small layer of gravel on top of the dirt-filled Hesco, we significantly mitigated the dust during windstorms. I carefully inspected his work to ensure it met the expected standard. Surprised by his efficiency, we employed him to level the terrain around the front gate and install a concrete chicane. Watching him complete the work with unparalleled zest and zeal, I realized Ali possessed a unique mindset - not just in Afghanistan but also in Canada. If you looked up the word entrepreneur in Pashto or Dari, you'd find Ali listed as an example. Without fail, he found a solution to any problem set and continuously moved with an unparalleled alacrity. While working out plans to create a pad for sea containers, dig a pit for burning garbage, or grading the HLZ so it drained properly, I realized he possessed vast talents and that I grossly underestimated his utility. In just a matter of days, his small contracting crew became an integral part of our team around Sperwan Ghar.

While working around the camp, he taught us how to use heavy equipment in the harsh desert environment and various hand tools with surprising precision. In exchange for teaching us construction Afghan-style, the sappers taught him English army-style. Great phrases like "happy as a pig in shit" and "you're pulling my leg." We even had words of the day such as pension and retirement. Many of our common words were a completely foreign concept.

"Master John, you retire, collect pension, not work?"

He paused in uncertainty, bearing the resemblance of a comedian waiting a half second to deliver the joke punch line.

"Master John, you pull my leg?"

His charisma and work ethic were a breath of fresh air, and I looked forward to our chats. Although he spoke broken English, we never struggled to communicate. A bit of a clairvoyant, he had an uncanny ability to read my mind and anticipate upcoming projects. His response to the most random questions was always the same: "No problem, Master John."

"Ali, can you rebuild the vehicle inspection point with concrete barriers?"

"No problem, Master John."

"Ali, can you help procure wood for our observation post stairs?"

"No problem, Master John."

"Ali, can you get us recently released movies from the local Bazaar?"

"No problem, Master John."

The black market in Afghanistan thrived so much that pirated DVD movies appeared just a day after their theatrical release in Hollywood. In a casual chat about films, I discovered that Ali was a die-hard American movie buff with a particular love for *Rambo*. His eyes lit up as he talked about *Rambo III*, filmed in Afghanistan—a film that had cemented Rambo's legendary status there, rivalled only by *Baywatch's* Pamela Anderson. Pictures of the voluptuous blonde in her trademark red bathing suit covered the walls of their quarters.

In addition to contracted services around camp, we explored unique procurement options to augment our capabilities. One platoon purchased donkeys to help move a small police unit between combat outposts. They researched donkey rigging while living in a combat outpost using the same ruggedized laptop and tactical satellite system required for completing administration like PERs. Through ingenuity and innate soldier skill sets, they successfully moved a bunch of large pelican cases full of police gear between outposts on the backs of the donkeys.

Another initiative that materialized around this time was the *Small Rewards Program.* The program aimed to encourage and reward locals who reported IEDs to coalition forces. For every confirmed device, the individual would receive five thousand Afghanis, or about one hundred American dollars. During one visit to Sperwan Ghar, Major Packer gave me the money.

"You guys are always in the shit. See if you can make use of the program."

He handed me a tube of cash about an inch and a half in diameter. For some reason, bazaars and cash transactions in Afghanistan commonly involve cash in rolls, similar to coin tubes, rather than using unfolded bills.

"John, just be sure you complete the proper paperwork if you use the money."

I glanced at the single sheet of paper that Major Packer handed me as part of the Small Rewards Program. It seemed odd to have a contractual document in English for a local Afghan who probably didn't read or write their native language, let alone English. Even if they were literate, they'd have to overcome the contagious fear of being eviscerated by the Taliban before they would approach one of our outposts to commence a conversation. I couldn't fathom how we would complete this piece of administration. Uncertain of the program's utility, I put the cash tube in my tactical vest to avoid breaking up the conversation.

The visit from Major Packer also provided some interesting battlefield insights. He'd just driven by a contracted road project behind Masum Ghar, a more significant combat outpost a few kilometres east of Sperwan Ghar. The goal of the project was to give "fighting-age males" gainful employment, so they were less inclined to work for the Taliban. At the time, we also falsely believed that paved roads made it more challenging to emplace IEDs; we'd later learn the Taliban's tunnelling abilities under asphalt covered roads were just as proficient as their digging skills in dirt roads. Hearing how the project exploited manual labour to maximize the number and duration of individual jobs, instead of optimizing the project timelines, demonstrated an unusual tactic to fight a war. By creating a make-work project, hypothetically we minimized the recruiting pool of our adversary. The logic being that if they had gainful employment with the coalition forces, they wouldn't seek employment with the Taliban. Beyond its military advantages, project managers highlighted the road paving project's ripple effects: opening markets, improving livelihoods, building trust in coalition forces and creating positive transformation amid the conflict.

"Some of the poor buggers look like fly tape," said Major Packer, concluding his observations of the road project, referring to the hot asphalt bitumen that splashed on worker's clothes while they transported it by wheelbarrows and placed it with shovels.

While preparing for a patrol the following day, I received a call to report to the Sperwan Ghar headquarters. I entered the room to see the duty officer in a tither.

"John, why the hell do we need all this heavy equipment at the front gate?"

Preoccupied with our daily camp maintenance tasks, I couldn't grasp what he meant as he continued speaking in a raspy tone.

"They're plugging the gate and we have a supply convoy coming."

Thinking Ali was up to something, I hopped in the John Deere Gator to find out.

As I pulled up to the front gate, an eclectic mix of about thirty heavy equipment vehicles blocked the road. Vibrantly coloured and elaborately decorated with tassels, Bollywood music rang out as the operators gathered in the shade of a gravel truck, waiting for instructions. Via the interpreter, I learned that contracted equipment arrived to complete a project at the camp. Puzzled about how I could have missed a project requiring thirty vehicles - equipment that could barely fit into the camp, let alone have space to function - I returned to my office to confirm the details with Hollywood. His response didn't help.

"No clue. Good luck with that. Big Chi, little Mo, Sir."

Stepping out of my office, I bumped into Ali, who was also alarmed.

"Master John, I do good work. Why new contractor?"

Fraught with paranoia, he thought the heavy equipment arrived to replace him.

"Just a misunderstanding, Ali. Don't worry, we love your work. Keep it up."

Slightly placated, he sprang back to work with a heightened verve to ensure we remained happy with his services.

Rounding the corner as I returned to the main gate, the unfolding scene shocked me. A hodgepodge of vehicles, some towing others with cables, marshalled at the camp's lower assembly point. Sputtering diesel engines, air brakes, and Bollywood music echoed off a Hesco wall as they parked. I soon learned that one of the truck drivers was the cousin of the ANA gate guard, so he let them into the camp. Through the interpreter, I spoke with the foreman of the motley crew. In his mid-forties, his skin showed years of hard labour in the sun. After sharing pleasantries, I told him there must be a mistake; he was at the wrong job site, and they needed to leave. Calmly he stated another problem, one so simple he could sum it up in English.

"No fuel."

He then walked down the row of trucks and kicked the fuel tanks with his sandaled foot. Each one boomed out an empty echo so loud it reverberated above the Bollywood music blasting from the road grader stereo. The convoy couldn't move without sufficient fuel as it risked running out on the road. As the construction company supported coalition forces, being stranded on the side of the road at nightfall in Taliban country could be a death sentence. After some back-and-forth conversations via the interpreter, the foreman spoke enough English to summarize the requirements.

"Need fuel, need food."

Hearing the foreman's crafty response, I got a weird vibe about his English fluency. By observing his face and mannerisms, my instincts told me he spoke English just fine. Just like I feigned washing my hands, he feigned the role of a poor Afghanistan contractor who could not understand English. At this junction, I didn't care about potentially being ripped off by a charade. I aimed to get them off the camp before they became a liability. After confirming they would vanish if we provided them with fuel and food, I departed back up the hill on my John Deere Gator.

I popped by the command post to see if they had any news about the rogue contractors. The look from the camp sergeant major sitting beside the radio said it all. *I don't care what it takes, get those glue bags off my camp, or you'll be filling sandbags!*

Getting the message loud and clear, I drove to see the camp storeman. A happy-go-lucky corporal helped me load a few boxes of military rations and about two dozen twenty-litre jerry cans of fuel. Bearing the resemblance of an overloaded jingle truck cruising along the local highways, the John Deere Gator puttered back to the assembly area with the goods. I helped splash a little diesel in vehicle after vehicle to help expedite their departure. With some fuel, the trucks at the end of the tow cables sprang to life as if by magic. The crews swiftly and skillfully wound up the tow cables, their practiced efficiency making it clear this wasn't their first time unhooking those trucks.

Resembling an Oscar-winning actor, the foreman held his poor contractor charade to the end. As the circus-like act of vehicles started to roll out of camp with Bollywood music blaring, the boxes of rations tucked into the foreman's truck versus spread out to his starving employees, I felt all but certain that a crafty con artist had just scammed us. We never discovered the alleged contract, the supposed scope of work, where the contractor came from or went after leaving. But to sustain the camp's security, we paid a bill of a few hundred litres of diesel and some military rations to make them leave. Comparable to our road paving project, it appeared that contractors could also develop make-work projects.

While Ali continued to provide exceptional contractor work around camp, other contractors cut corners. One week, the camp started to get sick. High numbers of troops reported to the medical inspection room with gastroenteritis. Due to the volume, an investigation ensued to find the root cause. After a couple of days, we discovered the culprit: the new portable toilet contractor.

From unawareness of the task or just laziness and plain stupidity, the portable toilet contractor used the same truck to empty the portable toilets and fill the kitchen hand-washing stations. He would empty the toilets, depart to dump the load and return with a load of hand-washing station water in the same truck. Nobody inspected his work as they just assumed he knew the expected duties. Consequently, the troops washed with diluted effluent for a couple of days before eating. I showed up for breakfast on a particularly bad morning when many had lost their appetite due to the sickness. Equally hit by the outbreak, the kitchen became short-staffed to the point that the karaoke singing kitchen officer needed to take a shift behind the grill to keep the mess open. He didn't say anything, but he looked a little under the weather as I gave him my standard morning order.

"Two over easy, please."

He paused before he cracked the eggs. My healthy body and energy punctuated the sickly camp vibe. He didn't say a word, but I could feel the potency of his thoughts.

*"You son of a bitch, you still don't wash your hands."*

With a mischievous grin, my face said, "Nope."

Eating my breakfast alone in the mess tent, I chuckled at the similarities between contractors in Canada and Afghanistan. Comparable to the American dollar, contractor issues crossed international borders and cultures. We dealt with quintessential contractors like Ali, crooked contractors like the construction foreman, and lazy contractors like the portable toilet guy.

I also chuckled about the backward nature of Afghanistan: you can do everything right and still be wrong. Outside the camp, we meticulously followed standard drills for efficiency and safety. Yet, the very procedures meant to protect us created predictable patterns that our adversaries attacked without mercy. Inside the camp, the kitchen officer strictly enforced protocols to maintain cleanliness in the kitchen. He strictly adhered to his training and protocols. Ironically, the very hand-washing rules meant to protect our health ended up making many sick. Throughout our military careers, we trained relentlessly to meet standards and earn qualifications—vehicle qualifications, leadership qualifications, and weapon qualifications.

Yet despite everything, I never became Afghanistan-qualified. Whenever I thought my apprenticeship was complete so I could get my check-in-the-box, Afghanistan added to the unyielding-curriculum in the most unexpected ways.

In what other training establishment will a portable toilet guy remind you of the universal truth for working with soldiers, contractors, or anyone else in life?

You get what you inspect, not what you expect.

# 15

# Life in a Wheel Barrow

As the springtime flowers bloomed, so did the enemy activity. The budding started with our daisy chain compound and Sia Choy patrol, which continued to spread throughout the summer. What had been minor, sporadic skirmishes with the enemy quickly flourished into larger-scale, organized operations across the battlespace, with the most notable being the Sarposa prison break.

In early June, approximately half of the prison staff came down with food poisoning. In jest, I half-expected our portable toilet contractor to be on the penitentiary payroll. Nobody detected or suspected this was the vanguard for a main assault. One morning in mid-June, a large fuel truck approached the jail's front gates. Once in the vicinity of the infrastructure, an insurgent fired an RPG into the vehicle. The ensuing explosion levelled the main entrance and security towers. Through a well-orchestrated assault, the inmates resembled ants as they scurried into a hodgepodge of vehicles that had been pre-positioned in the surrounding neighbourhood. In total, approximately 385 well-trained insurgents, many IED facilitators, escaped, refilling the Taliban ranks for the summer.[1]

The prison break stunned the coalition forces, from the soldiers to national governments. We were usually so occupied with the tactical minutia that we didn't pay too much attention to national headlines and high-level strategies, but this event also impacted us. Going forward, we would be operating in an IED-rich environment against an adversary that had just bolstered their ranks with a fresh batch of combat veterans. Reading about the prison break in the intelligence reports, it seemed like they were making an all-star team with the old gang. I wished we had more alluring options to deter the convicts from rejoining the Taliban team than employment with our make-work road paving project.

As part of some preliminary work for future operations, we partook in Operation NOLAI. The main effort of this operation rested to our north with other battlegroup elements, so the primary objective of our participation was to help overwhelm insurgent command-and-control networks. By providing superfluous activity in the same battlespace, the enemy wouldn't be able to confirm our true objective. As part of our feint, we would scout additional routes and wadi crossing points in our area of operations. We were desperate to find additional mobility options as we'd been tied to the Arghandab River and Route Fosters to resupply our tactical infrastructure in the Horn of Panjwai. Operation NOLAI provided an excellent reconnaissance opportunity.

Approximately thirty vehicles rolled out of Sperwan Ghar on the morning of the operation. We appeared to be a big deal, composed of tanks, armoured vehicles, and ANA trucks. To mitigate the IED threat, we started plowing new routes through the countryside. This approach involved the AEV dropping the blade, taking a compass bearing towards a point on the horizon and driving. Like a massive bulldozer, the AEV plowed over or pushed through everything in its path: adobe walls, ditches, farmer crops. The remaining convoy would follow behind on the freshly created path. Although exceptionally destructive to the local landscape, it significantly reduced the IED threat. As the route remained unknown until the last moment, it made it practically impossible for an insurgent to target a convoy with IEDs.

By late afternoon, we arrived in a large, flat field. After exploring several alternative route options throughout the day, we had one last wadi to inspect before nightfall. As the intention was to remain overnight, the convoy formed a leaguer. Approximately one hundred and fifty metres in diameter, a circular defence provided the best protection for our stay. With tanks marking each cardinal point, the remainder of the armoured LAVs and ELAVs filled out the circle, spread equidistant from each other. The soft-skinned ANA vehicles were marshalled inside the perimeter under the protective watch of the outward-facing armoured vehicles. With clear arcs of fire in all directions, we were well-placed to defend the position.

While forming the leaguer, our vehicle ended up facing north. In the distance over the open field, we could just make out a paved highway running perpendicular to our position. To our east and west were open fields, and to our south was a flat field that ran for a couple hundred meters before it abruptly hit a distinctive wadi. The only sign of life in the area was a nomadic village a few hundred metres to our west. I could see a cluster of animal-skin tents in the open plain in the early evening light. Their abode weathered surfaces blended with the earth tones of the surrounding landscape. Simple hand tools rested by their tents, while stooks of hay in neatly arranged bundles contrasted with the flat terrain. Some goats, sheep, and dogs scurried in and around the various shelters. The entire camp layout in the middle of a harvest was a testament to their rudimentary farming practices and the community's resourceful way of life. The hay stooks reminded me of museum photos of Canadian farmers settling the prairies. After getting established in the leaguer, I turned to Wally.

"I'm off with the recce section to look at that wadi to our south."

Wally gave me a thumbs up while trying to light a cigarillo with a feeble lighter.

With my patrol pack, I walked over to the recce section led by Sergeant Kirby Vincent. Sporting a bushy mustache, his calloused hands showed the countless hours he had spent in the wilderness hunting and fishing during off hours. We had a simple plan: conduct a short patrol to our south, inspect the wadi for potential crossing points and return to the leaguer. As we were in the middle of an open field, the threat of an attack seemed low, but I could see a real danger of being exposed to friendly fire. With the only cover for a potential attack lying on the other side of the wadi, our patrol would position us perfectly to be caught in a crossfire. After checking in with the command post, I spoke to each southward-facing vehicle about our patrol. I was particularly concerned about the tanks with their 120mm smoothbore cannon. Even with well-aimed shots in a crossfire situation, standing in front of an active tank main gun could result in injuries from the overpressure. In one engagement, I witnessed a section of infantry get caught in front of the Leopard tank as the main gun fired; they all dropped to the ground in unnerving unison similar to heavy sacks of potatoes being dropped on a storeroom floor. Although they continued in the fight, something told me the concussion from the gun caused concealed injuries.

With the sun starting to set, we proceeded on our patrol. The air reeked of marijuana from wild growing plants as a small homeless dog trotted along behind us, searching for a place to belong. Though I'd done everything possible to prevent a crossfire, I remained anxious. Looking back to our vehicles from the wadi, the leaguer appeared ominous. Only the armoured vehicles and their weapon systems were visible. With the unfamiliar view from the outside looking in, I immediately understood why the army commonly called a leaguer a "ring of steel." Our timing also put me on edge because our patrol would run up to the stand-to-hour, a defensive drill to man all weapons systems during the most likely attack periods. In our doctrine, and based on our experience in Afghanistan, this was the hour before first light and the hour before last light. With only ninety minutes of light remaining, our movement outside the ring of steel flirted with this witching hour. Fortunately, my concerns were all for naught. We quickly completed the wadi recce, with the copious amounts of marijuana plants being the only notable detail. Potheads back home would have killed for just one plant, let alone hundreds growing freely in the wild.

After forty-five minutes, we returned to our vehicles and joined the stand-too drills. While manning the LAV turret with Wally, I brought him up to speed on the recent patrol.

"It will be a tough spot to cross, but we could make a route with some time."

"I'm good with anything that breaks up our patterns," replied Wally in a semi-focused tone as he stayed vigilant for threats.

While looking around with my head outside the turret, I noticed the requirement to change the infrared glowstick on our LAV. To help mark friend from foe, we used infra-red markers. Invisible to the naked eye, they glowed brightly when observed through the infrared optics of aircraft and armoured vehicles. We taped a small water bottle upside down on the antenna mast a few feet above the turret to mark our LAV. The reflection inside the water bottle amplified the infrared signature and provided an easy container to hold the glow stick. By simply unscrewing the water bottle cap, vehicle crews could easily exchange the expired glow stick with a fresh one; each had an approximately eight-hour lifespan.

The attack started while standing on the LAV with my arms outstretched to change the glowstick. From across the wadi we'd just left, I saw three green tracers arc through the air around my head. As tracer rounds are typically every fifth round in a belt-fed machine gun, that meant a lot of bullets were being aimed directly at me. If the muzzle of that machine gun had aimed just a thousandth of an inch lower, or if the operator had sneezed, the burst would have sliced me up and introduced me to my maker. Another reminder that drove home the brutal reality: War is a battle of inches.

At the same instant, a mortar round landed with alarming accuracy thirty feet behind our vehicle, inside the leaguer. Upon impact, the explosive round unleashed a powerful blast, scattering lethal shrapnel over a wide area. Between the gunfire and mortars, my body instinctively went straight as a board as my arse puckered. In an instant, I descended comparable to a submariner going down the tower ladder into the protection of the armoured turret. As my head dipped below the turret, I saw another mortar round impact inside our perimeter and toss an ANA soldier like a rag doll.

Inside the turret, adrenaline surging from my core, the radio came alive with chatter.

"Contact."

"Dismounts to the south."

"Section minus engaged and destroyed."

Battle updates continued to pour in as the armoured vehicles returned fire with awesome lethality. To our astonishment, the enemy shattered the quiet night by launching a dismounted assault against an armoured leaguer. Small groups with AK-47s attempted to attack the leaguer by sneaking through the open field. In a suicidal attempt to attack, pinpoint accuracy machine gun fires cut down the assailants one after another. The insurgents had to be high on a cocktail of drugs to get the audacity to rally against armoured vehicles in a flat, open field. While Wally rapidly traversed the turret to find a target, I saw several adversaries running with AK-47s get mowed down by machine gun fire. One of the vehicles cutting down insurgents was the ELAV. After the fact, I learned of another design flaw with the new vehicle. Since the remote weapon system only held one box of ammunition, when it ran out, it required the operator to fully expose themselves to reload. The sappers quickly enlarged the ammunition capacity to prevent a similar occurrence later in the tour.

While the mayhem continued to ensue, Wally paused on a target. In our thermal sight, four men with AK-47s were seated in the back of a truck. Wally instantly used the laser range finder.

"Nine-hundred and seventy-two metres. Ready to engage."

As per the gunnery drills, he armed the weapon and waited for the command to fire. Only an eighth of an inch movement of Wally's trigger finger separated those men from certain death. Based on previous engagements, I knew Wally didn't miss.

As I peeked above the turret to get situational awareness with my own eyes, the night sky resembled a laser show at a rock concert as red tracer rounds ricocheted into the distance. Medics triaged the ANA casualties to our rear while armoured turrets continued to engage the onslaught. During this time, my mind repeatedly asked, where is the threat? Our rules of engagement only allowed us to engage targets that were a lethal threat to us or other coalition assets. As the effective range of the AK-47 is only four hundred metres at best, those four men at nine hundred plus metres didn't pose a lethal threat to us or any of our coalition brethren.

In contrast, the other dismounted attackers being annihilated around the leaguer were no more than three hundred metres away. Armed with the intent to harm coalition assets, they became legal targets to kill. All of this flowed through my mind in nanoseconds before I spoke to Wally.

"Hold fire."

His head perked up. By now, I knew his mannerisms so well that we could communicate without speaking. Glued to the weapon sight as the gunner, he didn't have the benefit of observing above the turret, so I elaborated.

"They are too far away to engage us, outside our ROE."

Something also seemed wrong about our target's mannerisms. While mayhem surrounded us, those four men dressed in traditional garb just sat in the back of a Ford Ranger pickup truck.

They were either exceptionally stupid and failed to recognize the signal to attack, or they were involved in something entirely different. We didn't have time to debate, as the radio provided a stark update.

"Machine guns have set the fields on fire."

Tracer rounds are phenomenal for bringing belt-fed machine gun fire to bear on a target. When shooting the pintle mount, I hardly used the sight. Instead, I just walked the red laser line formed by the tracer rounds onto the target. Unfortunately, the metallic fuel that burns and provides the tracer round illumination can also start fires. In this case, we were parked in a dry wheat field. If the wind changed directions, the fire could run through our position and engulf our vehicles in flames.

"Prepare to move," came over the radio.

A quick set of convoy orders followed. One platoon would escort the medical evacuation of the ANA casualties from the mortar attack via the road. At the same time, the remainder of the convoy would establish another leaguer a couple of kilometres to the north. Well practiced in maneuvering as a unit from earlier in the day, it didn't take long before we were slowly on the move. As the fires burned to the west, we scanned the area for follow-on threats.

The ensuing scene is seared in my memory. While we methodically withdrew from the leaguer, turmoil unfolded in the nomadic camp. Caught in the crossfire, tracer rounds from the belt-fed machine guns ignited the surrounding fields in dozens of locations. The organized tents and systematic stacks of hay became threatened by fire. Flames engulfed the outlying stooks of hay, burning so intensely that the crackling inferno drowned out the roar of our LAV's diesel engine. The light evening breeze blew the thick grey smoke directly through the camp making it an opaque cloud to the naked eye, but it remained unobscured through our thermal imagery.

Heat signatures filled the frame in our monochromatic green sight picture. Sometimes slightly blurred due to differing heat gradients, the images can have a ghostly appearance because of how the collage of heat contrasts are depicted on the screen. Through our aperture, we witnessed a middle-aged man scurry around his tent. He placed a wheelbarrow immediately adjacent to the tent, synonymous to parking a car in front of a North American-style house. Over the next ninety seconds, he threw a few belongings into the wheelbarrow along with a child. He then briskly scurried to the north while pushing the loaded wheelbarrow and pulling a goat on a rope. His entire life was in that wheelbarrow. Before long, his image receded behind the knoll of a slight rise in the field. As we continued to move out, I wondered what, if anything, he would return to after the fires.

I didn't have much time to reflect. Moments later, we approached the Ford Ranger truck containing four armed men. These were the same four individuals Wally and I almost shot during the firefight. As if a psychic in the patrol read my mind, a message came over the radio.

"All call signs, Ranger truck with armed soldiers are friendlies. They are ANA soldiers moonlighting as a security detail for a commercial convoy."

What a lesson in restraint. One of the young ANA soldiers dressed in traditional garb sat in the back of the battered pickup truck with his AK-47 resting casually across his lap. His sun-darkened face was marked with weariness beyond his youthful years, and a missing tooth added a rugged edge to his messed-up smile. The only thing more screwed up was the concept of moonlighting as a security force with an AK-47 in a warzone. As AK-47s were often used to help identify friend from foe, those lads chose a risky side hustle to make some extra cash. As we pulled away, I stared at them in disbelief. Their distant gazes indicated one of two things: they either ignored what had just happened or had grown so accustomed to gunfights that destruction and burning fields felt routine. Either way, they had no idea how close they were to being part of the devastating losses that night. War often comes down to inches. In this case, they lived because Wally didn't move his trigger finger an eighth of an inch.

About an hour later, we established another leaguer a couple of kilometres north of the burning field. As the nightly security routine recommenced, we again scanned our arcs of fire with our thermal imagery. This time, no ghostly green human images appeared in the surrounding opium fields, only an ominous stillness. While smoking a cigarillo with Wally in the turret, we finally had a chance to reflect on the recent events.

Our counterinsurgency training stressed the importance of focusing on the population to win the war: win the people, win the war. By garnering and fostering support for the host nation's government, we could counterbalance the insurgency by creating traditional markets, processes and governance. A common saying to express this approach was "dollars and ballots versus bombs and bullets." At the time, one central part of our strategy was establishing and sustaining the combat outposts. Through this infrastructure, we established a presence in the local populace to fight the counterinsurgency. The U.S. Army's *Counterinsurgency Field Manual* outlines these types of tactics. The book also states that counterinsurgency operations can be counterintuitive and paradoxical. Sometimes doing nothing is the best reaction when doing otherwise will create more enemies than it removes.

The counterintuitive idea of doing nothing is the best reaction resonated that night. Being attacked by an armed force within the effective range of their weapons made them a legal target. I wondered what would have happened if we didn't shoot. Would a dismounted enemy in an open field really overrun an armoured position? They only had a couple of magazines each for their weapons. I couldn't fathom they would charge with bayonets or attempt to butt-stroke the tanks; if they did, we could have driven over them. I suspect they would have realized the futility of their shoot-and-scoot tactic within another sixty seconds and chose to disengage. We'll never know.

What I did know is that by engaging, the conflagration caused by the crossfire burnt up the livelihood of a nomadic village. Although I felt our mission was morally correct, the events that night showed me there is a razor-thin line between being an asset or a liability. We undoubtedly removed dozens of enemy fighters that night, but at what cost? Comparable to an overzealous pesticide, we wiped out the pests, but in doing so, we poisoned the very crop we were meant to protect. Like a phoenix rising from the ashes, those fires brought an old adage to life with haunting clarity: you can win the battle but lose the war.

My heart went out to that nomadic village. That wheelbarrow carried more than just belongings – it carried an entire life, shoved into a heap and wheeled off into the unknown. Just a father, his child, and a goat fleeing a firestorm they had nothing to do with. Without insurance or government support, they faced a tough road to rebuilding. In the process, would they support the host nation government or any leadership that let them live in peace? Would they seek employment with our road paving project or bolster the ranks with the recently released Sarposa prison convicts? For the first time, I wondered if we were making any lasting change in Panjwai. Although we had made progress in some areas, it could quickly be negated by the secondary and tertiary impacts of our actions. Similar to trust, it could take years to earn and only seconds to lose.

*The Counterinsurgency Field Manual* aimed to fill a gap in military doctrine. It meant to make sense of the harsh, unconventional tactics and paradoxical actions we saw during counterinsurgency operations, like an organized prison break, a dismounted assault on an armoured leaguer across an open field, and soldiers moonlighting with an AK-47 in a warzone. However, sitting in the turret that night surrounded by clouds of cigarillo smoke, Wally and I sat in silence as we tried to make sense of it all. For the most part, the manual met the aim of filling a doctrinal gap, but there was still a chasm in our comprehension. Unlike the structured certainty of our training environment with its established standards, reality offers no perfect solution - only choices with consequences. In the end, we only knew one thing for sure after the events that night. The counterinsurgency manual needed a new chapter entitled: Somethings you never understand.

# 16

# Wedding and a Funeral

Wally departed on HLTA just before our most significant and longest dismounted patrol. Sergeant Dwayne Waller, one of my section commanders, became the acting troop warrant. A short, blonde, stocky man, he loved hockey and getting big in the gym, although he always sustained chicken-like legs. Full of common sense, he didn't hesitate to speak candidly. His willingness to share honest insights and propose solutions in a professional manner became an invaluable asset during the tour.

To reinforce our presence and show our resolve in the Horn of Panjwai, our most extensive patrol ever aimed to walk to each combat outpost, one after the other, over several days. This would result in approximately seventy-five soldiers composed of Canadians and ANA walking roughly ten kilometres from Sperwan Ghar to Mushan, straight through the heart of Taliban country. After resting for a day in Mushan, we would reverse the process via a different route back to Sperwan Ghar.

While preparing for the patrol, I also wanted to set the conditions for Wally's return from leave. From the moment we arrived in Afghanistan, Wally had one mission outside the war - buying a monkey. Thinking it would make a tremendous welcome-back gift, I kept the idea in the back of my mind. He'd hardly left the camp when I approached Ali about the potential procurement. After countless demands, it was the one and only time I stumped him.

"Hey Ali, can you buy us a monkey?"

"Master John, what is monkey?"

I made my best monkey-like gestures to overcome the language barrier by bending my arms so my hands could scratch my armpits.

"You know, a monkey. Ooh-ohh, ah-ah."

His sharp wit immediately connected the dots.

"Ahh. Master John, you want bandar. Three hundred American."

I'm unsure if I was more surprised by his guess of the animal from my charade or by the fact he knew the cost of one off the top of his head.

"Master John, why?"

I explained Wally's dream of buying a monkey and that we were conducting market research to find one for his return in two weeks.

"Wally have strange dream. No problem, Master John."

As I handed over the cash, I had to trust Ali understood my monkey pantomime because I could not translate the word "bandar."

As Ali disappeared to handle his usual camp dealings and to buy who-knows-what with my three hundred bucks, Waller and I huddled over maps and logistics, ironing out every painful patrol detail. With less than eight sappers available to support the patrol, we discussed options for best splitting up to ensure we could provide mobility support. We finally decided pairs placed throughout the patrol was the best option as I could move throughout the patrol column with my radio if required. The patrol aimed to move between combat outposts under the cover of darkness to avoid the midday heat and minimize our visibility in daylight. Fulfilling his troop warrant officer duties to the letter, Waller helped set up a map and assembled the troops in our common area for patrol orders. Before I commenced, he even gave them the riot act.

"Troops, pay attention. No screwing around. Sir."

To align with Waller's tone, I commenced giving the patrol orders as if General Patton sat in the audience. After about three minutes into a thirty-minute brief, Ali walked up behind our common area.

"Master John, bandar!"

In Afghanistan, many things can interrupt orders: contact with the enemy, a call from the Commander, or artillery guns firing. Usually prepared for every contingency, Waller was even astonished by the interruption of orders by the arrival of a monkey. After a moment of disbelief, I spoke.

"Uh, Ali, not now. Busy."

Somehow buy a monkey in two weeks got lost in translation into buy a monkey in two days. What wasn't lost in translation was Ali's face. It said, *take bandar now!* A little larger than a house cat, the somewhat aggressive monkey strained against the collar around its neck. With a repurposed chain from a child swing set, the monkey held the corrugated shackle with one hand to relieve the tension. It made quick, jerky movements with the free hand as it lunged towards anything in reach. Its fierce, restless energy was an anomaly, a strange fusion of defiance and desperation.

Sensing the stalemate in my communications with Ali, Waller spoke.

"Uh, sir. Let's pause orders for a few minutes while we deal with this."

By now, any resemblance to formal orders had been lost. Pandemonium spread through the sappers as they pulled out cameras and approached the monkey with the fascination of kids on Christmas morning. Waller had done his utmost to cultivate a professional setting. Of all the people to screw up orders with a monkey frenzy, it was me, his troop commander.

Someone yelled out, "Let's call him Whitie."

Unanimously accepted in an instant, the sappers each took a turn orienting Whitie to our common area while he continually made flailing grasps at his surroundings. To placate his sporadic movements, sappers gave him beef jerky, candy bars, and cigarettes. Resembling a miniature tornado of destruction, Whitie would sniff, bite or lick everything before tossing it to the ground. Thinking he might be literate, the troops handed him magazines. No change. He jettisoned Maxim, National Geographic and comic books after a quick glance. After much trial and error, Whitie finally calmed down beside our pond, chewing on a cherry pop tart and staring at a Playboy magazine's cover.

One sapper yelled, "Whitie has great taste!" which was met with uproarious laughter.

News of Whitie's arrival spread like wildfire throughout the camp. The engineers bought a monkey—no, they only have a donkey. To be sure, other soldiers filed by with their cameras and ended up taking photos of Whitie, the pop tart-eating, Playboy-connoisseur monkey. Decades of managing soldier shenanigans had prepared the camp sergeant major for almost anything—but not the purchase of Whitie. He popped his head into our quarters, took a double take to confirm we did, in fact, buy a monkey, then laid down the law.

"You got an hour. Otherwise, I'll kill it myself."

Not washing hands could spread bacteria, but a vermin-filled monkey could spread anything. We didn't need any further elaboration; Whitie needed to go. While the sappers showed Wally's quarters to our primate guest, who despite recently receiving a death sentence, remained blissfully unaware, I ran to find Ali.

"Ali, bandar needs to go back."

Thinking I wanted my money back, Ali explained the situation.

"Master John, sale final."

"No Ali, keep the money. Monkey can't stay. Please make it go away."

It took some explaining to tell Ali we were overjoyed with the purchase; we just couldn't keep it. Slightly perturbed to be handling a vicious monkey again, he tossed the restive critter into the back of the dump truck and departed for the local bazaar. In a cloud of dust and diesel fumes, Whitie unceremoniously departed Sperwan Ghar. After a ninety-minute circus-like interlude, we returned our focus to the upcoming patrol.

The patrol out to Mushan was relatively uneventful. We cut through fields, climbed over adobe walls, and traversed through graveyards to avoid the traditional IED-laced choke points along paths and roads. The only point of note was how the Afghanistan summer nights at thirty degrees Celsius could be frigidly cold. As we'd sweat profusely during the day, our cotton clothes became a pasty mess after multiple days. Without a change of clothes in the evening, this paste would cool. With just a thin air mattress and blanket, some of us, myself included, shivered uncontrollably throughout the night as we prayed for the warmth of the morning sun.

Situated on the edge of our area of operations, Mushan was the epitome of a combat outpost. The circular tailfin of one of the countless mortars fired at the position was pinned as the "O" in the "Welcome to Mushan" sign that hung at the front gate. A fine, powder-like dirt called "moon dust" permeated everything and turned it brown: tents, sea cans, equipment, weapons, and skin. Without an established resupply route, Mushan relied heavily on air-dropped supplies from helicopters or C-130 Hercules transport airplanes. During our first morning in Mushan, we helped collect water bottles from the morning airdrop in the back of ANA Ranger trucks. Working with the ANA, they continually proved helpful in unanticipated ways. When interacting with the locals, they could distinguish good from bad, discern dress, mannerisms, and language dialect instantly. In what looked like a homogeneous mix of inhabitants to us, outliers stood out in technicolour to the ANA. The latest unexpected benefit of working with the ANA became their cooking.

Tired of military rations, someone suggested we have a BBQ during our one-day stay in Mushan. The idea caught amongst the Canadian and ANA troops, but we needed food. I didn't think anything of it until one of the ANA observer mentors approached me.

"Sir, I understand you carry cash. We need some to buy grub for the BBQ."

I always felt more comfortable carrying some cash, but I didn't think others were aware of that fact; the patrol members knew me better than I thought. They also knew I had a propensity to buy animals based on Hughes and the recent monkey purchase. Assuming others had already contributed to the BBQ kitty, I handed over a hundred dollars American. The ANA observer mentor became crestfallen.

"A hundred bucks won't buy enough food for everyone."

When I realized I had somehow become the *main* sponsor for the BBQ, my only other option was to dip into the Small Rewards Program—funds meant for paying locals to report IEDs. Sensing the urgency to commence with the festivities, I handed over the roll of afghanis, which increased the total BBQ kitty to two hundred American dollars. As locals had reported IEDs in the past without receiving compensation, I figured we could sort out the Small Rewards Program administration later.

Delighted, the ANA observer mentor darted to a group of ANA soldiers. In a flash, a group of them shot out of camp in a Ford Ranger truck with a large Russian machine gun mounted on a standup tripod in the back. Within the hour, they returned with three large sheep in the back. Haltered to the machine tripod mount, each animal had florescent dots spray-painted on their rear quarter. I assumed the marks represented a brand or sign of ownership in Afghanistan. Surrounding the animals in the truck bed rested dozens of two-litre bottles of Coca-Cola and various local fruits. At that moment, I realized the prolific depths of American capitalism. Mushan may have been too isolated for a Tim Hortons, but in its biblical like surroundings, unchanged in generations, the American dollar and Coca-Cola thrived.

With the camp buzzing after the arrival of three sheep, I saw the camp sergeant major walk over to me, Master Warrant Officer Rod Dearing. Tall with dark hair, he possessed an easy demeanour and subtle wit that bonded him closely with the ANA soldiers he worked with and mentored. Joining the military to have adventures after being laid off at the local sawmill, his service with the Princess Patricia's Canadian Light Infantry provided them in spades. After witnessing firsthand his tactical acumen under fire during the Sia Choy patrol, I never wanted to cross him. Thinking he was approaching me to discuss the gong show I had just created in his camp by buying sheep for a BBQ, I braced myself for the worse.

"Hey sir, while you guys are here, can you help us with some unexploded ordnance?"

Relieved that he didn't want to skin me similar to one of the sheep, I also smirked because unexploded ordinance could be IED parts. I'd just justified spending the Small Rewards Program.

"No problem, sergeant major. We can handle those later today after the BBQ."

Preoccupied with other camp maintenance tasks, he didn't notice the sheep abattoir forming on the Hesco walls at the camp's entrance.

"Where having a BBQ?"

Finally having a moment to take in the situation, he surveyed the camp as fruits were being cut up with bayonets on the tailgate of a pickup truck.

"Right on." Sergeant Major Dearing was the kind of soldier who could foster camaraderie anywhere in the world.

With the efficiency of a finely oiled machine, the ANA platoon prepared the food. While some soldiers slaughtered the sheep according to halal practices, others started a fire in an earth oven; they used wood from broken forklift pallets recently retrieved from the morning resupply drop for fuel. Before long, the outdoor mud kitchen bustled with activity as the freshly butchered sheep boiled in a large aluminum cooking pot, a spitting image of a witch's cauldron. Smoke from the wood fire curled into the hot afternoon air, carrying the rich aroma of a slow-cooking animal in traditional spices. When ready, soldiers filed by comparable to a soup kitchen line to get a ladle full of homemade sheep stew. In various states of dress, some in their underwear and a t-shirt while others were in their full battle rattle, the troops raved about the cultural experience of eating authentic stew and homemade naan bread. We called it "foot bread" among ourselves as they kneaded the dough with their feet before baking it in the oven.

As troops gobbled up the meal, I usually would have been preoccupied with the unwashed hands, homemade flip-flops made of cardboard and duct tape, or troops eating in their undies, but I remained fixated on the cooking pot. The Taliban used the exact same type, only they filled it with homemade explosives to make IEDs, not sheep to have a BBQ. It struck me as surreal how the same rudimentary cauldron that simmered with the scent of shared food and joy could also become an instrument of violence, tearing lives apart.

During the stand-to that evening, we didn't have assigned positions as the camp inhabitants covered off all the arcs, so we just donned our full fighting order in the event of an attack. With the troops spread out and under as much cover as possible in the austere setting, I made my way over to the 60mm mortar pit in the center of the outpost. A crown jewel in the defensive position, the manning responsibility rested with Sergeant Major Dearing. As I perched myself on the sandbag protective barrier, he explained the detailed range card that hung from the bipod kit.

"Everything has a nickname for quick communication: school rubble, intersection, the knoll."

As he called out the nicknames of the common points used by insurgents to fire upon Mushan, he pointed to them on the range card. Each spot was clearly marked with the bearing, distance, and the mortar charge requirement previously calculated using range tables. This basic layout and design had not changed much since the inception of the 60mm mortar in the early 1950s. With an effective range of just over three thousand metres, the weapon significantly bolstered Mushan's defences.

"We've also marked no fire zones, like the bazaar."

Sergeant Major Dearing indicated the point on his range card, which was the likely origin of our BBQ supplies earlier that day. I leaned in for a closer look before speaking.

"What about the mark…"

"Contact, knoll!" cried out from the observation post sentry.

The mortar crew sprang into action. Being hit so regularly, troops placed bets on the origin of attack. Having wagered the knoll as the anticipated point of contact, they had prepositioned the mortar tube to aim directly at it. With mortars already prepared, they fired three outgoing rounds onto the target in under thirty seconds.

Boom.

Boom.

Boom.

Although deafened by the charges firing the mortars out of the tube, I immediately fell in love with the 60mm mortar. It perfectly countered the shoot-and-scoot tactics of the Taliban. As they always watched us, they knew indirect fire from our artillery pieces would take a couple minutes to arrive. With a preestablished mortar tube, they could drop rounds in an area the size of a truck in under a minute. It changed the phrase from "shoot-and-scoot" to "shoot-and-get-mortared-before-they-scoot." I don't know which Canadian won the bet for guessing the contact point of origin that night, but I do know the Taliban lost. No further shots originated from the knoll after the mortars delivered their lethal payload.

We spent the following day resting in preparation for the night patrol. The aim was to walk halfway to the combat outpost at Zangabad and rest for a day before returning to Sperwan Ghar the following evening. To pass the time and attempt to stay relatively cool, we lounged underneath parachutes collected from the resupply airdrops. Repurposed as sunshades by fastening them to the Hesco walls, they provided the only reprieve from the scorching sun. The crystal-white fabric stood out sharply against the muted colours of Mushan's decor. After a mortar attack the previous week caused part of Mushan to burn, many of us were covered in black soot as we lingered in the ashy remains. Although we tried several times to blow up the unexploded ordinance as requested by the camp sergeant major, we consistently encountered frictions that caused delays. By late afternoon, everything finally lined up for an explosive range.

Before long, a few sappers and Sergeant Major Dearing carted a mix of unexploded ordnance into Mushan's exclusion zone. Sappers prepared charges while Waller inspected the cache as he was qualified to handle IEDs due to his EOD training. As some of the conventional munitions had been tampered with to function differently than designed, they met the definition of IED components. With the sun starting to set on the horizon, I finalized the range clearances on the radio. I could not stay for the detonation as I needed to return to the Mushan command post for patrol orders. With all the delays throughout the day, our explosive range bumped right next to the scheduled patrol orders, the stand-to and subsequent patrol departure. Usually a master of concurrent activity, my multi-tasking plan resulted in an inglorious failure.

While proceeding to the patrol orders, I notified one of two platoons inside the outpost about the forthcoming explosion. Although news of the upcoming explosion was disseminated through the camp sentries and command post, it didn't reach the second platoon. During patrol orders, I took notes as Major Lane outlined the plan.

"We'll depart at... KABOOM!"

An immense ear-splitting explosion rocked Mushan. The concussion blast pushed dust two feet outwards horizontally from the Hesco walls and caused the draped parachutes to rapidly quiver. The unnotified platoon screamed, "Contact!" and scurried to whatever battle position they could find as the explosion echoed through the outpost. Above the bastion walls, I could see a mushroom cloud of dust rising into the early evening sky. Alarmed by the intensity of the detonation and follow-on confusion, my gut sank when a piece of shrapnel rang into the outpost, bounced off a sea can and dropped onto the exposed head of the forward observation officer sitting beside me.

I felt sick. Trying to do too much at once, I failed miserably. I caused chaos in the camp, interrupted orders for a difficult patrol, and created a casualty that required medical evacuation.

It was an inauspicious start to the evening. Although our casualty would make a full recovery, we were forced to operate over the next two days without our primary forward observation officer to call in artillery fire or air assets in support of our return patrol.

While feeling nauseous and unnerved about the range calamities, the remainder of the evening routine in Mushan went per the patrol orders. We conducted the stand-to, thanked our hosts for their hospitality and departed Mushan under the cover of darkness. I found it challenging to get my head back in the game after the range mishap, but Afghanistan has a knack for dispelling lingering thoughts. To avoid IEDs on paths, we took a zig-zag route through opium fields, across wadis, and over adobe walls. At one point, we reached a wall approximately nine feet tall. One by one, soldiers scampered over, using anything for a handhold in a style similar to a free solo rock climber. Just before climbing over myself, the soldier in front of me paused. After a minute, he remained unmoved at the top of the wall. Anxious to avoid breaking up the patrol and cause another issue, I called out in a hushed voice.

"Hey, what's the hold-up?"

After a brief pause, I heard a reply from the other side of the wall.

"Waller's upside down. He's caught in a grapevine."

On the other side of the wall, Sapper Hamilton responded to the situation. While scaling down the wall, Waller slipped and became utterly inverted after one of the tall grapevines caught his pant leg. Being only five feet, nothing tall to begin with, he hung helplessly upside down resembling a bug in a spider's web. With Waller giggling about his predicament, I heard Hamilton grunt while using his he-man strength to bust the entrapping grapevines. Before long, I heard a sarcastic update from the other side of the wall.

"Waller's fat ass is walking again."

This doubled as a signal for the rest of us to continue the patrol. As we scurried to catch up, it felt similar to drunk buddies navigating obstacles as they returned home late from a bar in a foreign country. The humorous episode was so out of place that it felt as if a sitcom had accidentally wandered into a warzone.

An hour later, BOOM.

A random blast broke the stillness of the arid night. Every unexpected explosion became bone-jarring and got on my nerves because you never knew if it would be a near miss or a casualty. It felt like a constant game of Russian roulette; many explosions were harmless, but others were catastrophic. The patrol paused while Major Lane assessed the situation. Although it occurred to our north in the riverbed, we attempted to find the root cause. Did an animal step on a device meant for a dismounted soldier, or did an IED emplacement team screw up and self-destruct? As the patrol commander attempted to see if any overhead drones saw the incident, I took a knee inside a graveyard. As IEDs typically didn't occur in graveyards, I felt safe amongst the dead.

Crooked wooden poles marked the graves, standing like silent sentinels, their tips adorned with faded rags that twisted and fluttered in the night breeze. The place offered the kind of silence that pressed in around you.

I was speaking casually with the patrol interpreter when death rose.

Fifteen feet ahead of me, a shallow grave in the earth barely two feet deep came alive. Without warning, a man sat up.

I recoiled, my breath catching in my throat. The movement was slow and unnatural, as if unseen hands pulled him up. The dim light cast his face in shifting shadows, hollow eyes blinking against the darkness. It bared resemblance to something out of a Stephen King nightmare. My mind scrambled for logic as a cold prickle ran down my spine.

Before I could react, two ANA soldiers pounced on the spectre. He didn't resist. A tense, hushed cross-examination followed, voices sharp but quiet, as if speaking too loudly might disturb whatever else lurked among the graves. Then, just as suddenly, they let him go. Without a word, the figure melted into the graveyard shadows, his silhouette swallowed by the rows of crooked markers. The interpreter, his voice almost amused seeing my reaction, finally explained.

"Maintenance man. Sometimes sleeps in graveyard. Says he feels safer here."

I sat there, cold despite the heat, trying to process what I had just witnessed. Completely stunned by what had just transpired, I couldn't fathom a creepier place to sleep than in a freshly dug grave. Talk about terrible working conditions and freaky fringe benefits.

But in a twisted way, I understood. The burial grounds remained untouched in a world where anything could be a weapon. Despite the use of torture, rape, and murder as means to ruthlessly terrorize the civilian populace and the countless unspeakable tactics to attack coalition forces, even the Taliban tended to respect the dead, so they didn't weaponize graveyards.

A few minutes later, the patrol resumed after being unable to determine the source of the random explosion. It didn't take long for the fresh, warm Afghanistan air to soothe my nerves from the random detonation and the resurrected graveyard worker. As we continually weaved through fields and beside courtyards in the still night, you could see and feel the beauty of the terrain. At one point, we walked adjacent to a compound alive with music. The vibrant mix of rhythmic drumming, soulful melodies and ululations spilled into the night as we clandestinely walked by. Curious about the event, I turned to the interpreter.

"What's the party about?"

Watching his footing on the uneven surfaces, he didn't look up to respond.

"Wedding."

We were approaching Zangabad as the music started to fade in the distance. What usually would be a welcome milestone rested heavily on my mind. We became funnelled to specific paths and routes as we neared our destination. As we were constantly being watched, our attempt to move covertly under the cover of darkness was undoubtedly known to our adversaries by now. As the front of the patrol neared the final corner, a couple hundred meters from Zangabad, a blast cracked through the calm night. Seconds later, my radio came alive.

"Chimo up."

A few seconds passed before the stressed soldier corrected himself.

"I mean contact, wait out."

As we'd placed a half section of engineers towards the front of the patrol, I monitored our sapper net to see if they needed any support from rearward-placed elements. While waiting on pins and needles for the verdict of the blast, I reflected on the radio transmission. Intended to be a simple update, the radio transmission signalled another inflection point.

Throughout our training, "contact, wait out" had been engrained into our psyche to the point it became an unconscious response. Any engagement with the enemy immediately translated to "contact, wait out" on the radio. To hear the words "Chimo up" first meant two things. One, the blast caused a casualty; two, it symbolized the metamorphic change the sappers created through their dedication, hard work, and heroism. We'd gone from being practically ignored in the training fields of Wainwright to being the pointy end of the spear, so much so that we had changed the infantry's indoctrinated radio procedures.

A few minutes later, the radio came alive with a nine-liner. Corporal James Arnal stepped on an IED at a choke point approaching Zangabad. Despite first responders' best efforts, we received confirmation in the middle of the night that he had succumbed to the blast injuries.

Scattered around Zangabad to rest for the night, many troops stared into the darkness in varying degrees of grief and shock. Not known for being emotional, the rollercoaster ride of feelings over the last twenty-four hours left even me utterly exhausted. From the joy of a BBQ, I ran through the guilt of the range mistake, the elation of Waller hanging upside down in a grape field, to fear from witnessing the resurrection of the dead, feeling contentment due to the wedding to the gut punch of another IED casualty. I'm no doctor; however, the rapid swing of so many emotions in such a short period must place toxic occupational stresses on soldiers.

Unable to sleep, I thought about how Afghanistan made the world binary. You either communicated correctly about buying a monkey, or you didn't. You either conducted an explosive range properly, or you didn't. You either stayed off the paths completely to avoid an IED, or you didn't. You either produced results or looked for reasons why you didn't. Comparable to walking a tightrope between two skyscrapers without a net, you needed perfection. If you didn't do it right the entire way, you failed.

I sat in silence while others beside me attempted to rest in the uneasy stillness. My mind was on Corporal Arnal when the Afghan night added another shot to my emotional cocktail. In a surreal, stark contrast to the evening's lethal attack, through the still nocturnal air, the only sound I could hear was music. Celebrations from the wedding party.

# 17

# Freedom in the Void

We arrived back from the Mushan patrol just as Wally returned from his leave. With only a couple of months left in the deployment, the HLTA program started to conclude, and we commenced preparing for our redeployment. This change also meant that the operational reserve from Canada would not be available for much longer since it didn't make sense to deploy soldiers for only a matter of weeks. Without a fresh pool of standby sappers, we would no longer receive replacements for casualties or repatriations. Consequently, we would need to finish the tour with the sappers in theatre.

I updated Wally on the events in his absence: the patrols, the construction projects around the camp, and the monkey fiasco.

"Sorry Wally, I wanted it to be a surprise for your return, but I screwed up the procurement."

Wally shook his head in disappointment as the troops showed him the videos of Whitie eating pop tarts, gnawing on cigarettes, and sitting on his bed.

Around this time, Hughes the donkey earned national attention. A reporter had visited the camp a month or two previously to capture stories about the troops. Shying away from publicity, I didn't pay much attention to the odd media interview that occurred around Sperwan Ghar. I figured the sapper's exploits disarming IEDs and destroying weapon caches would attract the attention of the press. Much to my surprise, the lead story about the engineers became Hughes. Drawn to the press, the sappers shared a vivid account about how they bought Hughes to help carry heavy loads during patrols. In reality, Hughes was less a workhorse and more a court jester for the camp. He never carried anything beyond his crude bridle and spent most of his time happily munching on cannabis in his pen or the camp exclusion zone. Now archived in Veterans Affairs Canada, the article continues to resurface every few years in various forms, providing some humorous relief each time.

Thankfully the reporter wrote the story before Hughes was injured. One sunny afternoon, I received a call to report to the medical station. Thinking a sapper sustained an injury working around the camp, I couldn't believe my eyes when two medics were holding Hughes onto the ground while a third stapled the skin on his head back together. With blood gushing from a nasty gash, it resembled the scene from a dysfunctional operating room. They administered some sort of drug to try and assuage the pain; however, it seemed to miss the mark. While flailing his legs in a gravel parking lot, I watched the medics rigorously apply first aid.

"Hold him steady!"

As if preparing to apply defibrillator paddles, the three first responders exchanged nods, signaling they were ready.

"Ka-chunk."

A staple gun bluntly fired a stitch to sew up the gaping wound.

"Steady!"

They prepared for another shot.

"Ka-chunk."

Hughes's wiry legs kicked gravel in futile attempts to stand up and bolt from the makeshift operating room.

After the staple gun surgery concluded, I discovered Hughes had tried to escape from the camp but got caught in the razor wire surrounding our defensive perimeter. In the process, he cut a gruesome gash behind his ear. As he returned to his habitual proclivities of eating cannabis by the bail, he resembled Frankenstein with a dozen staples sealing the wound across his forehead.

A day or two later, I awoke to a yell.

"Hughes escaped!"

After a quick investigation, I learned Hughes had gone to the front gate. When I arrived, I saw Hughes about five hundred meters up the main roadway leading into the camp, slowly trotting away with his halter rope dangling at his side. Apparently, he walked out the front gate uncontested and headed on his merry way. I went to the Canadian sentries at the gate.

"Why didn't you stop the donkey?"

No response.

They just shrugged their shoulders, indicating they had played a small role in a clandestine scheme to eliminate Hughes. Tired of his sporadic hee-haw vagaries in the middle of the night, the random Houdini-like escapes from his pen, the recent medical emergency, or a combination of them all, the donkey novelty had waned. So, I suspected that my peers had furtively arranged his departure. Unable to retrieve Hughes without arranging a patrol, I stood helpless as he ambled away to find a new home. Initially peeved about losing even more money on animals, I later learned the donkey leaving was the universe whispering, "You're welcome."

As we returned to our routine of constant patrolling, I could tell other units were also struggling with low staffing levels. To bolster our ranks in the field for a final push before the redeployment, one approach became to pull individuals from the headquarters in KAF and push them into field units. To compensate for these transfers, headquarters utilized the operational reserve while it was still available to backfill their positions. This strategy minimized the onboarding time for replacements in the field as the KAF-based members were already cognisant of the battlespace from spending time in the headquarters. On the downside, this approach also meant we had to be on the lookout for fresh, well-intentioned staff officers who had just arrived from Canada. One day, while we were cleaning up an IED attack on our Mine Detonation Trailer in the Arghandab River, KAF headquarters called us directly on the radio.

"E21A, need t-shirt sizes for your troops."

This request was wrong on multiple levels. It never should have come over the radio during an operation as it could have plugged up the network required for more urgent transmissions. There were also multiple ways to get the information that didn't involve the radio. I didn't argue as it would have only jammed up the radio even longer, so I played along.

"Medium, one size fits all for everyone, over."

I had no idea about the troop clothing sizes. On patrol, we had more important issues than ensuring our troop received a t-shirt from some morale boost or fun run occurring in KAF, so I provided a terse response. A moment later, we received a curt acknowledgment.

"Uh, ack. Thanks."

Undoubtedly, the senior duty officer launched at the well-intentioned officer when he made the transmission. Wally and I just laughed at the absurdity of the request. The event also offered a bit of solace, knowing we weren't the only ones facing human resources shortages.

Around the same time, we completed the administration required for the Combat Action Insignia. Designed to be a badge for wearing on our fatigues, tracking became an administrative nightmare. With three levels, bronze, silver, and gold, the insignia criteria ranged from being inside the enemy's weapon template to directly engaging the enemy with your weapon. After each operation, Wally and I would log who received what level of insignia based on the operation. At times, it got silly. Was Sapper Joe Blow in the danger template of the incoming mortar, qualifying for the bronze insignia? Did Sapper Joe Schmo return effective fire on an enemy position while being in the effective range of their weapon system, qualifying for the gold insignia?

Since troops rotated out on leave, missed operations due to being assigned other tasks, or arrived late in theatre as part of the operational reserve, it took a bit before everyone approached the gold level. Beyond being tedious to track, it created stress on the soldiers, increased their cognitive load worrying about their status and encouraged poor decisions in attempts to achieve gold. During one firefight, I watched a soldier dismount from a armoured vehicle and engage the enemy – not out of necessity, but to qualify for the highest insignia level. To eliminate the unnecessary, and sometimes life threatening bravado displayed to obtain the badge, without saying a word, Wally and I looked at each other and said, *everybody is gold.*

Wally addressed the troops to mark the moment and end the incessant questioning about what levels had been obtained.

"You're all gold."

He let it hang in the air before he repeated himself.

"You've all received the *gold* action insignia. So, stop asking us what level you are from here on in. I'm sick of it."

You could feel a palpable burden lift from the troop as Wally's speech ended the speculation about who had what level. I discovered years later that the conversation about the merits of the badge continued back in Ottawa. Senior ranking officers expressed concerns with the insignia, as it would be tough, if not impossible, for most Air Force and Navy personnel to qualify, even though they played crucial roles in the conflict. There were also concerns that troops might be tempted to take life-threatening risks to earn one. This worry aligned with Napoleon's observation that "A soldier will fight long and hard for a bit of coloured ribbon." Ultimately, Ottawa binned the concept like bad leftovers, so all the angst, analysis and documentation surrounding the combat action insignia was in vain. Although it would be nice to acknowledge soldiers for their actions in combat, as tour experiences differ drastically between trades, Ottawa made the right call. The insignia program became a deadly distraction. Until I saw it with my own eyes, I never would have believed soldiers would make irrational decisions and expose themselves to enemy fire to get a bit of coloured ribbon.

In addition to removing some administrative burdens, we also needed to remove some infrastructure strains. In retrospect, the infantry company commander, Major Mike Lane, made the case that we were fighting a guerilla war, not a counterinsurgency. There was no development or reconstruction ongoing in our area, as the environment was not conducive to those types of operations. Tactical infrastructure initially placed to help establish a presence in the area became a liability because we spent most of our efforts defending the positions instead of moving amongst the populace surrounding the positions. The problem was further exacerbated by the decreased manning levels we experienced towards the latter half of the tour. After some analysis, higher-ups decided to decommission combat outpost Talukan to free up some resources in the battlespace. They used the word "decommission" as a euphemism for destroy, as a lot of blood, sweat, and tears had gone into its construction, and we didn't want to provide the Taliban with easy propaganda.

Situated between Mushan and Zangabad in the Horn of Panjwai, Talukan was a continual challenge to fortify and resupply throughout the tour. Logistic trucks brought construction materials during each resupply run, and we did our best to reinforce the position by building a bunker and filling Hesco cells. In the early stages of the tour, we didn't have enough time to properly fill the Hescos in one section. To give the illusion of a bastion wall, we just strung out the Hesco and filled what we could so the barrier would remain in place until we could return and finish the job. Although it looked formidable, portions of the wall were, in fact, a series of empty cloth cubes and reinforcing wire. In doing this, we only provided concealment to the outpost's occupants, not protection. While assuming this risk, the infantry got lucky during one attack. To make the recoilless rifle munitions more sensitive, the Taliban would sand down the tips. One attack resulted in the recoilless round detonating on the outer shell of the empty Hesco bastion rather than piercing the hollow wall and delivering its deadly payload deeper into the outpost. We were lucky.

During a visit to Talukan early in the tour, a preventative medicine technician had a metaphorical heart attack. Responsible for health assessments, hygiene, and sanitation protocols, she couldn't believe her eyes after inspecting the camp with her clipboard during a resupply drop. With troops defecating in bags, urinating into a funnel that drained just outside the camp, and eating in the same cramped area, she marked her entire inspection sheet with X's instead of check marks. In a flabbergasted, uncertain voice, she spoke with the outpost's warrant officer.

"Uh, you c-can't, s-stay here. It's not healthy."

Notwithstanding the routine gunfights that involved whistling RPGs and mortars, she was worried about hygiene. The platoon warrant officer, who hadn't bathed or shaved in weeks, responded with a large grin.

"No problem. Shut us down."

He tauntingly glared directly at the medical technician, searching for a word he could say that would end the platoon's *sejour* in Talukan.

"Just say the word, and we're gone!"

Helpless to enforce the standard, the preventative medicine technician simply deflated and returned to the convoy with the failed inspection sheet. I empathized with the technician – she was just trying to carry out her duties as she'd been trained. However, this wasn't training or a standard environment—operating in such a harsh climate required exceptions to the rules, including disregarding some preventative medicine standards.

Resupplying the position was also tricky. At some points, platoon commanders from nearby positions coordinated patrols with the soldiers stationed at Talukan. While suffering from multiple cases of dysentery, affectionately called "shits through the eye of the needle" by the troops, Talukan soldiers linked up with a Zangabad-based patrol to collect essential supplies such as shitter bags, toilet paper, and Imodium. The troops already had their hands full navigating an explosive-laced environment every day— the last thing they needed was to worry about explosive diarrhea. Tactical level challenges such as defensibility, resupply difficulties, and preventative medicine concerns, undeniably influenced the strategic decision to destroy Talukan.

Removing the outpost became a task embedded in a resupply convoy to the outposts. Named "Operation ROOM SERVICE" to align with the concept of a hotel providing ordered goods to guests, the resupply patrol generally went down the Arghandab riverbed. Consequently, the monthly trips garnered the moniker "River Run." The riverbed was a wild tapestry of rocks, pebbles, and sand. Being around two hundred metres at the narrowest point, with the actual river only using a small percentage of that space, the riverbed provided a nice stand-off from the surrounding infrastructure. It also afforded the armoured vehicles clear arcs of fire. We mitigated many of the IED threats by plowing a safe lane with the AEV, similar to our approach on Route Fosters months earlier. We changed our approach slightly for Operation ROOM SERVICE III, our third river run. Instead of going up and back along the same general path, we would travel to Mushan via the Dowry

River located to our south and would return via the traditional passage of the Arghandab River.

The operation staged out of Masum Ghar. While marshalling the vehicles, a design flaw in the EROC vehicle emerged: its tail lights. While everyone else maneuvered into position in the dark without any illumination, the brake lights of an EROC vehicle kept shining. The quick-thinking EROC crew taped over the lights, which pacified the cantankerous patrol commander on the radio.

"Shut that light off, or I'll shove it up your arse. You're giving away our position!"

I had mixed feelings about the tactical concern. As Masum Ghar sat on a forward-facing slope, sometimes referred to as "the catcher's mitt" because the geographical formation tended to catch rockets, I believed we lost the surprise advantage the moment we arrived. Everyone in the surrounding country could see vehicles marshalling and the taillights of a single vehicle didn't give away anything. However, I also believed that little details were a big detail, so I didn't object to covering the vehicle taillights even though most of the staging area remained in full view.

Under the cover of morning darkness, we departed Masum Ghar. After travelling only half a kilometre, I heard a muffled explosion. Moments later, the radio came alive.

"Contact, IED."

One of the AEVs plowing our route struck an IED. The crew evacuated without injury; however, a vehicle fire ensued that lit up the morning darkness as bright as the sun. Being an older vehicle chocked full of petroleum products, small fluid leaks that accumulated in the armoured hull were common. Even though the crews conducted regular maintenance of hydraulics, engine components, and tracks to keep the AEVs serviceable, they were tired beasts that continually leaked flammable materials. In this case, fire engulfed the vehicle within a few minutes, transforming it into a raging inferno. The vehicle carcass disgorged billowing, black smoke into the air as we bypassed the strike and continued the operation. After Wally snapped a photo, he looked at me.

"They're targeting engineers."

We couldn't prove it, but it made sense. Seeing how the AEV plowed new routes and disturbed their IED placements, the AEV had become an absolute menace to the Taliban. By destroying critical engineering equipment that provided mobility around the battlespace, they could cripple the battlegroup's freedom of movement. My mind raced with contingency plans as we had lost one of only two AEVs in the opening minutes of a long patrol.

Thankfully, the rest of the voyage to Mushan went smoothly. The Dowry River provided a virgin route and spectacular views of the Registan Desert's red sands. With the vehicles juxtaposed against the untouched terrain, it looked like we were driving on planet Mars. To approach Mushan, we plowed through a few fields and adobe structures. Another nomadic village watched as we passed within a couple hundred metres. As the kids stood in awe watching our massive vehicles drive by, I wondered what they were thinking. They must have thought we came from another world. While cutting through an opium field, I also thought about a recent mishap. During a patrol through an opium field, the hose of a soldier's water camel pack brushed against the plants for an unknown amount of time. With the tip laced with plant residues, the soldier got pretty messed up, and it took a couple of days for the opioid to clear his system.

We only stayed in Mushan long enough to unload supplies and wait for the morning sun to arrive. As always, Mushan rolled out the red carpet of hospitality for us, and so did the Taliban with a few traditional mortar and machine gun engagements. By mid-morning of Day Two, we'd moved up the Arghandab riverbed to Talukan. In efforts to minimize the duration of our stay, most of the convoy remained in the riverbed, secured by armoured assets. Only the essential vehicles required to destroy the position made the short trip south to the outpost.

The in-situ platoon had already completed a lot of preparatory work. The team preloaded all serialized kit, such as radios, and essential items like crew-served weapons from the observation post into a sea can so a truck could quickly pick up the cargo. Concurrent with the sea can removal, the remaining AEV started pushing over walls and tearing down the observation post. During previous resupply runs, the team dug a large pit in the camp to burn garbage. While dismantling the outpost, we dumped so much ruined Hesco, plywood, and boards into the pit that it started overflowing.

One key objective of establishing an outpost deep in enemy territory was to demonstrate to the local population that we were there to stay and that we were unafraid of the insurgents who had dominated the area for years. It felt off to be changing strategies after putting so much effort into creating the outpost. The removal also created an opportunity for our adversaries. As the Taliban would undoubtedly try to spin the Talukan withdrawal into a defeat of coalition forces, we needed to destroy as much abandoned material as possible to avoid providing them with war trophies.

While one of the observation towers crumbled to the ground, the robust structure required to support the vast overhead protection caught my eye. Military field defence manuals specify the thickness of sandbag defences to protect against certain munitions. Mortars required a certain thickness, while heavy artillery necessitated additional layers. I never understood why we applied the artillery thickness to our force protection. As the threat was predominately RPG and machine gun fire, it seemed like we over-engineered our observation towers.

The design became even more troubling as RPGs tended to be the weapon of choice against the towers. Since they were robust wooden structures with solid columns to support a sandbagged covered roof, they provided a massive detonation area for the point-initiated RPG. Based on the threat of direct fire munitions, instead of protecting the troops, the hearty structure enlarged the potential kill zone. By simply hitting the robust columns or the underside of the roof, the RPG would unleash lethal shrapnel into the sentries. As an alternative, a simple sunshade could shelter the sentries from the sun and eliminate the large detonation area. In a brief chat with an infanteer, I mentioned my observation, but he remained resolutely tied to his training.

"Sir, gotta follow the field manual. We need overhead protection."

While the AEV spewed diesel fumes into the atmosphere, crushing everything in sight, I had a dialectic discussion with the infantryman who was entrenched in the view that we required fortification suitable for artillery rounds even though the enemy didn't possess the capability. An exceptional astute solider, he seemed to be a zealot for traditional force protection irrespective of threat. I wondered what would be necessary to break his old habits and entrenched thoughts to form new ones based on the threat, or maybe I was the one who needed to conform to the field manual standards.

As the outpost crumbled, I wandered over to the last standing bunker. It contained all the surplus items, such as rations, empty sandbags and metal pickets. The Alamo of the position, we planned to set the bunker on fire just before our final withdrawal. During the first hour, the area buzzed with activity as logistic trucks removed stores, soldiers removed stakes and wire entanglements, and the AEV levelled wall after wall. With everything going to plan, I had just popped my head inside the bunker when I heard, "Contact!"

Then all hell broke loose. In response to the machine gun fire and RPG rounds that whizzed through the air, security elements returned fire with a vengeance. As quick as a fire drill, tanks roared into position and began engaging the enemy. In the heat of the engagement, Waller came tumbling over an adjacent wall. Surprised to see me in the bunker, he dusted himself off as he said, "Hey, sir."

The skirmish continued longer than usual as armoured vehicles jockeyed around the position to bring effective fire to bear. Scared about fratricide as bullets flew everywhere, I stayed put in the bunker with Waller. The tank rounds concussed the ground so much that they raised repulsive smells from the latrine. It was an odd situation where staying put and doing nothing was the safest option. Surrounded by food and despite the fetid aroma, I felt a bit hungry. Sitting beside boxes of sealed military rations, I started popping them open with my knife to retrieve the token candy bar from the lunch packets. Helpless to do anything while the fray ensued outside, Waller and I ate a couple of Coffee Crisps while awaiting our opportunity to depart.

A few minutes later, I heard orders on my patrol pack radio. "Commence withdrawal."

Still under contact, it created a precarious situation. By this time, a couple of other sappers had joined us. Comparable to hiding from a sudden summer rain, we all crouched inside the bunker, waiting for the blistering firefight to conclude. With the order to abandon the outpost, we immediately doused the bunker in diesel fuel to make it burn easier. With the overpowering fumes filling the confined space, I feared an explosion. To prevent injury, I cautiously tried to light cardboard and toss it into the structure. After several failed attempts, I tried using trip flares because they burned hot when lit. Again, I failed. Scared to hold the flare when it ignited because it could melt to my hand, I threw it prematurely towards the bunker entrance before it lit. In doing so, when the device ignited mid-flight, the pop of the trip flare igniting drastically changed my throw's trajectory. After my fourth and final failed attempt, it felt similar to playing a rigged carnival game - one you can't win. In the middle of a fighting withdrawal, we had a bunker saturated with diesel fuel and several trip flares burning away just outside the bunker doorway like a Hawaiian Luau party. Standing in the middle of a desert, equipped with diesel and trip flares, for the first time in my life, I couldn't light a fire. Things were going to hell in a handbasket.

As I searched for another way to light the bunker on fire without killing myself, Wally sensed we needed an armoured escort back to the river, so he crewed the LAV up to our position. On route, the driver hit a ditch, which caused the front end to buck until it was vertical, resembling a car in an action movie. I could see the axles and suspension of the LAV articulate as it crashed back to the ground, after crossing the obstacle. Still recovering from the jarring jump as he pulled up, I screamed.

"Wally, we can't light a fire!"

While we continued to try everything at our disposal to create a spark that would ignite the bunker, the LAV sentry prepared the vehicle for dismounts. Moments later, Wally ran by like a jousting knight with a burning cardboard box impaled on a picket. He tossed it into the bunker, and it immediately responded with a WOOF!

As flames finally roared from the bunker, Wally bellowed, "Mount up!"

There was one problem. Throughout the events, thirteen soldiers had gathered at the Alamo position. We didn't have enough space for everyone since LAVs are designed to carry only seven passengers in the back. But as the security vehicles continued to return fire with a vengeance against the enemy forces surrounding the position, getting shot accidentally was the biggest threat. To get everyone back to the riverbed under the cover of armour, I yelled, "Get in!"

After the first eight soldiers entered the back of the LAV and sat along the bench seats, the remainder crawled in horizontally on their laps. One after the other, we dog-piled in. As the last man in, I squirmed my way on top of the bodies while my back slid against the roof. Squeezed in like a human sardine, my face ended up beside the crew commander, slightly pinned against the roof. Wally looked down with a cigarillo in his mouth.

"Hey, sir," he said as he ordered the vehicle ramp up and navigated our band of merry men back to the vehicle column in the riverbed. We all shared a few laughs as we dismounted from the LAV; Wally asked me with a grin:

"How many scared sappers can you fit in the back of a LAV?"

After waiting a moment, he delivered the punchline.

"Thirteen."

Back in the turret, we watched thick smoke curl into the sky from the ruins of Talukan. We could already see every local in the area scrounging anything they could from the spoils. I saw numerous men scurrying by with sheets of plywood on their backs bearing a resemblance of ants scampering to move their eggs after someone kicked the top of their ant hill.

With the late afternoon sun on the horizon, we continued our return journey up the Arghandab River. Being veterans of multiple supply missions, we were conversant with the traditional hostile points as we manoeuvred through the river bed gauntlet. Through our weapon optics, we scanned the horizon for any ignoble activity or insurgents brandishing arms.

At one choke point we were engaged on both sides. While I engaged a couple dismounts with AK-47s to our south, hot casing from the pintle mount machine gun rained down the back of Wally's neck. With his face glued to the gunner site engaging an RPG team to our north, he couldn't react to the small burns forming on the back of his neck. As soon as the engagement concluded, I couldn't stop laughing as he did the hot ammo flop inside the turret trying as he attempted to jettison the hot shells from his collar. We had a few other small skirmishes at the habitual hot spots along the rivers edge, but over all we made steady progress. With the shadows getting longer as the sun set on the horizon, a call from a logistics truck came over the radio.

"Anti-tank mine on the side of the route."

As the AEV helped spearhead the advance by plowing a lane in the riverbed, someone observed what looked like a tank mine on the furrow beside our route. Pressed for time to avoid being sitting ducks in the riverbed at nightfall, the patrol commander responded.

"Likely a road wheel from a tank. Proceed."

To an untrained eye in poor light, tank road wheels had the same general appearance as an anti-tank mine. Accustomed to giving unassailable direction, he resolved the situation—or so it seemed. After a short pause, the logistics truck responded in an assertive tone.

"It's a tank mine. Over."

Everyone could feel a collective gasp as the observer opposed the patrol commander. Another short pause ensued.

"How do you know it's a mine?" barked the patrol commander.

As if he had been waiting for this opportunity to speak, the observer responded in a sassy tone.

"Because I'm an engineer!"

Unbeknownst to us then, a sapper had jumped in the logistics vehicle as a co-driver, so he knew precisely what an anti-tank mine looked like. With the poor lighting, over a dozen vehicles had unknowingly passed the device on the side of the route. At this point, Wally and I sprang into action.

"Sir, I'll go and have a quick peek."

I gave Wally a thumbs-up and got on the radio.

"Chimos on the move to the AT mine."

As Wally descended from the vehicle, the sun sank behind a jagged rock formation in the distance. The encroaching twilight cast long shadows, creating an eerie stillness. With the convoy flanks exposed, we became exceptionally vulnerable to an attack while sitting idle. The patrol commander vehemently opposed tactical pauses.

"E21A, make it quick."

Wally linked up with Waller's section of engineers to examine the device, but in the process, I lost radio contact with them. Aware of the threat posed to the convoy while stationary, I jumped on the radio to the patrol commander.

"Engineers on scene."

I waited a few minutes before providing my next best assessment of the unknown situation.

"Engineers scanning for secondary threats."

Finally, after thirty minutes, Wally came on the engineering net.

"Hey, sir, preparing to blow up the anti-tank mine."

I immediately passed the information on the higher radio net and requested a restricted airspace over our patrol. I'd been slow to implement this because it would limit our defences. If aircraft, unmanned aerial vehicles or helicopters couldn't fly over the patrol, they couldn't help us engage insurgents in the event of an attack. I'd requested dozens of restricted airspaces throughout the deployment, and they only took a minute to establish. But in this case, no response. After a few minutes, Wally came on the sapper net.

"Ready to pop smoke."

The term indicated that he would initiate a time fuse that would detonate an explosive charge. But without a restricted airspace, we couldn't proceed. Pausing to think, the patrol commander questioned my delay.

"E21A, what's the hold-up?"

I faced dilemma with two options: adhere to the standard, wait for a restricted airspace and further expose the convoy to the risk of a Taliban attack, or just detonate the device and risk damaging an aircraft. It only took a couple seconds of processing before I broke with the conventional process. It was just an anti-tank mine, and by far, the more imminent danger was an attack from the river's edge. After a quick scan, I got on the radio with no aircraft in sight.

"Pop smoke."

I remained anxious about my call to proceed while waiting for the explosion. As an aircraft could still fly over the convoy in the couple minutes it took for the charge to detonate, I kept my head above the turret, scanning the horizon. In the initial darkness of the night, I could just make out a long convoy of stationary vehicles sitting like a sizeable resting snake. The sound of diesel engines idling and exhaust filled the calm air as we waited.

KA-BOOM-BOOM-BOOM

The explosion transformed night into day. The convoy became clearly visible as the searing fireball roared upwards. The shockwave rippled up the riverbed, leaving everyone trembling in stunned silence. Rocks the size of softballs rained down on the vehicles as I ducked my head under the turret. Murphy's Law: Two Kiowa helicopters flew overhead, returning from a patrol to the east, barely missing the blast's epicentre. The patrol commander spoke first after twenty plus seconds of rocks thumping onto the convoy.

"Uh, E21A, that's the *largest* anti-tank mine I've ever seen."

I responded as if he had never spoken to avoid incriminating myself for not knowing exactly what we had blown up.

"Conducting a post-blast investigation to ensure we got everything."

I'm not sure if it was physically possible to have miss anything. After the atomic bomb-size blast, we blew everything straight into next week. Fifteen minutes later, as if nothing happened, Wally strolled back to the vehicle.

As he climbed into the turret, I stared at him, "What was that?"

Surprised by the question, he did a double-take before responding.

"You knew it was an IED right?"

I lightly shook my head, miming, "Nope."

Having missed something in the telepathic communication, Wally elaborated on the recent events once re-established in the gunner's seat.

"Sorry. Found three TMA-4 mines that looked like large cheese wheels on top of some jugs of homemade explosives."

Slightly disappointed that I misunderstood the nuance of *tank mine* in this context, I didn't overly care about the mishap. We did the right thing. Waller was qualified to deal with IEDs, so we didn't break any rules in that regard; we just had a miscommunication about the device. Three TMA-4 mines on top of an unknown amount of homemade explosives was a far cry from a single anti-tank mine. It would be comparable to telling your spouse that you wanted to buy a firework package from the local gas station for a private party, but you end up setting off a spectacle that rivals the Canada Day celebrations on Parliament Hill.

Comfortably settled back into the turret as if nothing out of the ordinary had transpired, Wally spoke over the intercom.

"What's the hold-up? Let's ditch this place like a used prophylactic."

The convoy recommenced the return journey without incident. In the post operational reports, we responded to a few questions about the largest anti-tank mine in history, but the inquisition didn't last long. Everyone knew we did the right thing. We couldn't sit in the riverbed overnight waiting for assistance, so questions about the incident quickly dwindled.

Ultimately, everything leading up to and including Operation ROOM SERVICE underscored the insidious impacts surrounding opportunity costs. Like a vessel, our minds have immense cognitive capacity, but there is a limit. Consequently, small items such as the Combat Action Insignia administration, sustaining Hughes the donkey, and maintaining too many combat outposts added up. Individually, these items are manageable, but collectively, they create risk. In a stressful environment, the additional cognitive load creates an opportunity cost. By focusing on insignificant items, we occupied our cognitive capacity with small matters and risked overlooking significant items. For instance, did a dozen vehicles pass the largest anti-tank mine in history unobserved because their minds were loaded with smaller matters? By ruthlessly ditching the insignificant items, we could focus our limited cognitive capacity onto items of significance.

In the military, this required a cultural change as we suffered from an endemic of addition bias. When faced with a problem, the solution often became to add something like a policy, protective infrastructure, or a new piece of equipment. One sapper summarized the proclivity with, "We just throw paperwork at it." Although this approach appears to address the item on the surface, it can create significant opportunity costs.

Sometimes, counterintuitively, subtraction may be the best approach.

One unforeseen benefit of lacking sufficient sappers was that it forced us to find ways to reduce demands. It compelled us to fight addition bias. In doing so, this created secondary and tertiary benefits of simplification, reduced bureaucratic glut, and, most importantly, it minimized our cognitive load. I recalled reading about the Constitution of the United States of America. There has only been one subtraction from the Constitution's history: the 21$^{st}$ amendment repealed the 18th, which instituted prohibition. Conversely, there have been twenty-seven additions to the document. Only the pull of alcohol was enough to motivate a subtraction. Similarly, due to our culture of addition bias, we liked to get drunk by adding too much policy, protective infrastructure, or equipment to resolve issues when many times subtraction offered a better solution. In our case, elimination of excessive items created cognitive capacity where the sappers tactical intuition could blossom. While being coached on how to improve my crappy writing, a talented peer told me on several occasions, "John, with writing, less is often more." For the remainder of the tour, I mercilessly shortened the list of demands on our cognitive load because, in more areas than just writing, less is more.

# 18

# Chimo Requiem

There are many ways to describe Afghanistan, such as hauntingly beautiful, heartbreakingly resilient, and endlessly unpredictable. From a soldier's perspective, Afghanistan became a place where you could always expect the unexpected. A few weeks after demolishing Talukan, I was buried in paperwork at my desk when the radio crackled to life.

"Contact Haji. Wait out."

Just a couple kilometres away, machine gun bursts and explosions erupted, their echoes rattling through the surrounding countryside. As the details came in, my heart sank. We sustained another casualty, Master Corporal Erin Doyle. With his massive red beard, Doyle resembled a Viking misplaced in time. I often wondered how he got away without shaving but never asked despite having multiple conversations with him throughout the tour. During a couple of patrols, we discussed tactical movement. He showed me how he liked to use the ground to his advantage when moving through fields, compounds, and adobe walls. Killed by RPGs exploding in the observation tower while returning fire into enemy positions, I couldn't shake the thought—would a simple sunshade, instead of heavy overhead cover, have changed the outcome? We were caught up once again in the endless risk mitigation trade-offs—reducing one threat only to heighten our exposure to another

We moved to Masum Ghar a few days later to prepare for an operation. While staging out of the area, we took the time to review our vehicle extraction drills. With so many units gathered at Masum Ghar, the camp resembled a military car dealership, displaying nearly every vehicle platform Canada had deployed in theatre. Given this variety—and our role as first responders to IED strikes—reviewing primary and secondary evacuation procedures for each vehicle was critical, as it could mean the difference between life and death.

For instance, an IED blast could warp a vehicle's frame, preventing the rear ramp from lowering. In a fire, troops could be trapped inside if alternate escape hatches weren't quickly accessible. Tanks had their own challenges; extracting an unconscious driver could require a 19-millimetre socket to unlock the escape hatch if it was combat-locked. Knowing these details in advance was critical to provide a rapid response. During medical evacuations, they always stressed the golden hour. This referred to the significantly higher survival rate if casualties could reach medical support in KAF within the first hour of injury. Being capable of quickly extricating wounded soldiers from their vehicles was crucial in meeting that timeline.

During the tour of a Leopard II tank, an armoured warrant officer spoke verbosely about the 120mm munitions and how they used a combustible, disintegrating shell casing. This new type of ammunition fascinated gun enthusiasts, who obsessed over its features like collectors admiring a rare coin. The only thing I found neat about the latest round was the cup left over after firing. The size of a cereal bowl, they made excellent ashtrays for poker nights. After he thoroughly explained how the modern round provided better accuracy and eased the handling of empty casings but was more fragile than traditional brass-cased rounds, I finally interrupted to shift the focus to extraction drills. He looked at me in surprised disgust.

"What, you don't want to see my sabot round?"

He held the large munition like he was holding a baby.

"No," I responded. "I want to see how to extract your driver in the event you hit an IED."

A tank driver lingered near the front of his vehicle, dust-covered from a recent operation. Strapped high on both thighs, his loose tourniquets were a grim reminder of the brutal reality of war. As an IED could severely injure a driver's legs, a standard procedure became to put on prepositioned tourniquets as part of their pre-departure routine, comparable to fastening a seatbelt when you get into a car in the event you get into a collision. Reaching the driver could take time after the vehicle sustained a blast, so mitigating blood loss as fast as possible became a crucial life-saving measure. With prepositioned tourniquets, the driver could self-apply them if required to prevent bleeding out while waiting for help. The driver happily showed us extraction options from the tank while we let the warrant officer, who now had a cordial dislike for me, place his sabot round back into the munition rack.

As Afghanistan didn't have first responder capabilities like police, firehalls, and ambulances, we needed to create them for our own unforeseen situations. We called this capability the Quick Reaction Force and it staged out of Masum Ghar. Consisting of a composite mix of infantry, armour, recovery vehicles, an ambulance and engineers, the "patrol packet" remained on call 24/7, comparable to an emergency response crew in a typical North American city, prepared to respond to the needs of its citizens.

In some cases, patrols were large enough to contain their own recovery assets. For example, a Husky engineer vehicle got stuck in the soft riverbed sand during previous a river run. In the process of being pulled out by a tank, the Husky was torn in half. The blast-protected vehicle, designed to break apart during an explosion to shield the driver from the full shock, relied on shear pins for this functionality. However, these same pins could fail if you were not careful when recovering the vehicle. As the patrol was large, embedded logistics vehicles recovered the Husky without requiring external assistance. For all the small patrols that operated ubiquitously throughout the battlespace, the only first response element available was often the Quick Reaction Force stationed in Masum Ghar.

After concluding our extraction drills, I spoke with an engineering Quick Reaction Force Section Commander, Sergeant Tim MacCormac. Born into a military family, the Forces were the only life he and his twin brother knew. Consequently, destiny ensured he also joined the army as a combat engineer. Short, with an unassuming build, he could be a firecracker in a discussion. He always prioritized the welfare of others over how he came across in a conversation; if a question or issue arose, he ensured it was resolved before proceeding. In garrison, his confidence in seeking clarity or voicing what others were thinking but too scared to say, garnered some mentorship regarding tact. However, in Afghanistan, his conviction saved lives. As our casualties grew,

I became increasingly fond of frank conversations with straight questions and sharp responses.

During rehearsal of concept drills conducted before an operation, commonly called ROC drills, MacCormac's natural abilities to speak up, pose questions, or be a catalyst for others to do the same helped commanders leverage knowledge from the audience. This created a collaborative response to complex problems in an uncertain environment. In relating the story about how ROC drills had evolved significantly from training to theatre, he applauded the value of collectively seeking solutions instead of just listening to a single-minded approach.

"One mentality risks a lot of fatality."

Operating separately from us and predominately in different areas throughout the tour, I found it interesting to hear about some of his exploits and the terms they used. For instance, "drunken spacing" referred to how convoys should continually mix up speeds and distances between vehicles to make them a more challenging target for command wire IEDs and ambushes. We did the same, only using terms such as "mix it up" or "don't set patterns."

During a response to an IED strike, the Quick Reaction Force needed to use the AEV arm to rip the driver's hatch off of a tank. It had struck an IED with the barrel positioned over top of the driver's hatch. The tank sank into the mud before the driver could be extracted from the bottom escape door. The driver couldn't climb through the turret either, so the only option was to mechanically remove the upper hatch to extract the driver. I couldn't imagine the pucker factor of the driver as the tooth of an AEV excavation bucket scratched at a hatch just above his head.

While describing a gunfight that required him to mark his position with red smoke to prevent fratricide, MacCormac outlined how the approach could be a double-edged sword.

"Friendlies knew our position, but so did the enemy. Heavy volumes of enemy fire came onto us because of that smoke grenade."

During our chat, he described a dark humor mishap. Being inside the Buffalo when it struck an IED, after ensuring the crew was okay, he dismounted to clear for secondary devices. In the process, he didn't give much thought to the back of the vehicle being completely red. However, to the first responders coming to the blast scene, the sight was beyond horrifying. The sheer volume of red must have made their stomachs lurch as they braced themselves for the worst – a recovery operation. But then, through what appeared to be a blood-blanketed door, the crew emerged - alive, unscathed.

As it turned out, some design engineers had thought red would be a good colour for marking suspect spots on the road. This particular IED had struck a container of red chalk meant for the vehicle marking system. The blast had sent red chalk exploding across the back of the Buffalo, painting a grotesque illusion of carnage. For a few breathless moments, it resembled a massacre. But instead, it was only a cruel trick of colour, a grim joke in the chaos of combat.

MacCormac also described some tough challenges he faced. While responding to a vehicle that had caught fire after being struck by a rocket, he needed to restrain his sappers away from the burning vehicle because any rescue efforts would have been an exercise in futility. They didn't have any way to combat the fire that already engulfed the scene. Furthermore, exposing the sappers to the enemy gunfire surrounding the flaming vehicle would have added another problem to an already horrific situation. While we trained extensively for casualty situations, facing real ones tested our leadership in ways practice never could.

Additionally, he also noticed a distinct difference between engineering employment in theatre and during training.

"During work-up training in Wainwright, we were like a redheaded stepchild," he said. "No one wanted us or knew what to do with us. But over here, for the first time in my career, I witnessed two commanders adamantly fight for an engineering section."

Ultimately, the two operations were sequenced so that each received engineering support instead of one going without. Amending operational schedules based on engineering availability was unprecedented compared to the training environment. Upon hearing this, I realized one of the check-in-the-box training items for manoeuvre commanders in Wainwright should be: Fought vehemently for engineering assets.

At the time, talk occurred about a shuffle of engineering sections around the battlespace to avoid the perils of complacency and to prevent fatigue. It was thought that new terrain would make people more alert. There was a story going around that in one instance, a sapper shut off his mine detector because he was tired of the constant metallic hit noises in an area he had combed repeatedly. In another instance, a driver didn't wear his flak vest because it was too hot and they were only going for a short drive. While every position carried risks, the Quick Reaction Force faced the added challenge of exhaustion from being on call 24/7. I asked MacCormac about his thoughts about a section switch; he didn't mince words.

"Bad idea."

He took a moment to pause, choosing his words.

"There is risk to learning new terrain. During culvert searches for explosive devices on the common routes we travel, we know if a rock has moved. Rotating new people means they'd have to learn it all from scratch."

It was a fresh take on the concept of risk. Although there is an inherent risk of complacency stemming from doing the same thing repeatedly, MacCormac made a cogent argument about how staying in the same area is less of an overall risk to the unit and soldiers. Placing an experienced section into new territory made them fledglings to the terrain as well as to the Taliban's habitual spots and patterns. Learning the adversary's tendencies and the nuances of their subterfuge required time, time we didn't have and with consequences we couldn't afford if we got it wrong.

"Besides, this is the best job. Every day is different, so I'm always on my toes."

The Quick Reaction Force could be chaos incarnate, a perfect match for MacCormac's sharp instincts and restless energy. Undoubtedly, his sound reasoning and assertive challenge played a key role in quashing the section shuffle idea.

Back in Sperwan Ghar a few days later, I stopped by the ANA billets. They were in the process of killing two chickens for dinner. Watching them kill the hens with a bayonet that looked more like a hacksaw than a knife, I realized death is different in Afghanistan. They appeared to have become more callused to it because bloodshed occurred more often in their everyday lives. Even I became more accustomed to death, having lost track of how many chickens, sheep, and goats I had seen slaughtered over the last few months just before a meal.

To conclude the butchering process, it was common to witness chefs wash the blood off their hands before continuing culinary preparations. Besides fishing trips or boiling lobster, I couldn't recall a time in my life when the animal was alive only minutes before cooking it. Furthermore, living in a nation torn apart by years of conflict, Afghans were far more exposed to the harsh realities of death than Canadians. I regret never asking them about death and whether the common occurrence caused fleeting impressions or if it still caused enduring reactions; for them, it seemed to be a constant shadow, whereas for us, it was an eventual visitor.

Unfortunately, in late August, death visited the engineers. We commenced initial preparations for Operation TIMUS PRIME in the same manner as any other mission. Rumour has it the name stemmed from staff officers thinking it would be funny to name an operation after the popular character from the pop culture Transformers brand. The cumulation of information gathering on previous patrols identified a target compound, Objective WEASEL. Intelligence believed Objective WEASEL was a key meeting location for several high-value insurgents. We aimed to destroy the target with a gargantuan bomb from a B2 bomber aircraft; it just became a question of when, as the Commander intended to blow up the compound while it was occupied with high-value targets. We were to play a secondary role whenever the strike occurred and form a blocking position to prevent insurgents from squirting out of the area.

Sergeant Major Cavanagh approached me while walking to get a drink in our common area.

"Engineer vehicle has been hit."

We moved directly to the troop office to monitor the radio and the MIRC chat. MIRC was an early version of group chat messaging. With MIRC, we could read through the entire log of events to get up to speed on the incident.

As I reviewed the past messages, I learned that a Canadian LAV in a convoy had struck an IED. There was a possible vehicle fire, the Quick Reaction Force had deployed from Masum Ghar, and they needed to be ready to open a vehicle hatch. Through our engineer net, I learned that Sergeant Terry Vandenberghe was the engineer section commander who responded to the event. An avid motorcycle enthusiast, he joined the army on a dare, as his buddies didn't think he had the balls to do it. In the relentless grind of 24/7 responses, Vandenberghe lived by a few unshakable rules.

"First things first: Vehicle, weapons stores, then you. The mission comes first."

He preached, "Always be prepared for the unexpected."

He also believed in allowing junior members to fill leadership positions occasionally as a form of on-the-job training so the section could still perform if he became a casualty. The events of the day would cause him to deviate from that belief.

Although the Quick Reaction Force response started the same as so many others throughout the tour, this one felt more urgent. His sixth sense detected something different. Darting out of Masum Ghar faster than usual, he didn't have time to collect his second in command, who was on sentry duty at the main gate. Despite the peculiar rush, I later learned that Vandenberghe didn't know an engineering vehicle was involved in the strike when he departed.

In less than half an hour, they arrived on the scene. The on-scene convoy elements had established a security permitter around the hull of the damaged vehicle. As he approached, he was confronted with an upside-down LAV with the turret sheared off. A fire had engulfed part of the vehicle, but it was controlled with the help of the AEV by using dirt to smother the flames. Putting the radio transmissions together en route to the scene and seeing the AEV attempting to flip the vehicle over as part of the rescue response, Vandenberghe figured out the vehicle call sign: E21B. It was our reconnaissance section that had been supporting the recce squadron throughout most of the deployment. Sensing this could be a recovery versus a rescue operation, Vandenberghe positioned his vehicle so his crew could not witness the subsequent events. He even had the foresight to place his driver in the rear of the ELAV so he wouldn't just sit and watch a potentially horrible series of events.

"They're too young for this shit," he said to himself as he approached the vehicle with the medics and EOD team. With the ground smouldering and patches of fire still burning, the pungent smell of smoke filled the air as the odd round cooked off inside the vehicle. As suspected, in short order he confirmed it would be a recovery mission for three fallen sappers killed by the blast: Sergeant Shawn Eades, Corporal Dustin Wasden and Sapper Stephan Stock. The fourth member of their section, Master Corporal Jim Pattison, remained in critical condition as the nine-liner filled the radio network to coordinate his medical evacuation. Making this response even more visceral, Wasden was one of Vandenberghe's best friends. The bottle cap off Wasden's last Pilsner beer still hangs in Vandenberghe's shop at home.

In combat, tragic situations don't always give you time to pause. In this case, the threat of an attack grew the longer they remained in place, so they sprang into action and followed standard recovery procedures. The team placed the bodies into body bags, loaded the LAV onto a recovery vehicle, and blew up unstable items like damaged ammunition on-site. They used so much C4 vaporizing the volatile items that they set the adjacent compound on fire—the day had wrung them dry. Indifferent to the fire, they just drove away and let it burn as soon as they completed the recovery mission.

Back in Sperwan Ghar, we began piecing the situation together, and our worst fears were confirmed when ZAP numbers came over the radio. To avoid using names, service numbers—known as ZAP numbers—were used to identify casualties. Sitting in the command post with all the nominal roles at our fingertips, it only took moments to confirm the details. The engineer family and the families of the fallen would never be whole again.

The void caused by the loss of Sergeant Eades, Corporal Wasden, and Sapper Stock became palpable. Troops immediately became emotional. Even though many had responded to or dealt with casualty situations before, this one stung. Some had joined the military with the fallen sappers and completed career courses as peers, while others had just forged a close bond during their shared military experiences. But just like the summer heat, the unrelenting war didn't stop for mourning. Upon returning to Masum Ghar, Vandenberge took a short moment to share an embrace with a few friends who were also feeling the loss. It was a short tactical pause. As another Quick Reaction Force call could come at any instant, he reset the section for another response by adhering to his mantra: First things first: vehicle, weapons, stores, then you. The mission always comes first.

Unknown to us, over ten thousand kilometres away, 1 Combat Engineering Regiment families lived in the lurch. The press reported that combat engineers had been killed by a roadside bomb but withheld the names since the next of kin had not yet been notified. As the communication lockdown precluded any contact with family back home, and being utterly unaware of the ambiguous media release, we remained blissfully unaware of the angst and worry spreading like wildfire amongst our families. Spouses would call other spouses in uncontrollable panic.

"Have you heard from anybody?"

"No. Just the partial media release. I'll call you if I know more."

The phone cycle for information continued through the family network in different fashions. My parents were vacationing in their motorhome on Vancouver Island when their cell phone rang. A long-time university friend heard the news and reached out.

"Hey, is John okay? I just saw some news about engineers in Afghanistan."

An awkward silence and a short conversation followed. Unaware of the recent announcement and fearing the worst, my father contacted the regiment. By this point in time, the regiment was able to confirm I wasn't a casualty, but that didn't mean I wasn't severely injured. Before hanging up, Dad confirmed his contact information and location in case they were needed. Until the media officially publicized the names of the fallen sappers a couple days later, my folks spent their time preparing for the worst-case scenario. They'd peek at each passing car to see if a next of kin notification team composed of a Commanding Officer, an Assisting Officer and a Padre in full military regalia lurked by their campsite.

The following day in Afghanistan, questions about the ramp ceremony hung in the air as we concurrently dealt with the requirements of Operation TIMUS PRIME. Intelligence showed the time was right to strike, so the Commander gave the order to proceed. Doing our final preparations before kicking off our patrol, we learned that the ramp ceremony for our fallen would occur in 48 to 72 hours. Therefore, if everything went smoothly on the operation, we could return to KAF and pay our respects.

There is something about Afghanistan that strips aways the noise of the world and compels you to become firmly anchored in the present. While walking to form our blocking position on Objective WEASEL, we cut through farmer fields during the grape and raisin harvest season. In the process, we stepped on so many grapes our boots bulked up with crushed fruit similar to children's shoes after they walk through the mud in the spring. Each one must have weighed an additional five pounds. Smushing the gooey mass with each step, the capillary action of our pants wicked the crushed grape juices up to our knees, attracting the most annoying flies. I could hardly think about anything else as I wanted to crawl out of my skin from all the bugs biting me as they were drawn to the sweet fluids soaking my pants. With sweat pouring out profusely from under our body armour in the blistering sun, it was the only day in Afghanistan when I truly craved a shower—just to escape the grimy, sweltering mess I had become. Because of that day, it took me over a decade before I could eat raisins without getting itchy all over liked I'd rolled naked in a field of poison ivy.

We explosively breached into a locked compound to hunker down for the night. Wally and I had to rig up a basic charge as fellow engineers were dispersed throughout the patrol. Being a bit rusty on explosives because we didn't typically handle them in our leadership positions, we overestimated how much was required. Instead of just blowing the lock off a set of metal French doors, our small satchel charge dislodged the entire door frame from the adobe wall and hurled it across the compound. After clearing the position, we established a rotating sentry shift and slept.

My fireteam partner for the sentry shift, our driver Corporal MacMullin, woke me up in the middle of the night.

"Hey sir, I need a hand."

It took me a moment to fully wake up, mainly because I had to do a double take at his attire. Under the Afghanistan moonlight, it appeared as if he was shirtless.

"What are you doing?"

"Sir, these bugs are killing me. Can you rub this lotion on my back?"

I wasn't sure which part was more jaw-dropping, my fireteam partner half naked in the middle of the night while on patrol or the fact he still had military-grade deet insect repellent cream. I'd tossed my tubes months ago to save weight on patrols. Not waiting for me to help, he looked like a monkey trying to hump a basketball as he tried to contort his body to rub lotion on his own back. As he chomped on a massive wad of tobacco,

I generously slathered insect-repellant cream on him, channelling the vibe of a high-end spa treatment as I soothed his itch. Under the moonlight, with his Herculean muscles glistening as if he'd been baby-oiled, he looked more like a Mr. Universe contestant ready for the stage than a soldier gearing up for a sentry shift in the middle of a warzone.

"Thanks, sir." Treating the battle with the bugs as just another activity in the sapper job description, he spat a huge wade of saliva on the ground as he dressed for our sentry shift.

On top of the compound roof during our watch duties, the stillness was deafening. Beneath a sky thick with stars, the majestic agrarian landscape of grape huts, fields, and adobe compounds stretched out in patchy patterns as far as I could see. The only audible sound came from the nearby graveyard flags flapping occasionally in the warm summer breeze filled with the aroma of drying grapes. Looking at my watch, I knew in a couple of hours, the JDAM bomb from the B2 bomber would break up the peaceful tranquillity.

Just after the sun broke the horizon, Wally and I listened intently to the radio. We huddled tightly behind a mud parapet on top of a roof to get a good view of the strike.

"Bomber inbound," came over the radio.

With Objective WEASEL clearly in sight, Wally triple-checked his camera to film the drop.

KABOOM.

The precision-guided mission provided a direct hit. The resulting concussion wave passed through the adobe structures and their patched-worked roofs, lifting them as if a surge of water had passed underneath. After experiencing the bomb detonation up close, I looked at Wally.

"Now that's the largest anti-tank mine I've ever seen," I joked.

The JDAM bomb on Objective WEASEL was the only blast I'd seen that was bigger than Wally's anti-tank mine. With the deadly payload delivered and no squirters observed, we made a solemn voyage to KAF.

Preparing for the ramp ceremony, I scrambled like a madman to find a clean set of combats because everything I owned was stained with some combination of fluid, grease, or grape juice from the last operation. I learned afterwards that others did the same, but their uniforms were stained with blood from close-quarter engagements during Op TIMUS PRIME. Moreover, selecting the sappers to escort the fallen home to Canada was a deeply emotional process. With only three able to go and dozens of volunteers, squadron leadership was faced with the heartbreaking task of making the final decisions.

In one of the KAF chapels, three aluminum caskets, each draped with a Canadian flag, lay in silent honour. On top rested a photo of the fallen and a combat engineering beret. After a short solemn ceremony, we departed for a meal before the evening ramp ceremony. Three LAVs, bearing the remains of the fallen, rolled slowly down the tarmac, flanked by soldiers standing in silent respect. Near the rear of the open C-117 Globemaster, the stirring melody of *Amazing Grace* resonated in the still air from a small stereo.

I was familiar with the lyrics, as the song was one of my father's favourites. I hummed the words to myself as they loaded the caskets into the belly of the C-117 Globemaster. On this occasion the words held a different meaning.

*Through many dangers, toils, and snares.*

*We have already come.*

*'Twas grace that brought us safe thus far*

*And grace will lead us home.*

As the ceremony concluded, I prayed for grace to lead us home, as we still had a month in the theatre.

Walking back to the shacks that night, I reflected on the unexpected. I never anticipated fire would become a formidable adversary when responding to vehicle IED strikes. I didn't foresee questioning timeless doctrine about overhead protection in the face of evolving threats, rubbing bug repellant on a fellow soldier in the dead of night, or constantly analyzing our actions to avoid creating patterns the enemy could exploit. We all learned some poignant lessons from the loss of E21B: the fragility of life, the value of connection, and a life's legacy. As we embarked on the final weeks of our tour, one of Vandenberghe's signature phrases rang in my head.

"Always be prepared for the unexpected."

# 19

# War's Golden Thread

As I was preparing to depart KAF the morning after the ramp ceremony, I passed by the headquarters to speak with Hollywood. He provided a detailed brief of all the convoy movement that morning, emphasizing the recent threat.

"Command wire IEDs with secondary devices are becoming common on Highway 1."

This tactic, employed on major roads, allowed insurgents to specifically target vehicles in a convoy by holding the trigger mechanism in their hand. By timing when they pressed a button or flicked a rudimentary switch, they could detonate a device on demand when a specific vehicle passed over the IED. With practice, they refined the processes to include aiming markers because they learned there was a second or two delay from initiating the switch until the electrical current detonated the device. This delay often stemmed from weak power sources frequently made from dozens of discarded batteries connected in series to garner enough electrical current to initiate the detonator. With the command wire initiation strategy, the Taliban avoided indiscriminate attacks. The local daily traffic could pass unimpeded on the highways while the Taliban lurked for a military convoy. If they used pressure plate devices, such as landmines, it would close the road to all traffic as those types of IEDs didn't discriminate between targets.

The secondary devices referred to anti-personal landmines placed around habitual IED locations. Coalition forces inspected commonly used IED sites before passing through, as insurgents repeatedly reused these locations. Witnessing this strategy, the insurgents started targeting the inspection teams in the ditches and along the sides of the road with explosive devices, continuing the morbid cat-and-mouse game. Since the locals drove by and didn't walk on the edges of the road, the secondary devices posed minimal threats to resident traffic. Pointing at a map, Hollywood concluded his threat brief.

"Recently found secondary devices at these two culverts."

"Thanks Hollywood. I'll send out the missionary's wife to inspect."

He smiled and gave me a wink.

"Big Chi, Little Mo! Stay safe out there."

Back in the vehicle compound, I passed on the threat assessment to Wally and Waller. We all became uneasy about the numerous patterns earlier convoys had set that morning, inspecting the traditional hot spots. With increased activity, the high-risk areas could be seeded with mines before our convoy passed. To minimize the threat, we needed to mix it up. Thinking a little outside the box, I suggested an unconventional idea.

"What happens if we just gun it back?"

I could see Wally and Waller processing. Insurgents didn't always sit in the firing point waiting for a military convoy. They employed lookouts who would make a phone call so an IED team could arm the device before a convoy passed. The enemy's coordinated process—from making the phone call to preparing the IED to detonating it—was precisely timed to match the standard convoy speed of fifty kilometres per hour. If we drove at ninety kilometres an hour, we could outpace the insurgent's warning and preparation system, and we wouldn't expose dismounts to the secondary threats on the road's edge. But sheer speed also introduced new risks. The downside was that if a vehicle at the front of the convoy hit an IED, follow-on vehicles wouldn't be able to stop in time, so we'd create a nasty multi-vehicle collision on top of an IED site. Based on the current threat assessment, this appeared to be the more unlikely of the two risks. And so, since we had just said goodbye to three sappers killed by a command wire IED, we decided on the intrepid approach.

At this point in the deployment, some drivers became reluctant to get into the driver compartment of vehicles because they tended to get the worst of it in an IED strike. Extraction drills were often required to get them out, and the driver space looked comparable to a metal coffin. Similar sentiments were felt towards the other vehicle positions. If the vehicle rolled, it could crush the turret crew, or if the turret sheared off, it would slice the turret crew in half. I could empathize with these apprehensions because the uncertainty and randomness of IEDs became fatiguing. To combat this feeling, any opportunity to make a decision, even a small one, felt like regaining a foothold in unpredictable terrain. In this case, we had agency to decide the convoy speed. During the standard convoy brief, instead of saying the normal fifty-kilometre-hour speed, I paused after I said, "full speed."

Some of the drivers immediately perked up. My driver, Corporal MacMullin, raised his hand to seek clarification.

"Sir, you want us to just give'r?"

I paused for a second to look at the drivers.

"Yes."

Harnessed through the tour by standard road move procedures, we drove back to Sperwan Ghar like unbridled stallions. Flying through Kandahar City and the surrounding country, we set speed record after speed record. I'm surprised the duty officer didn't say anything as we clocked past checkpoints so fast they didn't have time to acknowledge one before we passed another. If we were on a North American road, we would have averaged three demerit points per kilometre as we weaved between traffic, blew through intersections and drove on the wrong side of the road. Usually, the radio mast antennas on our vehicles remained predominately vertical. During our move, they bent over at a sharp angle and often swung around like a sword when we turned corners. The smell of diesel exhaust that typically filled the air didn't have time to rise above the exhaust manifold before being whooshed away by the wind. Being an avid motorcyclist who loves highway rides, bombing down the road in the warm Afghanistan air, with the countryside blurring beside us, I almost forgot about the war for a few fleeting moments. Undeniably observed by the Taliban, I've always wondered what they thought as our bullet convoy of engineers outran their IED warning systems.

Back in Sperwan Ghar, the shortages of troops had become acute. As an officer, normally, my role wasn't to pull the trigger on a rifle but to provide leadership, command and control, and coordinate with other units in our operational area. However, since we were at the tail end of the tour and replacements were no longer arriving in theatre, we were forced to take an all-hands-on-deck approach. To secure the camp, I filled the odd sentry duty shift. Just before my observation post shift, I learned how to operate a .50 calibre machine gun for the first time. At front gate duty, I reconnected with Doug and Tex as they inspected food trucks entering the camp. During a lull in the activity, I took the opportunity to pull Doug's leg.

"Hey Doug, we could get you on a patrol again tomorrow. Wanna come?"

For some odd reason, he had grown exceptionally fond of gate duty since our last short patrol to Sia Choy.

"No thanks," he said. "Tex and I have some big fish to fry here."

On another occasion, I filled the duties of a sapper with an EOD exploitation team. As they conducted the post-blast investigation, I helped recover biomass in a bright yellow plastic bag. I struggled to find material until I noticed all the yellow jackets, the pesky meat-eating bugs that ruined many BBQs back home. They assembled on the dispersed soft tissue strewn across the field which helped me identify items that needed to be recovered during the gruesome task.

After losing Hughes the donkey and Whitie the monkey, somebody suggested we needed another pet to boost morale. Initially, I opposed another husbandry project because it would be an unnecessary distraction, and it would add to our cognitive load. However, the engineering common area and our random purchase of critters provided an unanticipated benefit: connection. I didn't realize it until the latter half of the tour; however, our common area provided an old-school coffee shop-type community where people socialized, discussed issues, and exchanged snippets of information as they smoked and joked. Before every patrol, I would check-in with the command post for intelligence briefs; however, more often than not, I was already cognisant of the current threats, issues, and events because of all the visitors who passed by our lines to check on Hughes, see what new primate we had purchased, or to sit on our red leather couches to watch TV or play poker. Consequently, Wally, Waller, and I worked through an animal purchase to nourish and foster the Zen Garden atmosphere and information marketplace.

"We need something with a lot less maintenance," stated Wally.

"Yeah, like a bird," replied Waller.

The conversation continued to develop until we homed in on the type of bird.

"We could get an exotic bird, maybe a parrot," suggested Waller.

"Yeah, and we can teach it how to swear and be rude," added Wally.

With the decision made, we approached Ali about getting an exotic bird. He immediately put us in contact with his taciturn deputy named Wali, his trusted avian advisor. Through some broken English, we exchanged sixty American dollars with the directions to buy an exotic bird.

"No problem, Master John," said Wali as he departed with our cash.

We were psyched about the arrival of a vibrant, rainbow-coloured parrot, and the forthcoming masterclass in profanity. We all shared a good laugh imagining our interactions with a profane parrot.

"Hey asshole, raawk"

"Morning asshole, scree-aaawk."

Three days later, Wali showed up with two pigeons.

"Good race bird."

He beamed with pride at the purchase of an *exotic* bird. We tried to hide our dumbfounded reaction and disappointment. As it turns out, parrots are exotic to the Western world, and pigeons are considered exotic to Afghanistan. Until then, I didn't know that pigeon racing was a popular pastime in Afghanistan, making them a unique animal. Not wanting to offend Wali or his enthusiasm for pigeons, which he expressed in broken English while raving about his father's pigeon-racing exploits, we built a cage and welcomed the birds into our humble abode.

Cultural distinctions between Afghanistan and Canada extended beyond our respective definitions of exotic birds. Throughout the tour, we hosted Ali and his crew for a couple of meals in our common area: spaghetti and meatballs, Kraft dinner, and a Surf and Turf night. On a special occasion, we received lobster and steak for the Canada Day celebrations. Since we ordered food for an entire camp and folks were always absent due to operation or leave, we always had extra food to share with Ali and his men.

"John, this is lobster?"

"Yes, Ali, popular in Canada."

Since Afghanistan was landlocked, Ali had never heard of a crustacean, let alone seen or considered eating one. After a litany of questions, neither Ali nor any crew member knew the word for lobster in Pashto or Dari.

"So, it's like a shrimp," I suggested, in efforts to find a reference point.

Blanks stares.

"A shrimp is like a tiny lobster," as I tried to explain another new word.

More confusion.

"Okay, imagine a sea bug that people pay way too much money for."

Ali squinted. "Like eating grasshoppers?"

Not being much of a culinary expert, I could see we were reaching an impasse, so I gave up.

"Sure Ali, something like that, but wet."

Although the crew didn't say anything further, they must have thought we came from another planet as we shared "wet grasshopper" with them in Afghanistan.

To reciprocate our hospitality, Ali invited us over for supper as well. One evening, Wally, Waller, I, and a few sappers walked over to Ali's barracks. Located on the south side of the camp, it only took a few minutes before we entered the lodging for camp contractors. The small concrete building housed a large sparsely furnished room. Beside the door sat a pile of supplies to support the construction company. Around the edges were mattresses placed directly on the floor. A large picture of *Rambo* hung on the wall. In the corner of the room, an old TV with an integral VHS system played *Baywatch* episodes quietly in the background. A large, dark red rug laced with traditional textures and patterns filled the centre of the room and doubled as the dining area. Various twenty-four packs of water bottles sat scattered throughout the room, with some stacks serving as nightstands. The room was well-kept and faintly smelled of dust, concrete, and a wood-burning fire from the adjacent earth oven. Shortly after entering, we all sat down on the floor cross-legged resembling kids in kindergarten while Ali fulfilled the role of host.

After serving us soda in cans with pull-off tabs—different from the pry tabs used in North America—he instructed a young man in charge of cooking. Another crew member kept popping in the doorway to get a glimpse of Wally, before quickly disappearing back outside. His unusual interest in Wally continued, as he took every opportunity to stare at him. I finally looked over at Ali and asked, "Why does that guy keep staring at Wally?"

Ali's face lit up with a big smile.

"He think Wally a king. That's why you buy him animals."

The senior members of Ali's crew concocted some story about Wally being a member of the monarchy in Canada. All our animal purchases made it easy to corroborate the story. Since the young man grew up in the local area and had not travelled much beyond Kandahar, he lacked context, making him an easy target for a practical joke. A bit of a dynamo, keen, and eager to learn, he thought it could be a once-in-a-lifetime opportunity to see royalty, so he wanted to get a good look at the "big deal." We shared a heartfelt laugh as Ali let us in on the prank.

"Young, easy to trick Master John."

Throughout the meal preparations, we didn't understand the words spoken between Ali and his crew, but we could follow the skit. As if he was serving a caliphate, every action the young man performed was an act of reverence and adulation while he was in the presence of the revered Wally. Watching the scene play out while enjoying my soda pop, I told Ali about some pranks we play on young, easy to trick sappers.

"We ask young sappers to find a left-handed wrench."

Ali paused momentarily to translate the phrase before the metaphorical light switch clicked and he realized wrenches are ambidextrous. Another big smile crossed his face.

"Very nice, Master John."

The way he said it tacitly implied that he couldn't use the trick. Based on Afghanistan's austere, rugged, and independent nature, I suspect every kid learned how to use a wrench at a young age, while many adults didn't know how to use a pencil. We were the exact opposite in Canada. Every child learned to use a pencil at a young age, yet some adults could still be easily duped into searching for a left-handed wrench.

The sharing of practical jokes stopped with the arrival of the food. Ali and his crew served up a local Afghanistan feast. They placed a large aluminum cooking pot filled with animal stew in the middle of the rug on the floor. The succulent aroma of the meal permeated our noses and filled the room with the smell of rich earthy spices such as cumin, coriander, and turmeric. The slow-cooked meat had simmered all day on the wood-fueled, earthen stove. Mixed with the lamb were garlic, onions and tomatoes. Beside the main course, they placed a plate of boiled green vegetables resembling spinach, small potatoes, and a large stack of freshly baked, homemade naan bread. They passed around Styrofoam plates so we could serve ourselves a meal.

Hospitality is deeply rooted in their culture, and Ali exemplified it perfectly, leaving no detail overlooked as the host. He even bought plastic utensils to respect the North American eating style. After allowing us to serve ourselves first, Ali and his crew used naan bread to soak the meal off their plates while we used forks and knives. As we ate, the voice of Pamala Anderson could be intermittently heard, as a *Baywatch* VHS tape played on repeat in the background. Curious about the nostalgia around *Baywatch* and *Rambo*, I asked Ali about movies.

"Do you like other shows other than *Baywatch* and *Rambo*?"

"Yes, Master John. But not as much as Baywatch and Rambo."

Ali went on to explain how these two-pop culture shows just stuck in his world. Despite having access to contemporary hits such as *Slumdog Millionaire* and *The Curious Case of Benjamin Button,* nothing dislodged their adoration of *Rambo* or Pamela Anderson. Maybe it was the construction industry, young males working a physical job; he couldn't explain it, but I could relate. Hunting, playing the lottery, and sports were perennial topics in the construction industry back home.

Towards the end of the meal, the conversation turned to the Taliban. As Ali operated a construction company that supported coalition forces, I asked about the challenges he navigated due to the war.

"Ali, how do you work in the heart of Taliban country?"

He paused for a moment as he soaked up the last of the stew into his naan bread.

"Master John, Taliban part of life."

He then ate the last bite of his meal and chewed quietly. I didn't probe further as the tone in which he responded said so much. The response felt comparable to asking a Canadian about the challenges of completing construction projects in the winter. Cold weather and potential snow delays were built into the plan and work schedule, treated as routine obstacles to overcome as part of the job. If you can't handle winter, you shouldn't work in certain parts of Canada. Every business has challenges imposed on them by the environment—government sanctions, regulations, weather, or, in Ali's case, the Taliban. Yet, after evaluating the situation, I realized that working in the face of those challenges was the best option for him, his company, and his family. With all the health and safety protocols of the Canadian construction industry, I couldn't fathom operating under the threat of a warring party. But then again, I didn't grow up in a place that was synonymous with words like tough, self-reliant, and resilient, as was the case with Afghanistan.

As we started to clean up, another young man drenched in sweat came to the main door. Throughout preparing the meal, he had been responsible for splitting wood, feeding the fire, and doing all the undesirable jobs behind the scenes to prepare the meal. His bedraggled appearance contrasted starkly against the rest of the group's relatively clean deportment. Ali gave him further instructions and he disappeared as quickly as he arrived.

"Ali, what is going on with him?"

"Master John, new guy. He get the bad jobs."

While peacefully sharing a meal, the new guy worked like a rented mule. As good-paying jobs were hard to find, he did everything he could to prove his worth. Comparable to a courtier seeking the leader's attention and trying to ingratiate himself in any way possible.

"No kidding Ali. We do the same in Canada. Our new guys fill sandbags and carry the heavy military gear on patrols."

We shared a warm laugh about the commonality of assigning crappy jobs to the new guys as we bid farewell. Ali placed his hand over his heart and acknowledged each guest with the traditional farewell that meant, "Peace be upon you."

"Salaam Alaikum, Master John."

"Salaam Alaikum Ali. Thanks for the meal, see you tomorrow."

We returned to our common area with the sun setting on the horizon. Listening to the troops play poker at the table, I sat and watched the pigeons peck the ground. As the two birds walked in unison to our water feature, the primordial similarities that our exotic fowls and people from across the globe all share struck me: connection, emotions, family.

Our cultural awareness training continually focused on the differences between the Afghan and Canadian cultures. The meal with Ali and his crew highlighted the similarities. It reminded me that we all experience the same universal emotions of love of family, fear of the Taliban or being ostracized from the tribe, hope for a better tomorrow, and the joy from movies, pulling pranks on the new guys and playing with pigeons.

Despite differing cultures and ideologies, the simple act of breaking bread together overcame our cultural differences and resulted in meaningful exchanges, cementing the idea that people are more alike than they are different. Shared laughter and a smile are the same in all languages and cultures, no matter the dialect spoken. Our sterile training sessions bombarded us with countless PowerPoint slides, exhaustive briefs, and drawn-out lectures, all designed to highlight our vast cultural differences—words such as religion, language, history, and traditions dominated the narrative. Yet, in the unpretentious warmth of a traditional meal with construction workers, Ali and his fellow contractors transcended those divisions, effortlessly revealing the profound cultural similarities that unite us. Their actions showed us what our cultural training never could, and they captured it perfectly in a single word: humanity.

# 20

# It's Just a Hole

Major Packer used to tell a not-so-well-received joke.

"What do you call engineers without their tools?"

He'd pause before boisterously delivering the punch line.

"Infantry."

He'd always laugh, even if he laughed alone. I didn't pay much heed to the joke beyond noticing that the infantry didn't overly appreciate the jab. However, towards the end of our tour, it proved prophetic. By this point, at most, only two- to four-man sapper detachments supported platoon-plus size infantry elements. Consequently, carrying all our engineering equipment on dismounted patrols became impossible. Since everybody wanted engineers with them on operations to respond to the never-ending explosive threats, previously unprecedented thoughts and actions became the standard.

During a company-level set of orders, the officer commanding noticed our absence.

"Where are the Chimos?"

Cognizant of all the current tasks and patrols, the duty officer responded.

"Just getting back to camp. Should be here in fifteen minutes."

As the duty officer recounted the story to me in our lines after the fact, the company commander wasn't impressed. Typically, commanders set the cadence according to their time. But seasoned from encountering innumerable explosive threats on patrols, he didn't want to proceed with patrol preparations without the engineers. As a result, he gave a unique order.

"We'll wait for the engineers."

Engineering availability had become a planning factor in patrol and order scheduling.

Similarly, on one occasion we advised that a two-man pairing couldn't carry a section worth of engineering kit. To accommodate the situation, we started to triage items according to the upcoming mission. The infantry didn't approve of this reduction in our capability, so they volunteered to carry our equipment to ensure we could perform all facets of our trade. Although laden with copious amounts of ammunition, water, and equipment already, the infantry found space for additional engineering gear. Ensuring the patrol had sufficient engineering capabilities far outweighed the discomfort of carrying a few extra pounds on top of their existing seventy-plus-pound combat load.

Down to the bare bones of available combat engineers, I became a fire team partner with Sapper Chris Hamilton on patrol. A dashingly handsome specimen better known as Hammy, his peers kidded that he should have been a Calvin Klein model with his looks instead of joining the military. For our patrol, I had my traditional radio and some explosives in my backpack. Hammy carried the mine detector, some prefabricated explosive charges, and some initiation sets. Extra C4 blocks, a set of bolt cutters, and a hook-and-line kit for pulling on suspect devices ended up in the patrol packs of the infantry soldiers we were supporting; as we needed different items, we'd simply call for them as required.

Towards the end of the patrol, we passed through Haji. A couple of kilometres away, we could see the imposing hill of the Sperwan Ghar. Just to the south of Haji, a mature set of trees impeded observation from the sentry tower. This location also doubled as a firing point for insurgents before they vanished into the surrounding adobe structures. Soldiers had tried to cut the trees down, but like everything else in the country, they were tough and resilient. They were so hard I didn't know if I needed a botanist or geologist to identify them. Chainsaw blades quickly dulled when attempting to cut the petrified wood. Hearing we still had patrol packs full of explosives, the reconnaissance sergeant from Haji sought our assistance.

"Hey Chimos, can you blow up those dang trees?"

We lacked sufficient resources to conduct a range by the book. In most any other circumstance, it would be inexcusable to proceed. However, once again, the Horn of Panjwai challenged the status quo. Evaluating the threat, I found it unimaginable that a well-concealed firing point remained within a couple hundred meters of the outpost. Coupled with the fact we had recently lost soldiers in Haji from RPG fire, I found it inexcusable to depart when we could help mitigate the threat. As we were en route home, we could afford to expend the patrol load of explosives removing trees. So, I agreed to assist.

"If you provide overwatch security, we'll blow up some trees."

The exuberant sergeant darted off to prepare the outpost while Hammy and I set up an explosive range.

*Training Safety*, our bible for conducting ranges in Canada, classifies explosive ranges as complex. To mitigate the risk of the activity, the manual explicitly outlined requirements for conducting an explosive range. For example, you needed an Officer in Charge and a Range Safety Officer to comply with the standard protocols. They couldn't be the same person, and the Range Safety Officer had to be a senior non-commissioned member. In addition, you needed a medic, an ambulance, a storeman qualified to transport dangerous goods, and a dedicated signaler to communicate with range control. Furthermore, you might need sentries to control the range danger template. At the Haji tree range, the explosive range team became me and Hammy.

"Hey Hammy, if you are the Range Safety Officer and medic, I'll be the Officer in Charge and the signaler. We can then alternate who sets off the charges."

Under-ranked and unqualified to perform his assigned duties, I gave him a "field promotion." Based on his aptitude and recent experience in theatre, he was more than qualified to handle an explosive range safely. Hammy quietly smiled and replied, "Chimo," as he got to work.

In theatre, *Training Safety* didn't apply. However, I loathed becoming too cavalier with the rules, as the manual provided an exceptional handrail for conducting ranges prudently. While Hammy assembled explosives, I advised Haji about our intentions and disconnected the claymore mines from their triggering devices. Designed as a weapon of last resort to wipe out a final push on a position, they contained hundreds of ball bearings that could quickly kill us if they detonated by mistake while we were removing trees. I also cleared the explosive range with our headquarters and established a restricted airspace over our position. With overwatch security provided by the machine guns of the Haji tower, I proceeded to assist Hammy with the charges.

"Hey sir, we should use up this dong charge."

Looking at fifty pounds of explosives neatly laid out in a divot on the ground, I didn't know which item my Range Safety Officer characterized as a "dong charge." An exceptionally intelligent sapper, Hammy sensed my confusion. He picked up a pre-prepared charge and elaborated on his lexicon.

"See this charge, sir? It looks like a dong."

Seeing the explosive charge, deformed with time in our backpack, I immediately got the blue humour.

With two people doing a three-man job, we used our arms and bodies to affix charges to the trees while standing on an uneven dirt surface. Throughout the process, we must have resembled two octopuses in heat with our limbs awkwardly wrapped around the trunk. Before long, we had a couple of dong charges strapped to a tree. We warned the tower, popped smoke, and took cover behind a dirt wall.

KABOOM!

Dust, bark and twigs landed around us as the tree awkwardly timbered over. I'd never seen a tree so tough. During an exercise in Canada, we blew up aspen, popular, and pine trees with ease. In some cases, we just needed to wrap a few strands of detonation cord around the tree base to cut it down. In Afghanistan, four blocks of C4 barely knocked over the average tree. Due to this toughness, we only removed half a dozen trees before we ran out of explosives. Though small, the clearing created a big impact by eliminating cover for a habitual firing point. With the entire patrol out of explosives, we cleared the range. Not long afterwards, Hammy and I returned to Sperwan Ghar with the infantry platoon and rejoined our troop.

A couple of days later, we were relaxing in our common area. The sappers were smoking and joking over an after-supper game of poker when the radio abruptly interrupted them. The snipers on top of the hill called in a target.

"Contact, man digging in an IED on Route Brown. Permission to engage?"

As if I'd won a high stakes poker game, I thought, "Jackpot." We'd caught an IED team placing a device within range of our snipers. It couldn't get better than this.

So, I thought.

After no shots rang out, my instincts told me something was up. Waller and I went to the command post to get the skinny. What could possibly impede the engagement of an IED team placing a device on the main road in and out of Sperwan Ghar?

Inside the small office, a flurry of activity occurred. The infantry company deputy confirmed the rules of engagement with a legal officer in KAF as Major Lane spoke with the Commander. The issue came down to the danger template of the IED. Since the IED was about one thousand metres from our location on Route Brown, there were no coalition forces in the danger template. Therefore, it didn't pose an imminent threat, so we didn't have the authority to engage lethally. Like the ANA soldiers moonlighting as a security force situation a couple of months earlier, their weapons didn't pose a threat to coalition forces, so we couldn't legally engage. While Major Lane beseeched higher command for a more permissive rules of engagement, the snipers continued to watch through their rifle scopes similar to ardent bird watchers as the IED placers worked unimpeded.

I understood the rules of engagement and why we had them as a professional military; however, in this case, I started to come unhinged. If we didn't kill the bomber, the follow-on implied task became my problem: Chimos, remove the IED.

I stood helplessly in the command post interposed between the IED and our rules of engagement. We couldn't take the legal risk of breaking a rule of engagement, but we were willing to accept the lethal risk of sending sappers to remove the IED. One or two sniper rounds would preclude us from becoming enmeshed in yet another IED. Furthermore, by shooting, we would eliminate a bomb-placing team and prevent them from moving on to their next job.

Waller shared my frustration and disbelief as a bomb was planted in the road with impunity. Since we built the road, I argued that it represented a coalition asset. However, the lawyer objected. My mind raced for options to neutralize the threat as the snipers provided an update.

"Plastic yellow jugs being emplaced."

I couldn't believe my ears. After dealing with countless IEDs and their aftermaths throughout the previous five months, I could only stand there helplessly and listen to the enemy build a trap in real time. At the start of the tour, we overcame the misapprehension that an observed road prevented the emplacement of IEDs. In my wildest dreams, I never imagined we would witness the emplacement of an IED unmolested. It was an unfathomable situation as we'd seen countless airstrikes from the footage captured by Reaper drones. In what became known as "Reaper Porn," countless videos showed the same scenario. An IED team would be as busy as a colony of beavers placing a device. Suddenly, the screen would flash as the Reaper's deadly payload hit the target. When the footage refocused after the blast, scattered debris covered the once-busy job site. With the ability to put a warhead on a forehead at our fingertips, and despite the precedence from similar IED situations, our rules of engagement compelled us to remain idle. In one last attempt, I made an outlandish insinuation.

"With plastic jugs of explosives, we could be in the danger template of the blast."

The conversation became stagnant as they repudiated my suggestion. An uneasy pause ensued. Although plausible that the jugs contained enough explosives to blow shrapnel into our camp, it remained doubtful. As the sun set on the horizon, the rules of engagement remained frozen like a statue. As a result, the insurgent IED team completed their job and moved on to the next; who knows where they would place their next IED. With the departure of our adversaries that night, my implied task for the morning became: Chimos, remove the IED.

Although we'd dealt with countless IEDs over the tour, this one struck a nerve. It felt like a completely unnecessary risk because it could have been avoided with a bullet fired by our world-class snipers. Adding insult to injury, we designed the road to help deter IED emplacement. Previous engineers on earlier rotations built the road straight as an arrow with wide shoulders to help facilitate observation. Yet despite the road design fully exposing the insurgent IED team, we couldn't capitalize. The road design that provided the snipers clear observation was for naught. Instead, our world class marksmen got a front-row seat to watch our adversary do their dirty work. Furthermore, handling

IEDs should be minimized as they are still a lethal risk even if you know their location. As per the empirical evidence captured in *Training Safety*, explosive accidents and incidents are usually a result of human error. Facing an adaptive adversary replete with devious stratagems, removing IEDs was like playing with fire; you can only do it so much before you get burnt. Although we'd gained some status based on our success removing IEDs throughout the tour, Chimos were not infallible.

Nothing allayed my angst as the countless stars appeared in the night sky. Being tasked to remove an explosive device whose kind had killed and marred countless coalition forces, after passively watching the emplacement, was an unbelievable nightmare. Equally infuriated, Waller took some time to think and contain his disapproval about the sequence of events. I racked my brain to try and find a fresh approach to the task. Thinking to myself, "Maybe if I took…"

BOOM, BOOM.

My thoughts broke with the shocking impact of the M777 firing from Sperwan Ghar. Every so often, their fire missions required them to launch projectiles directly over our lines. The resulting overpressure from the muzzles being pointed in our direction blew the doors open on the portable toilets adjacent to our barracks. The ensuing banging and clanging as everything returned to stasis added to the already bone-jarring explosions of the artillery working into the night. As the firing subsided, my mind ruminated on the next steps for the following morning. Tired and unable to think clearly, I fed our pigeons and caught a couple of hours of sleep.

An astute problem solver, Waller approached me early the following morning in a surprisingly chipper mood.

"Hey sir, can we get some ANA to help with the IED?"

Normally apprehensive about operating with ANA around explosive devices because their temperament could be a bit erratic, the idea surprised me until Waller explained his logic.

"There's a company of them in camp. We need security. They can help."

I took a moment to contemplate the idea and realized he was right. The ANA were an untapped resource that could alleviate many of my concerns. The ANA could flush potential triggermen from the neighbouring fields and establish a security cordon by conducting a patrol adjacent to both sides of Route Brown. With redundant overwatch security from the LAVs and snipers on the Sperwan Ghar hill, we could mitigate the security risk of the ANA departing the scene because they grew bored of the task. I dashed to the command post to seek authorization. Within moments I returned elated, and with two platoons of ANA at our disposal.

As we conducted battle procedure for our patrol, I watched Master Corporal Kyle Ho run his sections through preparations. Having been at the heart of many engagements, from the suicide child bomb, the Sia Choy patrol and countless IED responses, he left nothing to chance when preparing for the forthcoming patrol. He meticulously reviewed every patrol phase along with all the contingency plans. An intrepid warrior, he was the quintessential sapper and one of the finest soldiers with whom I had the honour to serve.

Years later, I learned about Master Corporal Ho's thought process when responding to dangerous situations similar to this IED. In short, he remained biased towards taking on difficult tasks himself, because it made it easier to handle mistakes. If a disaster happened, he didn't want to be the one explaining what happened to the families of his subordinates; he couldn't live with the thought. On the contrary, he could handle someone else explaining to his next of kin what happened to him if he didn't come home. Therefore, to avoid awkward conversations with his subordinate's families back in Canada, he placed a disproportionate burden on his own shoulders while operating in Afghanistan, a weight that became more acute as our redeployment date approached.

With orders and rehearsals complete, I watched the patrol depart from the walls of Sperwan Ghar through my binoculars. While Waller led the engineering team on the IED removal, we agreed it would be prudent if I stayed at the command post to corral additional resources, if and as required. The patrol plan played out smoothly as the ANA platoons efficiently swept each edge of the road while the small engineering section advanced towards the device. A rooster's crow could be heard in the distance on the sunny Afghanistan morning. Everything was going to plan until an impatient ANA soldier walked up to the device. I did a double take through the binoculars. I could see a few folks scurry for cover as reached down to grab the device.

Everything happened so fast as my mind screamed, "No, no no!"

One moment we were conducting a methodical advance, the next, the patrol hugged the ground while an ANA soldier pulled on the device like a gardener removing oversized vegetables from a garden. I could see the sappers taking cover in the ditch while Waller attempted to gain control of the situation. In under a minute, the ANA soldier pulled the device out of the ground by the wires and swung it like a shopping bag as he walked around the objective. I couldn't believe my eyes. I knew ANA soldiers could be erratic, however uprooting an IED and swinging it like a picnic basket in under sixty seconds left me speechless.

With the same impatience used to remove the device, it wasn't long before he dropped it. With some of the threat removed, new threats emerged. Waller now had to dispose of a disturbed and dismantled IED. After taking a moment to regain control of the situation, he sent a report over the radio.

"Will proceed to blow IED in place."

Waller used some tent poles to place charges next to the IED components. Knowing the tasks would require the placement of explosives, he decided to bring poles on the patrol to keep as much distance as possible from the IED. The poles became even more helpful dealing with a disturbed, potentially volatile device after the ANA soldier had rotter tilled the area. By establishing a restricted air space through me, we detonated the device and left a moon-sized crater in the middle of the road. After checking for secondary devices, Waller called over the radio.

"All clear. Now we need to fill this hole."

I'd already been concurrently working on a plan in camp, and the prognosis remained grim. Lacking in situ assets to repair the road, we needed to mount a convoy to get heavy equipment and a dump truck from Masum Ghar. As we could only move in three vehicle packets, I needed to wait for Waller to return so we could crew a third vehicle. Collectively short on personnel, we had just enough people in Sperwan Ghar to man a convoy after covering all the camp security requirements. Further exacerbating the issue, the dump truck and loader we needed were unavailable until late that afternoon. Therefore, the simple task of repairing a hole in the road would take an entire day. Adding insult to injury, and by far the most infuriating part of the event, I seemed to be the only one charged up about driving on IED-laden roads to collect equipment to repair a hole that could have been prevented in the first place with a couple bullets the day prior. I boiled with rage at the insanity of it all. The bureaucratic process and standard procedures compelled me to go metaphorically around the block instead of walking next door, and in this case, expose soldiers to explosive threats throughout. As the Sperwan Ghar command post helped knit together the administration for an escort patrol to retrieve the heavy equipment, I seethed with contempt. Feeling beat and disheartened by the lack of options, I had resigned myself and gathered my patrol gear when Ali walked in.

"Master John, you need hand with road?"

That simple sentence sent my brain into overdrive. How did Ali know about the road and the current challenges? Until then, he had not been in the vicinity to hear updates on the radio. We both stood in silence as my mind processed the question. But of course, he knew. As a relative magnate in the area, his business required intimate knowledge of everything that happened around Sperwan Ghar. With his flip phone, he had contacts all over the area. Like using the ANA to support the patrol, I had another epiphany: Ali was another untapped resource. I became intrigued as his demeanour subtly hinted that he had more to say.

"Ali, what do *you* have in mind?"

"Master John, you need gravel for road, I have truck loaded."

In my myopic planning, I'd only focused on using Canadian assets to fix the problem. Unbeknownst to me, Ali followed the day's events with his cell phone contacts. Anticipating a hot mess, he took the initiative to load a gravel dump truck with a front-end loader and marshal the vehicles. He and Wali, his stolid deputy, awaited the command to repair the road. Gobsmacked, I confirmed the details.

"Ali, you're ready to go now?"

His response was the most refreshing statement I'd heard in the last twelve hours.

"Yes, master John, it's just a hole."

My instinct was to respond, "Yes Ali, but you don't understand," However, as he stood there with a calm deportment, I realized he understood the problem perfectly. Blissfully ignorant of all our policies and standard operating procedures, Ali called it as it saw it. As a contractor who worked in the heart of Taliban country, he couldn't operate any other way. He lost money and risked insolvency if he didn't cut to the jugular of every issue. In one sentence, Ali untied the Gordian knot I'd created to repair the road with undeniable precision. I couldn't fathom explaining my mind-numbing, convoluted plan to him, that adhered to coalition protocols while ignoring some common sense. Instantly recharged by his pragmatic, results-based approach that simplified the issue back to just filling a hole, I almost embraced him as I spoke.

"Ali, if you're ready. Go fill the hole."

"Yes, master John."

With a wave of his arm, he wrapped a sun-faded scarf over his face and departed. He didn't say a word, but I knew he hid his face from the Taliban watching the site. In retrospect, I should have reported to the command post to outline my solution, but I didn't. They were still running around like chickens with their heads cut off, trying to pull together patrols to escort heavy equipment and a dump truck to our location. Spit balling an estimate, I'd bet that over twenty man-hours were expended by staff officers exploring options to amend schedules and adjust patrol matrices so we could coordinate the arrival of some heavy equipment to fill a hole. I could have stopped the mayhem, but I didn't want to jinx the situation, so I let the frenzy continue while I returned to the lookout with my binoculars.

Right on cue, Ali and Wali bombed down the road in a vibrant, hand-painted dump truck piled high with gravel, shining in the mid-morning sun. Behind it, a rugged front-end loader, scratched and sun-faded, bounced along in quick pursuit. Listening to my patrol pack radio, I chuckled as updates passed on the net.

"Dump truck of gravel and a front-end loader at IED site."

Moments later.

"Gravel dumped into the hole."

Five minutes later.

"Hole filled, assets returning to base."

In under fifteen minutes, Ali and Wali resolved what would have taken me ten hours and dozens of staff hours behind the scenes. Although no shots were fired, Ali and Wali deserved a medal for gallantry. Their deft response in the face of the Taliban, with only a scarf covering their face, was nothing short of phenomenal. They could have faded into their normal camp tasks that morning or claimed that some clause in their contract precluded them from working in the face of the enemy, but instead, they risked exposing their identity to the Taliban and epitomized foresight, initiative, and results. Reeling from their unwavering dedication to supporting us, I sat in humble gratitude as the troops returned safely to camp. Since the command post heard the updates on the radio, I never reported to them about the events that transpired. Before long, inquisitive headquarters staff walked over to our common area.

"Hey, John. How did you fix the hole so fast?"

Having relieved them of a tedious task, I suspect they had only completed a small fraction of the work required to do it the coalition way. I saw an opportunity to market the engineer's divine powers. In a laidback response, I plagiarized a line from Ali.

"It was just a hole."

As I hid my early frustrations well, they seemed slightly shocked at our efficacy that morning. In many ways, I felt like I'd just lived the phrase, "You need to be lucky to be good and good to be lucky." I'd been lucky enough to be surrounded by industrious individuals who exuded a get-things-done attitude. I just helped provide them with space to thrive.

Looking back, Ali's boldness was profound and went far beyond just filling a hole. The events surrounding the Route Brown IED gave us a taste of his everyday world. He needed to wring the most out of every resource to function, and he innately did it without thinking. Leaving no asset unused is more than just a strategy for him; it was a cellular response built into his core mindset. Potentially via osmosis or by passive observation, his ideology rubbed off on us as we uncharacteristically started using the infantry to move our kit, the ANA to assist on patrols, as well as Ali to respond to the aftermaths of an IED blast. By just filling a hole, Ali showed us the *sine qua non* of effective problem-solving in Afghanistan lay in harnessing untapped resources. By venturing beyond the standard approach, unconventional solutions emerge.

# 21

# The Maple Leaf Lottery

As we approached redeployment, by this time many of us had return flight dates, we began to tidy up loose ends before we departed. One night, the idea to clean up the discombobulated gym spontaneously developed in our common area. Over copious amounts of cigarettes, the odd Red Bull, and a boisterous poker game, the sappers developed a plan.

"We could make a building over the gym's concrete pad," suggested one sapper.

The next round of betting took place.

"We have extra wood in Beaver Lumber," added another.

To stay prepared and avoid future supply shortages, we never amended our bi-weekly material requests for wood. As a result, we received wood on almost every supply convoy to Sperwan Ghar. Throughout the tour, we amassed a vast stock in Beaver Lumber that would rival a small-town lumber yard.

"I'll draw-up a plan," concluded one sapper.

Before long, the camp sergeant major had blessed our plan and helped coral a work party to build the gym. Over the next twenty-four hours, the camp looked similar to a barn raising party in a Hutterite colony. Every available soul helped clear the concrete pad, construct panels, raise walls, install a roof, and re-install the gym equipment. With little direction, everyone worked harmoniously to leave an indelible mark on the camp.

There is a joy seeing evidence of progress made possible by harnessing your creativity. Throughout my career, I've always been drawn to projects that can be completed from start to finish with one group because they create a much greater sense of accomplishment. On the contrary, I find piecemeal projects are tougher to glean a sense of progress as it can be difficult to see how small pieces fit into the bigger picture. With the gym, in one massive surge over a day, the camp transformed a dusty concrete pad used by a bunch of muscle heads and iron addicts into an inviting, contemporary gym. The task transcended work and became a form of art, as everyone played a part and drew upon their initiative and respective cached resources to contribute. Electricians wired lights, some soldiers with a knack for interior decorating created a couple of workout posters, carpenters installed a window, and a techy installed a stereo system. I knew the camp contained a bunch of stashed items for just-in-case moments, however, the variety of available resources and the metamorphic changes they created surprised me. Of all our work we complete in Afghanistan, the organic development, free-thinking, and teamwork approach used to complete the gym remains a fond memory; not because of what we did, but because of how we did it. I don't know if he was known for his skills in the gym, but in the end, the camp decided to name it *Doyle's Gym* in honour of Master Corporal Doyle.

Around the same time, we decommissioned the Thunderdome. After tossing in a bunch of frogs for one last fight to the death with spiders and scorpions, we shut down the sideshow. With the power of hindsight, we never should have started the Thundersome in the first place. To remove all traces of the shenanigans before new sappers arrived, we tossed all evidence into the trash.

Just like us, Major Packer was also tying up loose ends. During one of our chats, he outlined his requirements.

"John, I needed your Small Rewards Program administration yesterday!"

Referring to the cash incentive program for locals to report IEDs, I initially tried to return the money early in the tour, but the system didn't want it back. In discussions with a logistics officer in KAF, he told me to find a way to "expend" the funds in accordance with the program because it would create more paperwork if I didn't use the money. As I'd spent one reward package purchasing animals for a BBQ, at a minimum, I needed to complete one form. We had the name of a local who turned in an IED but declined the cash, so that submission would be easy to finish. I'd procrastinated on completing the paperwork because I still had a second reward package. This fact caused an ethical dilemma as a tiny voice in my mind spoke.

"Give the money to Ali."

His actions in responding to the Route Brown IED and minimizing the movement of coalition forces in an explosive environment justified a ten-fold reward. Just as he didn't care about all our convoy policies, he didn't care about our typical awards of medals, ribbons or certificates. He worked for cash. Consequently, the reward package equivalent to about one hundred US dollars became an alluring bonus to acknowledge his services. Furthermore, using the program money would be the simplest way to finish the outstanding Small Rewards Program administration.

Throughout the tour, several locals had reported IEDs but didn't take or accept the money from the program. So, we had ample examples for the administration, but I didn't have actual names. To officially account for the expenditure of the second rewards package, I needed to artistically bend some rules. After speaking with Wally, he agreed that Ali deserved a bonus if we could make one happen. His mischievous side appeared once again as he suggested a way to complete the paperwork.

"Go speak with the intelligence guy in the command post. You'll need an untraceable alias."

In the corner of the Sperwan Ghar command post sat an intelligence corporal. Bearing the resemblance of a police crime scene bureau, he layered the walls around his office with photos of high-value individuals. In some cases, string-connected the faces. In other instances, a sheet of clear talc overlayed pictures that contained various Staedtler marker-coloured lines, circles, and handwritten notes. Seeking a fictitious name, I couldn't fathom a better spot. It took a bit to explain my requirements. When he got it, his analytical, data-centric intelligence mind went to work.

"Sir, let's just pick three pictures. First picture first name, second picture second name, third picture third name."

The concept worked for me, so I randomly picked three photos, like a kid in a carnival picking prizes off the wall. The intelligence corporal keenly wrote each name down as part of the game. In the end, he didn't look enthusiastic after writing the final name.

"Uh, sir, we've got Mohammad Muhammad Mohammadullah."

Perfect. While writing the pseudonym on my Small Rewards Program form, he elaborated on his concern using my name as an example.

"Sir, that's like saying your name is John Jon Johnny."

I pondered his observation momentarily but continued to write. Although a highly unprobeable name, it was also untraceable. I called out playfully while exiting the command post.

"Thanks, Corporal. I'll keep an eye out for Mohammad Muhammad Mohammadullah."

Striving to be a consummate administrative professional, I meticulously covered all the salient points in the Small Reward Program document. Proud of my administrative prowess and the remarkable improvement I'd made completing paperwork throughout the tour, I showed Wally the finished product. He was incredulous.

"What? You can't submit that."

Blindsided by his abrupt about turn, I was speechless. Although we only discussed the plan briefly, I thought everything about fabricating a name for submission was clear. Before I could say anything, he grabbed the paper from my hand and tossed it on the floor like trash. In one seamless motion, he grabbed his mug and splashed coffee on it, then kicked dirt on the document before grinding it into the concrete with his foot. After his whirlwind moves subsided, he handed me a dishevelled piece of paper that looked as if it had been a doormat for the last six months.

"Now it looks genuine."

As everything in Afghanistan quickly faded with the sun and absorbed a taint of dirt colour, the document did look legit. I placed it in an envelope for the next mail run back to KAF. With the Small Reward Program administration buttoned up, we shifted focus to a farewell meal.

To celebrate the close of the tour before the redeployment cycle commenced, the morale and welfare staff pushed us the supplies for our second and final surf and turf meal. Once again, we invited Ali and crew to partake to show our appreciation for their hard work.

"Master John, you want fireworks?"

"No Ali, no fireworks."

His question stemmed from our first party on Canada Day. While cleaning out a deserted sea can, we discovered a few Afghan fireworks. They consisted of some homemade rocket-type projectiles crudely taped to a stick. Long story short, the design and manufacturing lacked any quality control. While igniting them during our Canada Day party, one blew up in my face, a second shot in wide circles before exploding, and a third rocketed sideways. This resulted in the firework streaming across our helicopter landing zone at eye level before exploding a few feet from our fueling point. With thousands of litres of fuel stored inside a fabric bladder, we narrowly missed a catastrophic event. Needless to say, we burned the remaining Afghanistan fireworks and vowed never to repurchase them.

"Master John, you bring trophy?"

"No Ali, just a meal."

His second question stemmed from a second major event in Sperwan Ghar: a morale and welfare trip to the outpost that involved General Rick Hillier, the Chief of Defence Staff, bringing the Stanley Cup. I didn't overly care to see the cup, but it was nice to have morale and welfare events travel to us. As the VIPs flew in helicopters, we minimized the risk to the troops travelling on the roads to attend the event in another location. Furthermore, by bringing the show to Sperwan Ghar, outside-the-wire-based members got some benefits from the perks that generally only occurred in KAF.

The most memorable part of the visit for me was the past National Hockey League players who joined General Hillier on the tour and the creative administration the general completed to make the Sperwan Ghar trip possible. Most notably, famed enforcer Bob Probert joined the visit. A big man at 6-foot 2 inches, his hands were the size of anvils. I'm unsure if he was there to boost morale or physically defend the cup from the Taliban, as he'd made a living fighting in hockey. Shaking his hand, I couldn't imagine being on the receiving end of a Bob Probert punch back in his prime.

Years later, I learned that General Hillier pushed the boundaries to make the visit possible. Fearing a mishap in a warzone, the National Hockey League insisted the Stanley Cup remain in KAF. This limitation would mean many outside-the-wire soldiers would not see the famous trophy. To expand the reach of the cup tour, the general signed an order increasing the footprint of KAF to include several combat outposts, one being Sperwan Ghar. This order only lasted a few days to facilitate the Stanley Cup tour around the warzone. With Sperwan Ghar now being included in the definition of KAF, the general creatively adhered to the National Hockey League constraint. For years I grappled with how I had completed the Small Rewards Program paperwork. Hearing about the Stanley Cup paperwork, it was comforting to learn that I wasn't the only one taking a liberal approach with administration.

During our third and final event in Sperwan Ghar, the aroma of steaks grilling, roasted garlic, baked potatoes, and boiling lobster filled the hot afternoon air. While cooking, we casually chatted about work and family. We also took the opportunity to thank Ali and the crew for their services over the deployment. Wali enjoyed checking in on our exotic pigeons as they bathed in the water feature, while Ali inquisitively watched our meal cook. He finally mastered the word lobster but still couldn't grasp that we ate ocean-based food in a landlocked country. The supply chain capabilities of the Canadian Forces forever remained a foreign concept to him.

Ali and his crew ate reservedly during the meal. Comparable to a child trying vegetables for the first time, they didn't want to overeat. While eating, one of the troops joked about needing to win the lottery so he wouldn't have to work anymore. Ali caught onto the word.

"Master John, what is lottery?"

I explained the concept of buying a lottery ticket for a few dollars to have a chance at winning millions of dollars. He asked a few follow-on questions about sweepstake lotteries, but the concept remained abstract. In the end, he added the word lottery to the list of foreign concepts we had discussed during the tour, such as life insurance, pensions, and the untranslatable idiom: happy as a pig in shit.

"Master John, why pig happy in shit?"

No matter how much I tried to explain the meaning of the phrase, he didn't make the connection to why an animal would be happy in poo. Being based in a predominately Muslim country, pigs are considered *haram,* meaning forbidden and not to be eaten. Consequently, pig farming or even just the presence of swine was extremely rare in Afghanistan, so he had no reference for the proclivities of pigs.

With the meal complete, all our guests except Ali departed after exchanging pleasantries. As the night was still young, the troops cracked out the poker chips, highlighting another cultural difference. Due to the religious norms of Islam, gambling and card games were generally discouraged. Under patio lantern lights, with Creedence Clear Water Revival playing and cigarette smoke filling the air, Ali watched intently as the troops played. I didn't play to avoid putting myself in a situation where I could take money from the troops. Ali knew the basics of cards, such as face value and suit, but he asked several questions about Texas hold'em poker. Although a junior player at best when I did play, I knew enough to explain the rules, the odds, and the rounds of betting that occurred as part of the game. Once he made the connection that the poker chips represented cash, he became especially fascinated and made an insightful comment.

"Master John, you bet on kings while you live like kings."

While Ali learned about poker, I gained a new perspective on luck. Based on the hardships of Afghanistan, his lifestyle was rooted in asceticism. The ten-to-twenty-dollar rounds of poker represented a day's wage for Ali. He used money to support life, to buy food and run his business, but never for pleasure. On the contrary, the sappers flouted cash in an entertaining game of poker while they smoked copious numbers of cigarettes and swore at each other like drunken sailors. A Canadian flag left over from our Canada Day celebration provided a backdrop to the poker game as it hung on the wall. I sat pensively, realizing yet another stark contrast between life in Afghanistan and the life I was lucky enough to know under the maple leaf flag.

My thoughts were interrupted by a bold card move.

"All in," someone said.

After watching a few rounds of poker, this was the first aggressive move. Some cards hit the table as players folded with profanity-laced language, while others anteed up to see the match through to the end. Ali leaned in to ensure he didn't miss a thing.

"Master John, all in?"

I explained that the move meant that a player was betting all their remaining chips. It generally occurred when they had strong cards or were trying to bluff others that they possessed a winning hand. The move reflected a mindset of confidently seizing opportunities, even when the outcome was uncertain. Unwittingly, I concluded the explanation with another colloquial expression.

"All in means you make the most of the hand you're dealt."

His eyes widened, and a subtle smile crossed his face as he realized the deeper meaning of the phrase.

"Poker interesting, Master John. Make most of the hand you're dealt."

Unlike with pigs in shit, he clearly understood this. As we watched the same game, Ali started to pick up the nuances of poker while I experienced an epiphany regarding choice.

Growing up, discussions about freedoms were a regular part of my education, but I didn't fully comprehend the depth of the word. Watching that poker game with Ali deepened my understanding of the word "freedom"- the ability to have choice.

Living in Canada is comparable to sitting at a poker table, where you have the choice to strategize, take risks when it makes sense, and fold your hand when you don't like the odds. It's a game where you can pace yourself, play smart, and choose how to play your hand. With our judicial system, you can play confident that the rules remain fair and that the other players face the same odds as you. In contrast, being born in Afghanistan is like being forced to go all in every single round, regardless of the cards you're dealt. There's minimal time to think, less opportunity to strategize, and no guarantee of fairness. In Afghanistan, it's a relentless series of high-stake moves with unfavourable odds, where the next hand could be your last. Yet despite lacking a fair justice system, Ali sustained a sanguine mindset while regularly overcoming insurmountable obstacles in a warzone. He did more than just survive; he thrived.

As the poker game ended, Ali rose to depart. Uncertain if I'd see him again, as he was leaving for a couple of weeks to oversee another job, I walked him to the edge of our lines. At the start of the tour, I grossly misjudged him with my sardonic view of his rag-tag staff and patchwork of heavy equipment. Seeing the motley crew, I was arrogant enough to think he would be another training burden on our overtaxed troop. Although I taught him a few English words and a little about Canadian culture, he was the sage professor, and I was the naive student - at best, a neophyte. Although he never talked about books or libraries, and I'm not sure how well he could read or write, I know that he possessed a level head, was keenly observant, thoughtful, and pragmatic. Despite having no formal education, he had an incredible intellect that let him cut to the heart of the matter. This, coupled with his street smarts, served him better than any formal education ever could. In a sense, he was one of the most educated men I've ever met.

From my pocket, I pulled out a tube of cash composed of the Small Rewards Program money along with everything Wally and I had in our wallets. The diameter of a Coke can, I handed Ali the wad, providing the final cultural shock of the night.

"Thanks Ali, I'll never forget you."

Not expecting a bonus, as they were outside the scope of Canadian contracts, he starred in slight disbelief at the cash. We must have given him two month's wages.

"Master John, thank you."

He did a double take at the money to ensure he wasn't dreaming.

"Salaam alaikum, Master John."

He paused again and smiled.

"I'm happy as a pig in shit."

I laughed and probably broke all sorts of social protocols by hugging him.

As his silhouette faded into the night, I stood in awe of an incredible soul. Ali lived in a war zone under the constant risk of death supporting coalition forces, yet he never missed a deadline. Some of our soldiers still struggled to arrive on time for their sentry duty, at a post that was fifty metres from their bed. With minimal government systems, no insurance, and only making a few American dollars a day, he thought he won the lottery by being the unexpected recipient of a handful of cash. If he could wake up every morning full of vigour, eager to tackle the day, and with a desire to win, what excuse did I have not to?

In a couple of weeks, I'd be off to the land of kings, to live like a king. I could enjoy as many surf and turfs as I liked, and I could exercise my choice of how I played my metaphorical cards. On the contrary, Ali would continue to run his business in the middle of a warzone. I'm unsure if an Oscar-winning movie writer could have scripted two more opposing realities.

In the end, the divide between us was rooted in something neither of us chose – our place of birth. Ali was born in Afghanistan, while I was born in Canada. From afar, it seemed to be a subtle distinction, but it made *all* the difference. Looking at the Canadian Flag hanging behind the poker table, I realized I'd won the lottery by being born under that maple leaf.

# 22

# Play to Win

In the final days of the deployment, focus began to drift.

The missions continued, the patrols went out, and the convoys rolled through dangerous terrain, but the looming thought of redeployment back home was impossible to ignore. With its heat, dust, and ever-present danger, Afghanistan started to be discussed in the past tense instead of the present. Long story short, the redeployment became a distraction.

Consequently, I feared complacency setting in, reinforced by the troop chatter shifting from tactical strategies to daydreams of sitting poolside with a cold drink in hand during the decompression stop in Cyprus. Some multi-tour veterans joked about the last time they went to Cyprus; boasting that they drank liquor at the pool bar all day and somehow never left to take a piss... Some found the activity humorous, while others found it off-putting; however, getting all the remaining sappers through the last weeks in theatre and into the cesspool bar in Cyprus became my goal.

The decompression phase in Cyprus encompassed three half-day classes designed to help reintegrate soldiers into the lives they had left behind. After six-plus months in Afghanistan, they didn't know what they didn't know about returning to a normal life in Canada. Sessions covered the challenges of transitioning back into society, the potential changes in family dynamics during their absence, and strategies for coping with emotions and reconnecting with loved ones. I particularly liked the analogy that we would be similar to a car merging onto a highway, where the traffic flow represented the family. The soldiers needed to adjust their velocity to merge into the family tempo; failure to do so correctly would result in an accident. But for most soldiers, the well-intended reintegration sessions were overshadowed by the anticipation of leisure, indulgence, and normalcy. It wasn't that they didn't value the classes, but after months of gruelling heat, relentless patrols, and constant vigilance, they longed for a furlough. Even with ongoing tasks and missions, we were so close to Cyprus that we could taste it.

Walking by the vehicle lines one afternoon, I witnessed a platoon warrant officer berating a section commander.

"Sort this out! It ain't over yet!"

As a bystander, I could see I wasn't alone in fighting a common enemy: complacency. In this instance, the warrant officer referred to some deferred vehicle maintenance. The section commander had neglected to maintain his LAV properly because it was so close to the end. By not adhering to proper maintenance protocols, a small hydraulic leak had slowly filled the hull with litres of fluid. Beyond reliability concerns and the eye-watering smell caused by the oil sloshing about in the vehicle hull, it created a tremendous fire hazard. To prevent us from deferring similar tasks, I continually sought unique ways to keep our heads in the game. Running sprints as a track athlete in high school, our coach always yelled, "Sprint across the finish line." It was an equally apropos way to conclude our tour in Afghanistan.

During lunch one afternoon, Waller mentioned an idea.

"We should run a non-conventional range."

In military lexicon, there are two types of ranges: a conventional range and a non-conventional range. A conventional range is typically a well-established site with arc markers, textbook firing positions, and standard targets. Although the aim can differ, generally, a range of this ilk focuses on improving weapon handling drills and marksmanship. On the other hand, the infrastructure of a non-conventional range tends to be less established. The same safety protocols apply, but the range typically lacks standard items such as arc markers and pre-established firing points. Often, these types of ranges are used in the field to help simulate combat scenarios and provide more realistic training for soldiers. Similar to the gym construction a couple of weeks earlier, the one comment became a catalyst for a mastermind group that resulted in many unorthodox range ideas being suggested by the sappers.

"We could shoot from the driver's hatch on the ELAV," touted one sapper.

To one-up the idea, another added, "We should fire from the John Deere Gator."

As the conversation built upon itself, I was happy that the troop's attention shifted from Cyprus to creating a stellar range practice.

"We have lots of shotgun and 9mm ammo," declared another sapper.

Before our lunch concluded, the sappers designed a range that manifested into a lavish scenario. To simulate fighting from a disabled vehicle, the ELAV's remote weapon system and the driver, from within the driver's hatch, would provide suppressing fire downrange. Concurrently, the mounted sappers would extricate themselves from the vehicle's rear and then leopard crawl around and under the ELAV to join in the firefight. After discharging a ridiculous amount of gunfire at targets made up of paper silhouettes, stale candy bars and expired fruits from the kitchen, a couple of sappers would mount onto the John Deere Gator to close with and destroy the targets from close proximity. After advancing from the one-hundred-metre mark to the fifteen-meter mark, sappers would engage the remaining targets with 9mm pistols and shotgun slugs at point-blank range. Once complete, they intended to rinse and repeat the scenario until we had fired a quarter of our body weight in ammunition. After giving me the back brief, a dozen sets of eyes looked at me for approval.

In almost any other context, I should have denied the idea, as creatively firing from vehicle platforms constituted an elevated risk. But I knew the threat was complacency, not getting shot by seasoned combat veterans. They'd been through countless gunfights and fighting withdrawals. In some cases, they expended so many rounds they had to hand-load magazines amid firefights to sustain fire into enemy positions. In the process, some had the grim foresight to keep a hand grenade ready – their final guarantee that if the bullets ran out, they wouldn't be taken alive. With this type of combat experience, a bland conventional range to work on marksmanship didn't provide enough spice. The creativity they put into designing the scenario pleased me and I wanted to harness their enthusiasm. Moreover, it was oddly satisfying to discuss dangers and plausible responses rather than listen to people drone on about activities and drinks in Cyprus. I fully supported the concept but glanced at Wally to ensure we weren't completely ignoring safety.

"Sir, you're on the line. But you haven't crossed it."

So keen to manifest their idea, the sappers resembled a pack of wild dogs ready to chase a rabbit. I looked at everyone and responded.

"Alright, let's do it."

Ninety minutes later, over the put-put engine noise of the John Deere Gator idling, all hell broke loose as the engineers disgorged their rifles and crew-served weapons during yet another sapper rifle range. Although the ELAV became the centrepiece of the range, non-participants in the main event provided suppressing fire from the flanks, so an unfathomable volley of munitions went down range. After completing the second serial, our new explosive search dog team walked over. Subbing in for Doug and Tex while they were on leave, the handler approached me.

"You guys mind if we watch real close? I wanna get the dog used to gunshots."

Waller shrugged his shoulders indifferently while jockeying the John Deere Gator for the next serial.

It didn't bother me, so I replied, "Sure, no problem."

By nature, sappers are an ingenious bunch. While reloading magazines after one range serial, the creative juices flowed. Noticing that the handler carried a 9mm Glock, significantly newer and cooler than our ancient 9mm Browning pistols (which legend has it, Noah used to defend the ark), they popped the question.

"Hey, can we use your Glock?"

The dog handler looked at me. I looked at Wally to see if I was crossing the safety line, but he didn't object. So, we proceeded to provide a few orientation drills to sappers about the handgun before we resumed the range. As our pistols used the same round, we had a lot of ammunition to try out the contemporary weapon. With the amended safety orientation complete, we integrated the dog handler, his explosive detection dog, and the 9mm Glock into the remainder of the range serials. After serenading the explosive dog with copious amounts of small arms fire, we shut down the range, and I returned to the barracks, content that we'd done our best to reignite the sapper's focus in the waning days of their deployment.

The last couple of days were a whirlwind of activity. Wally needed to be repatriated early to deal with the passing of a family member, so the handover responsibilities fell to Waller and me. As his section was scheduled to depart in three days, we had less than seventy-two hours with one of the incoming sections to conduct a "left-seat, right-seat" handover. The phrase represented a metaphor for how the military liked to perform a changing of the guard in theatre. In a perfect world, switching entities would pair up for a few days. At first, the new member would shadow the outgoing member to learn the nuances of the job that couldn't be covered in training. After a day or two, they would switch. The incoming member would be in charge, and the outgoing member would monitor and potentially mentor in the background before departing. With Waller's crew scheduled to leave in a couple of days, I let him take the lead on passing information. Since my flight was a week and a half away, I had ample time to address any follow-up questions with the incoming crew.

Waller's main orientation handover was as efficient as it was unceremonious. It took place in our common area under the harsh late afternoon sun. The outgoing engineers stood in a loose semicircle, their uniforms stained with sweat and grime, while the fresh section of engineers, still crisp in comparison, leaned in with a mixture of eagerness and quiet apprehension. The uniform of one incoming sapper was so new that it still smelled like the fabric factory.

"Alright, let's get to it," said Waller as he began the brief.

He went over the map outpost by outpost. Then he showed the new sappers the routes and outlined the hotspots in our area of operation. After providing the orientation, we collectively responded to a wide variety of fundamental questions, such as what kit we took on patrol, how much water we carried, and how we leveraged the intelligence crew to garner as much information as possible before departing on patrol. About to conclude the brief to allow the vehicle crews to chat about equipment, I received a question about the percentage split between mounted and dismounted patrols.

"We did about sixty percent dismounted," I replied to the slight shock of the new crew.

Similar to us, they had hardly conducted a single dismounted patrol in training. Naively, I thought the training system would have adapted to theatre realities. But that approach would have meant changing the pre-established training standard midway through planned exercises—an almost impossible ask based on the training bureaucracy.

After responding to a few inquiries about patrol frequencies and compositions, equipment, and camp life, they wanted to know more about medical items. Like us, in preparation for harsh environment they attended several mandatory briefs on medical threats and received so many inoculations that their arms looked as if they had been in a bar fight with a porcupine. One question stuck out.

"Hey sir, did you take the anti-malaria pills?"

The inquiry stemmed from a debatable standard of issuing medications such as mefloquine to prevent malaria. While effective, the drug was linked to severe side effects such as anxiety, hallucinations, and suicidal ideation. Although we received briefs on the medication, some soldiers felt they were inadequately informed about the risks. In later years, the controversy raised concerns about balancing the need for malaria prevention with soldiers' mental health. Some leadership argued for taking the medication to ensure our forces were fit to fight, as you couldn't be effective while suffering from malaria. That is a valid point, but I'd also argue that the potential to suffer from anxiety, hallucinations, and suicidal ideation also negatively impacted a soldier's ability to fight. Consequently, it created another give-and-take balance so often forced upon us in an environment replete with risks.

Being raised in a culture of strict adherence to the standard, I could feel and appreciate the slight tension in the air as young soldiers weighed the risks for themselves. The sapper who posed the question seemed particularly health conscious, as he had tube of Coppertone sunscreen and a bottle of Purell hand sanitizer beside his notepad. I kept my answer simple to avoid getting into a medical discussion or debate.

"No, I didn't take my pills."

After reading about the potential for nightmare side effects, I jettisoned my medication into the portable toilet. I figured

Afghanistan provided enough odious experiences; I didn't need to dream about them as well. A firm believer that a few germs never hurt anyone, I decided not to provide any additional context to my response. But if they knew my handwashing habits rivalled those of a toddler, they may have questioned my medical judgement.

Scanning the audience, I could tell another sapper had a question, so I motioned for him to speak.

"Uh, hey sir, why is your Situational Awareness System monitor being used as a door stop?"

It had been so long since we dealt with that fiasco that I'd almost forgotten about it. The thick green monitor, the size of an elementary school desk, was starkly juxtaposed against the water feature, wooden deck, and pigeon cage. I wished Wally could have been there to add to my response.

"In short, the system didn't work as designed, so we removed it."

Numerous questions followed regarding why we would use an expensive monitor to perform the same function as a rock. To provide context to my response, I told them how contractors arrived at the beginning of the tour to install the system. Due to its size and positioning between the gunner and crew commander, it grossly impeded our ability to communicate and operate the LAV's weapon systems. With the screen installed, it became impossible to fight the vehicle. Wally and I tried to prevent the installation, but the contractor adamantly objected because they needed to install the system to get paid for the delivery of goods. Therefore, we reluctantly acquiesced.

Be it fate, luck or a combination of the two, before our next operations we received word that the system wasn't working properly. That fissure in the design was all that we needed to justify the removal. With the screen protector still installed on the monitor, Wally and I removed it from the vehicle by using the driver's tool kit. Without any other utility, true to Wally's prophecy back in Canada, the screen made an excellent doorstop.

As I finished relaying the story, I saw the shock in some of the sappers faces.

"Who were these people with such disregard for military kit?"

Seeing their reactions to what appeared to be flippant disrespect, I came to realize an important truth: Sometimes you need to focus on results rather than avoiding mistakes.

Still fresh from the training environment, the new sappers were just breaking out from the check-in-the-box training atmosphere – where a mistake could mean missing the deployment. Consequently, the training standard habituated young soldiers to conform so they didn't miss out on a highly sought-after operational deployment. On the contrary, after being in theatre the last few months, we focused on achieving results even if it risked making a mistake. We still respected procedures but were more willing to push the limits during ranges to fight complacency, question medications to fight malaria, and remove equipment without permission to have better success fighting the vehicle. A subtle but distinctive shift in mindset that is often summarized in sports as "playing to win" versus "playing not to lose."

With everything on the line in Afghanistan, the tacit theme of our handover to the incoming sappers was: *play to win*.

# 23

# Alberta Bound

After another day of handover discussions, Waller and his section's bittersweet redeployment date finally arrived. The night before they left, I lingered in the common area longer than usual, listening to the muffled chatter inside our barracks as the sappers concluded the last of their packing. Someone was telling a story, probably a recycled tale that had grown more exaggerated with each retelling. The laughter was real though, and I was going to miss the lads I spent so much time with over the last year and a half.

I was happy to see them reach the end of the tour in Sperwan Ghar, but anxious about being the last member remaining. The new sappers were properly trained and didn't do anything to alarm me, but they were still fresh, and I would have to conduct a few handover patrols with them. Being so close to the end of my deployment, I would have strongly preferred to have a few of my sappers assist in the process rather than doing it solo.

The morning of the departure resembled a graduation party. The troop morale was over the moon as country singer Paul Brandt's *Alberta Bound* song blared from a stereo. One by one, the troops loaded their kit bags of sleeping gear onto a large truck that would join their convoy to KAF. Similar to cleaning out a cottage for the season, last-minute sweeps of dirt and garbage removal occurred so the incoming sappers could nest in the bunks. I watched and tried to pitch in where I could, but like a perpetual motion machine, the troops didn't need any additional encouragement to finalize their tasks before departing.

As we'd done countless times before, the troops received patrol orders and marshalled the ELAV into a vehicle convoy on the edge of the helicopter landing zone. The excitement was palpable, as several infantry sections in the convoy were also on their last trip to KAF. In some ways, their smiles conveyed an edge of disbelief. Could they really be so close to home?

As the convoy prepared to roll out, the energy was infectious. Soldiers clapped each other on the back; some exchanged final quips, while others just enjoyed reaching the milestone. One soldier even made an exaggerated air-guitar gesture with his rifle, ecstatic to be deploying home. As I shook hands with each departing member, I saw exhaustion in their eyes. They were seasoned professionals, and I saw no signs of complacency or overconfidence in their final preparations, but I worried. They were so close to being done, but still so far away. The convoy needed to pass through numerous hot spots before it reached the relative safety of KAF. Comparable to a close hockey game, you couldn't afford to coast or let up until the final buzzer. Anything less risked giving your opponent the chance to strike.

Despite their experience, I felt a quiet unease gnawing at the edge of my thoughts. A heavy sense of apprehension and foreboding weighed on me, watching the joyous convoy roll out on their final road move. It felt like someone had called 'End Ex,' military lexicon for signalling the end of an exercise in training. The problem was that this statement was usually called in the field before the return trip to base. As a result, soldiers dropped their guard as the exercise was over. I couldn't shake the fear that we had subconsciously ingrained the "End Ex" habit into our psyche, a custom that could have lethal consequences in Afghanistan when the final road move back to base still contained lethal threats. The cheerful buzz of Paul Brandt's *Alberta Bound* in my head couldn't drown out my unease.

*I'm Alberta bound...*

*This piece of heaven that I've found..."*

We were so close to safety, but the distance between Sperwan Ghar and KAF felt impossibly vast.

Alone in the cleaned-out barracks, as the other sappers hadn't moved in yet, I sat in stillness, listening to the patrol radio. Mixed relief and unease passed over me as the convoy called in checkpoints on their way to KAF. Similar to a project manager checking off milestones on a planning document, I followed the convoy's progress on the map.

"Passing road project."

This checkpoint noted the make-work paving project. As it could severely impact mobility, it also became a checkpoint during vehicle movement. Over the course of our tour, the project paved a few kilometres of road with painfully slow manual labour. I couldn't argue with the touted economic results, but I still shook my head at the concept, and I questioned the overall tactical benefits of the initiative.

The convoy progressed well. After a short layover in Masum Ghar to pick up additional people and resources, it didn't take long before they were back on the radio.

"Departing Masum Ghar."

A key strong point for coalition forces, the high ground the position offered played a vital role in stabilizing the region. Taken by force by a previous rotation, I had to chuckle at the bureaucratic challenges that battle created for contracting officers and lawyers on our tour. To properly compensate the proprietor for our presence, local meetings with village elders were held to try and identify the lawful owner. In response to the question, "Who owns the land?" you'd have thought we were giving away free beer – hands shot up from everyone who lived within fifty kilometres of Masum Ghar. Lacking a lease also created contracting challenges for our American allies. While trying to establish a small contract for services in Masum Ghar, the contracts officers required the lease before taxpayer dollars could be expended on the property. Since we took the place by force and had yet to establish a lease, contract negotiations ground to a halt.

The convoy calling in checkpoints as it continued to snake its way back to base broke my reminiscing thoughts. The patrol updates had become steady, almost rhythmic. A call sign, a position relayed. A routine so familiar that I nearly started to let out a breath of relief as they were only twenty minutes from reaching KAF. Then, my worst fear materialized.

"Contact, IED."

My stomach clenched as my mind processed the message. I felt sick.

Captain Rob Clarke's vehicle, the patrol commander and my peer through many of the tour's trials, had struck an IED. Second in the order of march behind Waller's ELAV, the device detonated under the engine; the ensuing blast concussion blew out the back door of the LAV. The combined physical forces of the convoy's momentum plus the blast caused the vehicle to flip backwards and roll off the road. A combination of instinct and luck allowed Captain Clarke to drop inside the vehicle before it rolled instead of being tossed into the air as part of the carnage. As a result, he somersaulted like a ninja inside the back of the LAV.

"I remember being weightless for a split second," Captain Clarke would tell me years later. "As we bowled over, I saw the view through the air sentry hatch changed from ground to sky, ground to sky, to dust."

A moment before the blast, the crew had been cutting up the driver's mom in friendly soldier banter. Seconds later, they were inside the wreckage of a LAV, some members catatonic from the blast, yet they needed to respond to the strike.

As smoke rose from the blown-up LAV engine, the remainder of the convoy acted in unison. After establishing a security perimeter, Waller and his section helped respond to the scene. I sat helpless in the Sperwan Ghar command post as updates came over the radio.

"One vital signs absent, nine-liners to follow for casualties."

On the scene, soldiers hammered the butt of the C6 onto the driver's hatch to release the locking mechanism. When they finally extracted him, he was saturated in hydraulic fluid. With 25mm ammo, water bottles, and axillary vehicle kit strewn all over, the convoy triaged the casualties and finalized the nine-liner submissions. After the casualties were evacuated, the remaining members helped recover the LAV. When the final situational report came in, Sergeant Prescott Shipway, an infantry soldier with the 2ⁿᵈ Battalion, Princess Patricia's Canadian Light Infantry, became the last casualty on our tour and the 97th soldier to die in Afghanistan since the start of Canada's mission. The last time I saw him, he had been counting down the days before he could return home to see his family.

Sitting in the dimly lit command post, I felt a crushing helplessness as the radio crackled with updates on the IED strike and recovery. The chair beneath me felt uncomfortably rigid. I ran my thumb over the edge of my notepad, tracing the same lines over and over as I listened to the radio. It was an old habit, something I did during briefings, waiting for orders. Only this time, there were no orders to give, no calls to make, as I was powerless to assist.

The room was quiet except the occasional murmur from the radio. Every transmission put me on pins and needles as I feared another terrible update on the last convoy move. We all knew Afghanistan didn't give you free plays, but seeing it actually unfold during a final task, hurt. When the convoy eventually resumed the trip to KAF, every second felt unbearably long. Since the IED strike had stopped them on the road for some time, I feared other IEDs could have been armed or placed by our ever-observant adversaries. All I could do was wait. The futility gnawed at me with each passing moment until the patrol radio finally confirmed the message I had been waiting to hear.

"Back in KAF, leaving these means. Out."

I exhaled sharply when the call finally came, but the relief didn't come as expected. Instead, an emptiness settled deep in my chest. My hand still gripped my notepad. I felt hollow, anxious and frustrated by the weight of the day's events. I should have felt relief. They were back and they were safe, but one wasn't.

With the convoy complete, the patrol started the arduous task of preparing for the ramp ceremony.

Unfortunately, a tone-deaf senior NCO who had been ensconced in KAF the entire tour took exception to the dress of a bedraggled sapper because their uniform was covered in a pasty dried mix of sand, oil, and blood. Long story short, the sapper, beyond furious based on events of the last hour, responded to the bombastic reprimand by telling the senior NCO exactly where to shove it. It any other circumstance this would have been a chargeable office, however the sapper must have shaken the senior NCO to the core, because nothing further came of the exchange.

A similar dress and deportment shock occurred when Hammy, my range safety officer from the Haji tree range, returned his equipment to the quartermaster. Still in a bit of shock from responding to the IED strike, he didn't notice distinctive stains on his uniform from hydraulic fluid, oil, and blood until an incoming sapper inquired.

"You guys got hit?"

Hammy paused, looked himself over and realized his uniform was a hot mess. Exhausted and not wanting to make small talk, Hammy provided a terse reply.

"Yup," and proceeded to return his equipment so he could continue to redeployment process.

Hammy's time in KAF also spawned a small-world moment. His father was a surgeon augmenting the medical team at the Role 3 hospital in KAF. While rounding a corner in KAF, Hammy saw his dad. Thinking it would be weird to call out "dad" in KAF, Hammy yelled out, "Hey Stewart", his father's first name. Surprised as hell to see his son, they quickly caught up and planned to grab a coffee later that day. The surreal rendezvous resulted in them lightly discussing the IED strike from two distinctively different vantage points. I've always wondered what I would have said to my old man if I had the opportunity to meet him for a coffee in KAF. Would I tell him the truth? Or skirt around my day-to-day activities, so he didn't worry.

On the verge of being home, the entire series of events required to repatriate a soldier just prior to their redeployment seemed surreal. Instead of returning kit, packing bags for Cyprus, and signing another reframe from Paul Brandt's *Alberta Bound*, the troops found themselves preparing for a ramp ceremony. What should have been a transition to well-earned rest became a final act of duty as they paid their respects to Sergeant Shipway.

But as hard as it felt for me in Sperwan Ghar, it paled in comparison to the families of the casualties and the soldiers who experienced the incident firsthand. In an instant, the emotional pendulum swung from an almost home sensation to a gut-wrenching funeral. After the ramp ceremony in KAF, the soldiers proceeded to Cyprus. I couldn't fathom the elixir of emotions they experienced there while surrounded by social activities and cocktails as part of the reintegration process. There, amid the lush vegetation and warm breeze in the reintegration resort, it must have felt surreal to be surrounded by normalcy – just days after navigating IED-laden roads and responding to a fatal

IED strike. I'm sure many sat at the poolside bar all day as did previous soldiers, only this time, they sat in disbelief at how their last convoy operation had unfolded.

The famous New York Yankee Baseball player Yogi Berra once said, "It ain't over until it's over." Serving in Afghanistan was no different - every mission demanded relentless focus and vigilance. There was no "End Ex," no free play, and no easy patrols just because the end was near. No matter how close we were to the end, it wasn't over until it was over.

# 24

# Nothing Sticks to
# Duct Tape Like Duct Tape

My penultimate task was a left-seat, right-seat handover with the incoming troop commander and another section of combat engineers. For my last two weeks in theatre, while the relief in place of the battlegroup occurred in earnest, I grew eyes in the back of my head. I double-checked everything and walked with even more care, for two reasons. Firstly, I wanted to ensure I provided the best possible orientation within the limited time. The incoming troops were competent and well-trained; they just needed to learn some of the Afghanistan nuances before embarking on their own. As I would be partaking in patrols with incoming soldiers as part of the transfer, heaven forbid a simple error or assumption on my part would result in a significant injury or casualty to them. Secondly, I started to faintly realize that I might get home in one piece. I didn't want to see anyone get hurt, but something about being injured in the last days of a deployment made it feel even worse.

As part of the transition, Major Lane provided an orientation brief to the incoming leadership from the Royal Canadian

Regiment. Usually, the briefing room had sufficient seating, but in this case, it was standing room only. I listened intently as the meeting progressed, struck by the stark contrast between our combat fatigues. The uniforms of outgoing members were sun-faded and worn compared to those worn by the replacements, whose crisp-coloured clothes looked fresh from the supply depot. As the briefing concluded, the floor opened for questions. It's a long-standing tradition for the Princess Patricia's Canadian Light Infantry and the Royal Canadian Regiment to engage in playful ribbing. Comments such as "we only need a section of soldiers to do what's a platoon's job in your regiment" were common. I never paid much heed to the joshing, but one question from the incoming leadership caught my attention.

"What do injured soldiers wear in Germany?"

Hearing concerns about the clothes soldiers wore in Germany while receiving medical treatment for wounds sustained in Afghanistan struck me as odd. I couldn't grasp the reasoning behind the question. As the room stirred with shared uncertainty, the questioner provided additional clarification.

"I heard soldiers in Germany hospitals wear regimental physical training gear, but we didn't bring any for our casualties. I don't want my troops forced to wear non-regimental colours."

None of us in the room could confirm or deny what soldiers wore in German hospitals. What I wore, or what my troops wore if they sustained an injury, never crossed my mind until that question was asked. Once the briefing room members admitted to being ignorant of the hospital dress code, I'm not sure anybody else thought about the question again. For most, we tried everything to prevent getting injured, that way we didn't have to worry about hospital clothes. But if I were a critically injured soldier and needed the medical treatment of a first-class hospital, my only concern would be how to get better. I would be happy to sport any regimental colours, or a mixture of them, or be as naked as a jaybird. I noted who the question came from and made a mental note to be extra cautious around him until he started focusing on preventive actions to prelude injuries versus developing responses to them.

A small round-robin of handovers occurred between closely located outposts to maximize the exposure of the troops to the entire area of operations. This format resulted in a rotation of engineering sections between Sperwan Ghar and Masum Ghar. In addition to orienting troops to the geographical battle space, this approach also maximized the opportunity to learn the nuances of the area through interactions and joint patrols with outgoing soldiers. In this particular case, it would also allow me to get reacquainted with my old explosive instructor from the Canadian Forces School of Military Engineering, Sergeant Kruse.

I'd heard a rumour that he was an incoming section commander, but I didn't know if we'd cross paths. Listening to the radio in our lines, I heard the convoy of vehicles announce their arrival in Sperwan Ghar, so I went out to meet them. As the dust settled in the parking lot, Sergeant Kruse appeared in the flesh. Apart from his tan-coloured combats, he looked exactly the same as he did back at the school. Dismounting out of the back of a vehicle, his mustachioed face and gangly movements stood out distinctly as I approached.

"Morning, Sergeant Kruse. Welcome to Sperwan Ghar. I'll show you our lines."

Once we had finished exchanging pleasantries, I guided the new sappers to our billeting area. If Sergeant Kruse had any prickly feelings from our previous interactions, he didn't say anything or let them show. Since his section would be operating out of Sperwan Ghar for the foreseeable future, they proceeded to settle into the recently vacated bunks. After giving them a brief tour of the camp's administrative area, we agreed to conduct a handover brief following lunch.

With bellies full of food and in the shade offered by the engineering common area camouflage nets, I reviewed the maps, drawings, and the key points I'd discussed with the other section a few days prior. As the brief progressed, I found their questions insightful. Often, they caused me to reflect on a deeper level about how much had changed since our training in Wainwright. For example, they knew IEDs were just as popular today as they were during the Soviet invasion of Afghanistan. They knew the mujahideen jerry-rigged conventional munitions and made homemade explosives to construct a wide variety of devices that could be used in isolation or as part of an ambush. But like us at the start of our rotation, they only knew the theory. They didn't understand the scale or the wrath IEDs unleashed, how the enemy always gets a vote in situations, and how our adversary often played by different rules. Despite all my experience with IEDS, I found it impossible to convey the destruction they left behind. The devastation was ineffable – beyond anything words could truly capture.

"Responding to an IED strike is like imagining a worst-case scenario, only worse."

The briefing closed with general questions. Similar inquiries arose from the previous handover brief regarding equipment, how to handle the heat, and to how we employed Hesco bastion to complete force protection projects. An observant group, they also inquired about the Situational Awareness System monitor doorstop, so I told them the backstory. To close out the brief, I outline the schedule for the next three days. Beyond orientation to the camp routine and acclimatization to the Afghan environment, we would conduct a couple of joint patrols over the coming days. As the troops departed to complete various tasks, Sergeant Kruse approached.

"Sir, you mentioned a rifle range. Can we use it?"

"No problem, sergeant. When?"

He started to think out loud while processing the necessary timelines.

"Draft range orders, draw ammo, setup range…"

He didn't say a number, but based on the engineering school's range protocols, the time estimate would have been measured in hours, if not days. To expedite the process, I offered a suggestion.

"How about in an hour, sergeant? I'll get approval and ammo; see you at the range."

It was as if I had told him I could build Rome in a day. The time it took to set up a range quickly showcased the new realities of operating in Afghanistan. He had a look of slight disbelief, pausing to ensure I wasn't joking before responding.

"Yeah, that works sir."

As I departed, I could feel his apprehension about being able to set up a rifle range in under an hour. But having conducted countless ranges to fight complacency and ensure we stretched the springs in our rifle magazines, for the Sperwan Ghar command post it simply became a question of when the engineers would shoot again. I spoke with the duty officer in the command post and stated our intention. The radio speaker chirped as I walked back into our troop lines to grab my gear.

"Chimos conducting a small arms range. Out."

As Sergeant Kruse prepared his gear, I gave him a thumbs up once the radio announcement had concluded and proceeded to get some ammunition with the John Deer Gator. Right on schedule, the incoming engineer section met me at the firing point of the range with their ELAV. I commenced the range brief once they established communications with the Sperwan Ghar command post. In under two minutes, I highlighted a few nuances of the Sperwan Ghar range, like medical support and arcs of fire. After pausing for questions, I concluded the brief.

"Range open. Proceed."

Stunned by the rapidity of the process, one sapper raised his hand.

"Uh, so we can start?"

I repeated my last three words.

"Range open, proceed."

Accustomed to numerous range safety officers hovering around to monitor every move comparable to an overprotective parent, they looked around for additional people. Other than me, now sitting in a John Deere Gator with my feet up, they were alone. It took them a moment to realize we had covered all the standard points outlined in *Range Training Safety*; we just did it at warp speed without any unnecessary bureaucracy. They were one patrol away from a two-way range with the enemy, so from this point forward, they would need to be their own range safety officers.

It didn't take the sappers long to adjust to the novel reality and fully embrace the newly empowered freedoms. After zeroing their sights one last time, they began to send volleys of fire down range. In the process, they became a bit creative with reloading drills. Sitting on the John Deere Gator as a silent observer, they looked over several times to see if they were crossing a line. I indicated everything remained kosher. Since it was their first range in Sperwan Ghar, I didn't let on that we traditionally turned the John Deere Gator into a weapons platform as part of the exercise. After the firing ceased, the troops started picking up the brass. At the same time, Sergeant Kruse apprehensively posed another question.

"Hey sir, I'd like to do some explosive training. Can we do that?"

Typically, ranges in Canada are templated and licenced for certain munitions. You can determine what type of activity can be conducted on each range based on standing orders. In Sperwan Ghar, they may have had something written about this, but I never read it. If the danger template of the desired activity fit within the space of our range, I simply stated my intention to the command post. They would do a double-check for safety and to ensure it didn't impact operations in be area before granting authorization to proceed. The agency to conduct an austere range in a controlled environment seemed like a natural progression to prepare troops for the countless danger template assessments they would have to do on patrol. It had been a while since we conducted an explosive range, but I didn't think it would be a problem. Provided it only involved explosives and not metal, as that would increase the danger template too much, I didn't see any reason to object as I looked at Sergeant Kruse.

"No problem, sergeant, when?"

He paused. Typically, it takes some time to switch between an explosive range and a small arms range, especially if nobody had pre-planned the transition. This time, he didn't say anything out loud, but since I knew him, I knew he was preoccupied with all the standard processes he needed to complete to get an explosive range approved. At this point, I was only curious about logistics, so I broke up the traditional explosive range planning process.

"Hey sergeant, do you have explosives in your ELAV?"

Surprised that I'd already proceeded to the concluding step of the planning process, he nodded.

"Yes sir, got a basic load back in KAF."

With that major milestone complete, I made an unorthodox suggestion.

"How about an explosive range now?"

Awestruck at the agility offered by the Sperwan Ghar range, he couldn't have been happier to get his section handling some explosives. Within five minutes, we requested and received permission to conduct a basic charge explosive range.

Not having the desire or patience to attend another explosive class from Sergeant Kruse, I placed him in charge of the range and puttered away on the John Deere Gator. As I crested the hill, I could see Sergeant Kruse going over some charge preparation drills while holding a roll of duct tape. I chuckled to myself, knowing that at some point during the demonstration, he would quip: "Remember troops, nothing sticks to duct tape like duct tape."

Relaxing in the early evening calm back in the common area, the peaceful silence was sporadically broken throughout the next ninety minutes as the engineers completed an explosive refresher range.

The following day, we conducted battle procedures for a short patrol around the village adjacent to Sperwan Ghar. Although the intelligence community concocted some great tactical significance for the mission, we all knew the main objective was to acclimatize the new soldiers. At this point, I had the gear in my patrol pack down to the gram. While observing the new section prepare, I noticed a few unnecessary items. One sapper strapped the largest set of bolt cutters I'd ever seen to his pack. Watching the handles stick high into the air, I wondered if we were going on a mission to break into Fort Knox. I also noticed a few other sappers carrying pistols in addition to their service rifles. I found our Browning-issued pistol to be more lethal if I threw it as a projectile than when it was shooting them, so I never carried it on patrol. I debated about interjecting, but I'd already talked a lot during the handover briefs. As the sappers were following their pre-patrol procedures, and there was little risk in carrying the extra weight, I remained silent and let Afghanistan's heat be the instructor.

As we broke into the patrol order of march, I did a double take on the number of sappers present. At the end of our tour, at best, we could scrounge up two to four sappers to support a sixty-man patrol. For this patrol, our ranks were replete with ten sappers. As we walked out the main gate, I chugged two half-litre water bottles and tossed the empties beside the sentry. A few other veteran soldiers did the same; the water didn't do anybody any good until consumed. Although I'd briefed the incoming soldiers about the heat and the copious amounts of water required to stay hydrated, some thought I was speaking in hyperbole.

I'm not sure if it was planned as part of the acclimatization, but we encountered the heat of the day by leaving mid-morning. I didn't realize it until being placed amongst incoming troops, but over the course of our tour, I'd become comparable a grazing cow while on patrols. Consuming so much water to stay hydrated, I often pissed like a racehorse standing in the chutes - so much so that I didn't even bother doing up my fly. While the new crew still exercised a little discretion when nature called, I barely sought visual privacy during a short halt to relieve myself.

If my animalistic deportment concerned anyone, they didn't say a word. What the new troops did find concerning was the lack lustre attention spans of the ANA soldiers. While the incoming troops cautiously inspected everything as they remained on high alert, a small section of ANA soldiers frolicked along the patrol path resembling lovers on a picnic. In another case, some ANA soldiers placed flowers into the muzzles of their AK-47s to make a bouquet. With their rifles slung haphazardly on their shoulder, they didn't have a care in the world. Within earshot of the patrol interpreter, a sapper asked about the ANA.

"Why are they so relaxed on patrol?"

I knew the answer but figured it would be better coming from the ANA. So, I motioned to the interpreter to pose the question to a flower-carrying soldier. After a short exchange, he translated the conversation.

"He said, 'Taliban sleeping. Only we stupid enough to walk in this heat.'"

That was significantly better answer than what I could have provided. The response also aligned with my observation that the ANA had a sixth sense about the Taliban. Consequently, it was common to see the patrolling ANA buy food from a market, hold hands and engage socially as if they were in a park. I explained to the incoming soldiers that reading changes in the ANA's temperament was far from an exact science, but it generally signaled trouble. The ANA had an instinct—they just seemed to know when the Taliban were nearby.

During a short halt in a nearby village, we stood before a small group of Afghan civilians. A couple of Canadian soldiers were joking with each other in English. As a result of their banter, one of the observing civilians laughed. An outgoing platoon commander immediately singled out the man for questioning. A short conversation between them followed but it didn't result in anything, so the man returned to the group. After witnessing the scene, a private asked the platoon commander about it.

"Hey sir, how did you know he spoke English?"

Accustomed to patrolling through villages, he offered up another trick of the trade.

"When he laughed at your joke, I knew he spoke English. He says he learned it years ago at school in Kabul."

As it wasn't a crime to speak English, and we had no other reasons for concern, we let the man return to his day as we resumed our patrol. After doing a small circuitous loop through the village and countryside, we returned to Sperwan Ghar.

With their first real exposure to physical activity in the Afghan heat, the sappers were bushed. The conversation quickly turned to ditching unnecessary equipment as they recuperated in our common area. Instead of leaving equipment behind, I mentioned another option.

"Don't hesitate to request infantry support to carry engineering gear."

They looked at me as if I told them water flowed uphill. That's when I realized combat engineers on the new rotation were still viewed with a training mindset; the incoming battle group had not yet undergone the tropism that occurs in fighting units after experiencing their first real IED strike. Just as when we arrived, the incoming sappers were seen as the red-headed stepchild versus an essential patrol element. They could not believe that the infantry fought for engineers, delayed orders so engineers could attend them and willingly carried engineering equipment on patrols if it ensured they received proper engineering support. I concluded the conversation with a warning from a previous mishap.

"Just don't confuse the explosive residue test kit with the hair trimmers."

I could see their bewilderment, so I placed the two plastic cases beside each other on the table. The two black boxes, each the size of a 2-litre pop bottle, looked almost identical.

The explosive residue test kit is a forensic tool we used to detect trace amounts of explosive materials. By swabbing the hands of suspect individuals, we could determine if they'd been recently handling explosives. When we received positive test results, follow-up investigations occurred. While hastily packing for a short-notice patrol in the dark, a sapper mistakenly packed the hair trimmer kit in their patrol pack. A few hours later, we proceeded to investigate a suspected IED maker. In full view of the suspect and a couple of other soldiers, when we went to do the test, we pulled out a hair trimmer instead. With the power cord dangling in the air, we all shared a collective "damn" while the suspect looked at us in disbelief. Unable to speak English and with no interpreter in sight, he didn't understand the screw-up. He just sat confused, wondering why we would want to cut his hair in the middle of a grape field.

The following day, we did another short patrol. This time, the troops departed without bolt cutters, pistols or the hair trimmer. Many also gulped several water bottles with me before leaving the main gate. Like the day prior, the main aim of the patrol was to help acclimatize the incoming soldiers to the harsh Afghan environment. Nothing was said when we returned, but I felt my handover was complete. The incoming crew had been well trained, they were smart, and they could see some of the challenges that lay ahead. I'd passed on what I could; they'd have to figure out the rest on their own. Just as when we arrived at the start of our tour, the outgoing crew is only appreciated for so long before they start to cramp your style, similar to when family guests overstay their welcome.

During my last night in Sperwan Ghar, I had a long conversation with Sergeant Kruse. A sponge for information, he filed everything in his head as we discussed tactics, IED responses, mobility support, and force protection tasks. In response to his questions, I outlined examples of what we did and why. As the conversation progressed, I realized most of his questions sought a response grounded in training and policy. Without realizing it, we'd tweaked the decision cycle while operating in the Horn of Panjwai because we often needed to find a solution to a problem that our training or policy didn't address.

The military planning process taught us to find answers to some key questions, such as what were your assigned tasks, implied tasks, constraints, and restraints. With these answers, you could identify your mission and start to bracket in a plan. With policy and training providing many handrails, we could quickly develop sound courses of action to support our plan. But like a tripod that becomes unstable when it loses a leg, fighting in Afghanistan could negate policy and training since we needed to deal with unique situations. Consequently, we required another question to help stabilize our plans.

That question became, what makes sense?

In asking it, unconventional responses often materialized. As a visual thinker, I tended to use a three-circle Venn diagram composed of policy, training, and did it make sense. In addition to providing some unique solutions, it also provided us with one of the best combat multipliers, simplicity, as complex plans can cause problems to compound and quickly spiral out of control.

For instance, consider the Situational Awareness System that we jettisoned from the LAV. There was no policy; we never trained on it and keeping it in the vehicle made no sense, because it limited our ability to function. Consequently, we simplified our lives by removing the system and making it a doorstop. Regarding the Sperwan Ghar ranges, conducting them provided exceptional training. As we could be on a two-way range at any time on patrol, our safety manuals didn't fully apply, so we needed to defer to what made sense. Conducting Sperwan Ghar ranges made sense and provided a simple solution to the problem of preparing for combat situations. Similarly, the infantry carrying our engineering equipment provided a simple solution. Although uncommon in training, sharing loads didn't breach any policy, and it just made sense in theatre. I used the same logic to explain my thoughts about speeding through a command wire IED route and whether overhead protection is required when the threat is predominately direct fire from RPGs.

Ultimately, my handover advice boiled down to two key principles: keep it simple and do what makes sense. As Sergeant Kruse quips, "nothing sticks to duct tape like duct tape;" a simple statement can provide immense utility.

That night was the last time I ever saw Sergeant Kruse. We didn't openly address it, but we buried the hatchet between us over the course of our interactions at Sperwan Ghar. We'd come a long way since my red chit for deficient performance because I had the audacity to question explosive standards. Ironically, many of the handover points I provided him stemmed from taking a non-standard approach. Unceremoniously, I departed the next day and arrived safely back to KAF.

Unfortunately, I can't say the same for Sergeant Kruse.

Three months later, I walked into a gas station while getting fuel during the Christmas holidays. There he stood, his mustachioed face staring back at me from the local paper's front page. Killed in Afghanistan by an IED explosion.

# 25

# The Standard

As I look back on my time in the military, I see the path as a series of unconventional choices. From the moment I took a fifty percent pay cut and slid the company truck keys across my boss's oak desk, through training and deployment, to the decision to write this book despite doubts about my writing ability, it became just another unconventional decision in a journey that has been laced with them.

Like so many others who served, my experiences were just that—experiences—moments in time, decisions made, and lessons learned along the way. I never set out to write a book. But as the years passed, I realized that the stories of those I served with were worth preserving for posterity. The combat engineers I worked alongside have moved on; many are now raising their families. One day, their children and grandchildren may ask, "What did you do in Afghanistan?" This book is a small part of that answer.

Beyond that, this book captures some lessons we learned— lessons that aren't always written in doctrine but are just as valuable. There is value in understanding the profession, not just from the perspective of doctrine and standard operating procedures but from the experience of those who carried them out. Through our story, I hope these pages serve as another tool in the sapper toolbox, providing insights to avoid past pitfalls.

More than anything else, this book is about the people whom I am grateful to have served with and learned from.

To my early instructors, who put me on the right path to see beyond the immediate task and focus on the bigger picture. To Sergeant Six-Inches, who drilled the importance of the most minor details, even if it was just the six-inch fold on a bed sheet. By enforcing the standard, he also taught that you get what you inspect, not what you expect.

To Major Noe, who reminded me that sometimes, the best way to lead is to challenge the rules when they don't make sense and, Capt Battey, who championed never step on enthusiasm.

To the non-commissioned officers like Wally, Waller, and Hollywood, who helped keep me on track and who fought for what was right, even when it wasn't easy. To Vandenberghe and MacCormac, only years later did I come to understand just how much they did behind the scenes to support the sappers. Their efforts meant more than I ever realized at the time.

To Major Packer and Bret, who gave me just enough rope to learn without hanging myself. There were many times I probably deserved to be hung, and if Afghanistan hadn't been so wild, I'm positive my career would have taken a *very* different turn.

And to *all* the sappers - the ones who carried the weight. I learned more from them than from any manual or classroom. Unfortunately, despite previous rotations recommending this approach, we didn't get a few months to decompress together after the tour back in Canada. Instead, we scattered across the country, continuing to help the ever-demanding military beast accomplish the next mission; the metaphorical green slug kept inching forward.

Throughout my career, the standard dictated how we trained, worked, and measured success. It was in everything we did—from making a bed precisely to preparing a demolition charge. We saw it in Wainwright, where the standard dictated that we train in a way that didn't always match reality, such as when we weren't allowed to dig proper defensive positions because of environmental policies, so we "built" them with words instead. We simulated river crossings with white mine tape instead of putting vehicles in the water. The standard existed for a reason. It provided structure, discipline, and a way to measure success so we could get our check-in-the-box. But sometimes, when you face an adaptive adversary who sees patterns as a vulnerability to attack, the standard isn't enough. Sometimes, what makes sense isn't written in a manual, and adapting is the only way forward. That's when the real lessons began because war doesn't always follow the standard. In many cases, it is the antithesis of it.

If I could go back, I'd tell myself to pay closer attention to the unseen costs of war. The mental toll, the concussions from blasts, the gradual erosion of hearing, the scars left not just on the body but on the mind. In our youth, we pushed through with ignorant bravado, dismissing injuries as badges of honour. But time has a way of collecting debts we thought we'd never owe. Winston Churchill once remarked, "A medal glitters, but it also casts a shadow." Unfortunately, that shadow continues to follow many of us long after the deployment ended. The military prepared us for war—but not always for what came after.

We won the lottery being Canadian, but that doesn't mean we left the battlefield unscathed. Many still carry their scars, while others are still fighting the demons that followed them home. The price of service isn't just written in history books – it's carried in those who served and manifests in different ways. For some, it means avoiding crowds and loud noises. For others, they are triggered by seeing a face or item that takes them right back to Afghanistan. For me, it's chicken wings. I've never seen one in a pub or at a family dinner without being taken back to our IED strike in Sia Choy, where the casualty's legs looked like an overside, half-eaten chicken wing. In a similar way, I still find myself keeping a bit of distance from people when hiking – a habit carried over from patrols in Afghanistan. On a dismounted combat patrol, spacing wasn't just protocol; it was survival. If someone beside me stepped on a mine, I'd be far enough away to avoid the blast and would be able to provide first aid. And if I stepped on the mine, the distance might spare those around me – so they could give first aid and maybe save my life.

I'd also say that some of the most valuable lessons don't come from doctrine, training exercises, or battlefield experience—they come from unexpected places. I lost count of the times sappers rigged something from lessons they learned from the farm as a kid or drew upon a Hollywood movie to concoct a solution. My lesson came from Joy, the mother of one of my best friends. A God-fearing woman, she could make even the most hardened drill sergeant crumble under one of her fire-and-brimstone speeches.

One day as young teenagers, while we were listening to heavy metal, she fiercely interrupted the headbanging session by saying, "This is Satan's music!"

She then delivered a searing admonition about the devil. I learned his name was Lucifer and how evil can manifest in the world. At the time, I laughed it off, thinking she had a screw loose. But in the years that followed, I came to see the sage wisdom in her words. She could have remained silent as I wasn't her kid, but she took me under her wing, for which I'll be eternally grateful. Through that one interaction, I learned a fundamental truth: the world is generally good, but evil exists, and you must be vigilant. That simple, seemingly innocuous lesson turned out to be one of the most profound tools in my toolbox for dealing with the fallout of operations in Afghanistan. Being unequivocally warned that diabolical evil existed somehow made it less daunting to face.

Forewarned is forearmed.

In the end, I've come to realize that combat engineering is a profession of inches, and combat makes them binary. The inches work for or against you, as the difference between success and failure, safety and catastrophe, can come down to the slightest details. While the standard gives us a foundation to help keep the metaphorical inches working in our favour, sometimes the situation demands something different. The best leaders, soldiers, and engineers know when to follow the standard and when to deviate from it, which is an art, not a science. In doing so, they harnessed untapped resources such as innate ingenuity, unconventional thinking, or even the right people at the right time, like Ali or the ANA. I saw it every day in the field when sappers found a way to get the job done, even if it meant bending the rules. When a problem couldn't be solved with the standard approach, they adapted – because combat engineering is about making things work, not just following the plan. That's what makes sappers great.

Standards are important. They provide structure, order, and a baseline. But sometimes, when confronted by adversity, the only way forward is through adaptation. Consequently, the lesson I leave you with—the lesson I hope this book imparts—is that sometimes, the unconventional approach *is* the standard.

Chimo!

**ABOVE**: Foot inspection after a long dismounted patrol. Credit J. Hallett

**BELOW**: The best contracting crew and problem solvers in Afghanistan, Ali and Wali. Credit T. Wolaniuk

**ABOVE**: Foot inspection after a long dismounted patrol. Credit J. Hallett

**BELOW**: Austere sleeping arrangements after finding no room at a combat outpost during a multi-day dismounted patrol. We were prepared to crawl under the LAVIII in the event of a mortar attack. Credit J. Hallett

**ABOVE:** Sappers reinforcing a bunker with sandbags at Sperwan Ghar. Credit T. Wolaniuk

**BELOW:** Improvised coffee cup with cozy to enjoy a "Mac Attack." Credit J. Hallett

**ABOVE**: "All hands on deck" to raise a heavy wooden wall as sappers build sleeping quarters at a combat outpost. Credit J. Hallett

**BELOW**: Ali and crew hosted us for a home-cooked meal in their quarters. Credit T. Wolaniuk

**ABOVE**: Afghanistan soldiers baking "foot bread" in an earth oven. Credit J. Hallett

**BELOW**: Escaping the sun under old parachutes in Mushan. Credit J. Hallett

**ABOVE**: Troop photo with Ali and Whitie the monkey.

**BELOW**: Sappers building a Hesco bastion barrier at a combat outpost. Credit J. Hallett

**ABOVE**: Building the Sperwan Ghar gym. Credit J. Hallett

**BELOW**: Typical graveyard in our area of operations. Credit T. Wolaniuk

**ABOVE**: Overview of Sperwan Ghar, our staging area for the deployment. Credit T. Wolaniuk

**BELOW**: Patrol through a typical local village near Sperwan Ghar. Credit J. Hallett

**ABOVE**: Looking north from Sperwan Ghar, same location where snipers watched an IED being planted. Credit J. Hallett

**BELOW**: Mushan BBQ, Sappers in their Sunday best, eating stew from a large aluminum pot - the same kind often used in IED construction. Credit J. Hallett

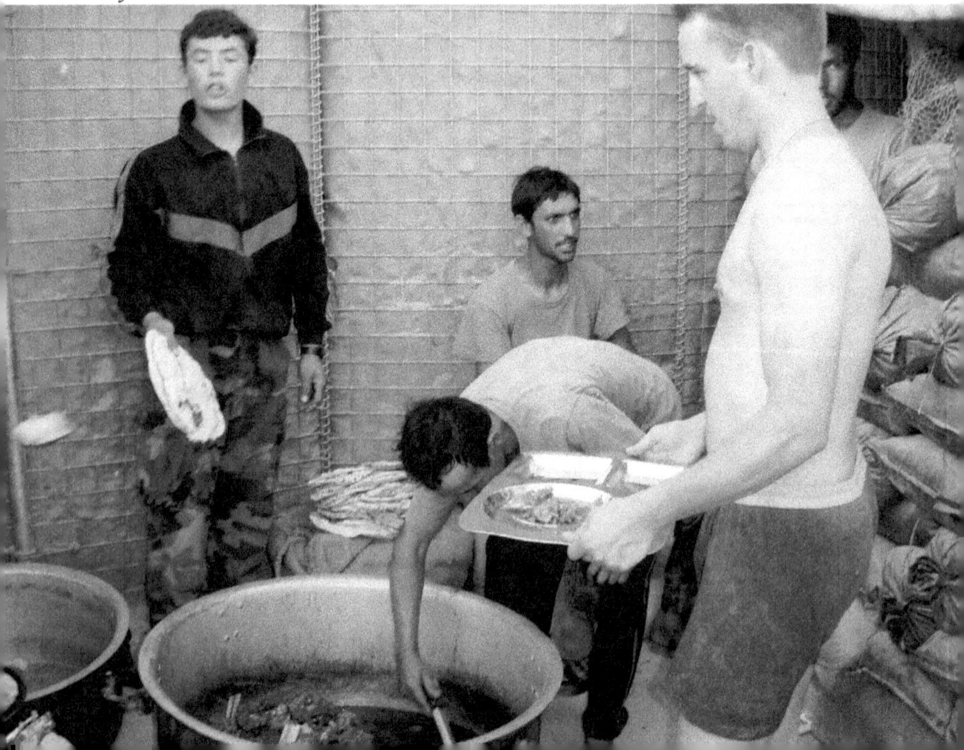

**ABOVE**: Sappers moving heavy steel beams during a bunker build at a combat outpost. Credit J. Hallett

**BELOW**: Hiding from 50 degree Celsius heat during a dismounted patrol. Credit J. Hallett

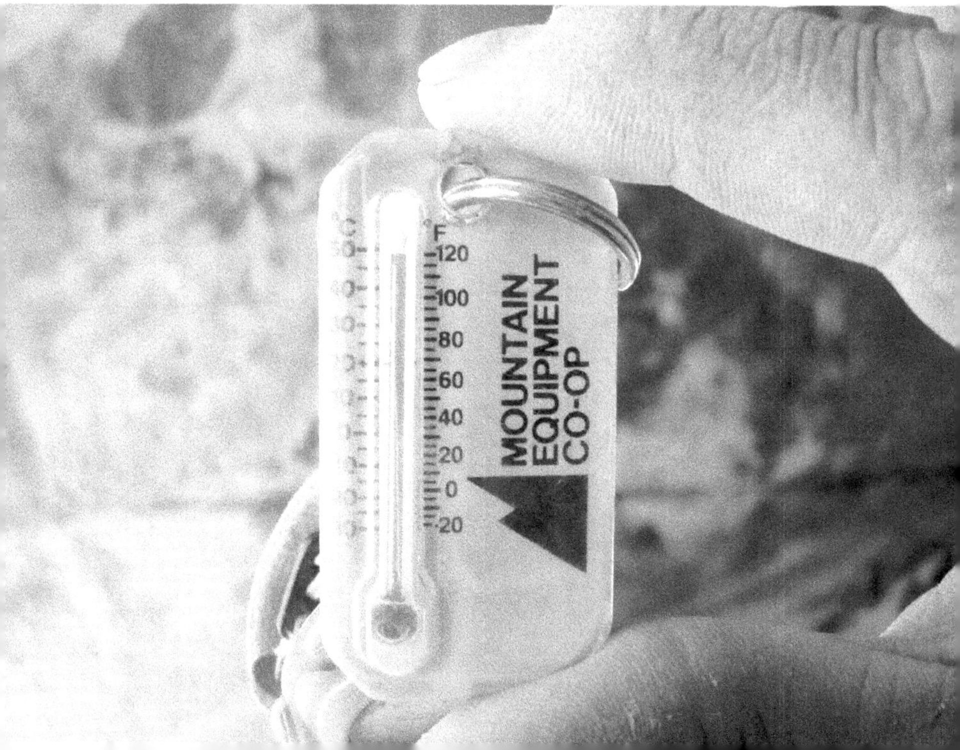

**ABOVE**: Sappers completing a rugged steel bunker at a combat outpost. Credit T. Wolaniuk

**BELOW**: Troop photo with Hughes the donkey. One of the only times the troop was together. Credit T. Wolaniuk

**ABOVE**: Wally tackling the never ending troop administration in our office. Credit J. Hallett

**BELOW**: E21B, Corporal Wasden, Sergeant Eades, Sapper Stock. Credit C. Hamilton

# About The Author

Born and raised in the Calgary, Alberta area, John spent his early years working a variety of construction jobs while pursuing a Civil Engineering degree at the University of Calgary. After a few years in the concrete industry, he joined the Canadian Armed Forces as a Combat Engineer, driven by the desire to gain the most experience in the least amount of time. Over the course of a 20-year military career, he served in postings across Canada and deployed twice to Afghanistan. Balancing military service with academic achievement, he completed a Master of Business Administration, a Master of Defence Studies, and earned a couple professional designations in Project Management and Facility Management. He is also a licensed Professional Engineer in the province of Alberta.

An avid outdoor enthusiast, he spends his free time exploring Canada's backcountry by motorcycle, ice fishing, and tackling the challenges of the 1000 kilometre Great Divide Trail, which he is currently working to complete. He lives in Calgary with his spouse and two children.

# DOUBLE†DAGGER
## — www.doubledagger.ca —

**Double Dagger Books** is Canada's only military-focused publisher. Conflict and warfare have shaped human history since before we began to record it. The earliest stories that we know of, passed on as oral tradition, speak of war, and more importantly, the essential elements of the human condition that are revealed under its pressure.

We are dedicated to publishing material that, while rooted in conflict, transcend the idea of "war" as merely a genre. Fiction, non-fiction, and stuff that defies categorization, we want to read it all.

Because if you want peace, study war.